BLACKOUT

BLACKOUT

World War II and the Origins of Film Noir

Sheri Chinen Biesen

The Johns Hopkins University Press, *Baltimore*

1   2   3   4   5   6   7   8   9

The Johns Hopkins University Press
2715 North Charles Street
Baltimore, Maryland 21218-4363
www.press.jhu.edu

Library of Congress Cataloging-in-Publication Data

Biesen, Sheri Chinen, 1962–
Blackout : World War II and the origins of film noir /
Sheri Chinen Biesen.
p.   cm.
Includes bibliographical references and index.
ISBN 0-8018-8217-6 (hardcover : alk. paper) —
ISBN 0-8018-8218-4 (pbk. : alk. paper)
1. Film noir—United States—History and criticism.
2. World War, 1939–1945—Motion pictures and the war.
I. Title.
PN1995.9.F54B53 2005
791.43′6556—dc22
2005001866

A catalog record for this book is available
from the British Library.

For my uncle and my grandparents
and all who survived the war
with courage and spirit

Contents

Illustrations

Acknowledgments

For years I have been fascinated by many questions about film noir. When and how did *noir* films evolve to become so shrouded and shadowy in their visual design and cinematography? When did full-blown film noir definitively come into its own, and what was *film noir* before the term was coined overseas in 1946? In other words, why were there so many brooding and distinctively *noir* crime films prior to 1946, during a time when America, and the world, was at war? In response to these questions this book began twelve years ago, in 1993, when I was researching a master's paper at the University of Southern California School of Cinema-Television. That paper eventually grew into my 1998 doctoral dissertation, "Film Noir and World War II: Wartime Production, Censorship, and the 'Red Meat' Crime Cycle," at the University of Texas at Austin.

I am indebted to many people over the course of this journey. I thank my editors and the staff at the Johns Hopkins University Press for their efforts and support of this project. Special thanks to Mahinder Kingra, Michael Lonegro, Linda Forlifer, Joe Abbott, Jennifer Gray, Kathy Alexander, Amy Zezula, and Melody Herr. I also thank especially my doctoral adviser, Thomas Schatz, at the University of Texas at Austin and my master's adviser, Richard B. Jewell, at the University of Southern California School of Cinema-Television. I am grateful to the archives and archival staff who assisted with the research for this book. Special thanks to Ned Comstock and the staff at the USC Cinema-Television Library Special Collections, Noelle Carter at the USC Warner Bros. Archive, Dace Taube in the USC Regional History Center Special Collections, the Academy of Motion Picture Arts and Sciences Margaret Herrick Library and Center for Motion Picture Study, UCLA Young Research Arts Library Special Collections, the Harry Ransom Humanities Research Center at the University of Texas, the New York Public Library for the Performing Arts Special Collections, Janet

Lorenz and Kristine Krueger at the National Film Information Service, and the Library of Congress.

I received support from the University of Texas at Austin, the University of Southern California, the University of California, the University of Leicester, and Rowan University to conduct research for this book.

I thank many friends, colleagues, and teachers and my students for their encouragement and support over the years. Special thanks to Brian Taves, Brian Neve, Thomas Doherty, Michael Anderegg, Charles Maland, Robert Sklar, Peter Rollins, James Welsh, Felicia Campbell, Charles Ramirez Berg, Joseph Kruppa, Drew Casper, Marsha Kinder, Michael Renov, Leonard Leff, Cynthia Baron, Nicholas Cull, Scott Curtis, Walter Metz, Fred Metchick, Judith Bushnell, Martin Vego, Githa Susan Srivatsa, Karah Ladd, Kelly Colla, Julia Hall, my family, Nate, John, and my grandparents.

BLACKOUT

Introduction

The camera slowly zooms in on a silhouette of a man on crutches until blackness fills the screen. Automobile headlights zigzag through a dark city street, where fog obscures the few dim street lamps. Tires screech, and a horn blares in the darkness as the car veers into an intersection, nearly colliding with a truck. A shadowy figure in a trench coat and fedora staggers out of the car. He enters a building and rides an elevator, trailing blood into an office. Its black interior swallows him. He snaps on a desk lamp, loosens his tie, pulls out a cigarette, fumbles for a match, and strikes a light. A disheveled, wounded Fred MacMurray slides his chair over to the office Dictaphone and recites a murder confession beginning with the date: July 16, 1938. Filmed in fall 1943 and released in 1944, *Double Indemnity* makes no explicit reference to the Second World War, but its cynical tone, brutal violence, and shadowy visual style all suggest the bleak realities of a world at war.

Dark, brooding, obsessive—*Double Indemnity* reversed an industrywide ban by Hollywood Production Code censors on James M. Cain's hardboiled fiction, a ban that had been in place for nearly a decade. Provoking great controversy, the moody screen adaptation of Cain's book, scripted by director Billy Wilder and novelist Raymond Chandler, paved the way for a new trend of films in Hollywood. From its first shot, even as the opening credits roll, the picture is undeniably film noir. *Double Indemnity* was one of a vanguard of Hollywood films emerging in the 1940s. Striking for their sophisticated "black" visual style and thematic duplicity, these films would be labeled dark cinema. In 1946 French critics viewing these wartime American films for the first time coined the term *film noir* (black film). The origin of film noir is linked to *série noire* (and later, *fleuve noire*) or "black" detective fiction, French translations of American hard-boiled novels by authors like Dashiell Hammett, James M. Cain, Raymond Chandler, and Cornell Woolrich. In this unique breed of Hollywood cinema, stars such as

Humphrey Bogart, Alan Ladd, and Robert Mitchum embodied hard-bitten cynicism in shadowy images depicting a fateful universe onscreen. Classic films noir such as *Double Indemnity, Laura* (1944), and *Murder, My Sweet* (1944) portrayed a world of menace and urban deviance, featuring rain-slicked city streets and murderers lurking in back alleys, seductresses bathed in the haze of cigarette smoke, detectives covered in the barred shadows of venetian blinds, crooked cops, and the sound of gunfire. Enhancing the distinctive look and cinematography of film noir, moody lighting and camerawork emphasized heavy expressionistic shadows, stark visual design with low-key chiaroscuro pools of light, claustrophobic interiors and confined spaces, high-contrast black-and-white photography, oblique camera angles, and asymmetrical compositional framing. *Noir* filmmakers also employed a variety of narrative techniques, such as visual flashbacks and subjective point of view, that created complex story structures. Obsessed, guilt-ridden characters confessed their crimes in psychological voice-over narration that conveyed an overwhelming sense of fatalism and doom for violent self-destructive antiheroes and lethal women.

Filmmakers conceived, produced, and released many films noir during World War II. A series of visually stunning and narratively provocative wartime pictures heralded the first definitive phase of the trend: *This Gun for Hire* (1942), *Street of Chance* (1942), *Double Indemnity, Murder, My Sweet, Phantom Lady* (1944), *Laura, The Woman in the Window* (1944), *Ministry of Fear* (1945), *Mildred Pierce* (1945), *Detour* (1945), *Scarlet Street* (1945), *The Lost Weekend* (1945), *Spellbound* (1945), *The Big Sleep* (1946), *The Postman Always Rings Twice* (1946), and *Gilda* (1946). The bleak vision in these films grew out of wartime American culture, the realities of making films in Hollywood during this time, and the way home-front—and battlefront—audiences saw these pictures. Many films were stockpiled—made during the war and held by studios with a backlog of pictures that were not distributed or promoted until later in the conflict. Not only were they made in Hollywood under wartime circumstances, but they were also limited to predominantly domestic reception, targeting North American home-front audiences and armed forces overseas while much of international distribution to foreign markets, with the notable exceptions of Great Britain and Latin America, was suspended over the course of the war. In fact, the American film industry and domestic press recognized these *noir* pictures as a growing movement before they were formally acclaimed in France in 1946. By 1944 Hollywood studio publicity and critics in the United States had already identified these innovative films as a bold new trend called the "red meat crime cycle." The crime and violence, particularly sexual violence, in these pictures grew out of changing patterns of censorship during the war, which was affecting American culture and Hollywood studio filmmaking.

Emerging out of the austerity, populism, and social critique of the Depression era and responding to the immediate challenges, concerns, and anxieties of wartime, World War II–era films noir would in turn inspire a cycle of postwar crime movies reflecting new fears about the cold war and nuclear war. Indeed, film noir is often identified as a predominantly postwar trend preempted by the war. Paul Schrader, for example, has suggested that "were it not for the war, *film noir* would have been at full steam by the early forties. The need to produce allied propaganda abroad and promote patriotism at home blunted the fledgling moves toward a dark cinema . . . *film noir* thrashed about in the studio system, not quite able to come into full prominence."[1]

Studio records, the films, and the history of how they were produced tell a different story. Wartime productions such as *Double Indemnity, Phantom Lady,* and *Murder, My Sweet* represent the most expressionistic, stylistically black phase of film noir.[2] Wilder's *Double Indemnity* is darker in visual style than his 1950 film *Sunset Boulevard;* Fritz Lang's *Ministry of Fear* and *Scarlet Street* are darker than his 1950s films noir, such as *The Big Heat* (1953). The *noir* aesthetic derived from wartime constraints on filmmaking practices. Brooding, often brutal, realism was conveyed in low-lit images, recycled sets (disguised by shadows, smoke, artificial fog, and rain), tarped studio back lots, or enclosed sound stages. In the postwar period filmmakers redefined *noir* realism, having more flexibility in location shooting and lighting. Wartime film noir is important to our understanding of culture and society during the World War II era because these films reflect a different set of anxieties from those we see in the films noir of the postwar era and result from a different set of circumstances in the Hollywood production system. These early *noir* films created a psychological atmosphere that in many ways marked a response to an increasingly realistic and understandable anxiety—about war, shortages, changing gender roles, and "a world gone mad"—that was distinctive from the later postwar paranoia about the bomb, the cold war, HUAC, and the blacklist, which was more intrinsic to late 1940s and 1950s *noir* pictures.

The global conflict affected American culture in unprecedented ways. The darker side of wartime permeated the home-front experience, characterized by agonizing uncertainty and fears—of German spies, Japanese submarines, and loss of American lives overseas, as well as on U.S. soil. These experiences culminated in an anxious combat and home-front mentality, in a cultural psyche obsessed with grave concerns about the conflict and possible invasion, and about the bleak hardship of everyday life, such as government rationing of basic daily items, war-related shortages, and the sheer deprivation of the war. Home-front worries certainly made audiences more receptive to the darker visions depicted in film noir. As city factories hired workers away from small towns, the urbanization that took place during the war made the urban milieu of film noir more familiar than it would have been a decade before. The after-hours setting was also familiar, given that military production required twenty-four-hour shifts. And the darkened backgrounds in film noir resembled the shadowy abysses of blacked-out wartime cities at night.

Wartime anxiety also found cultural expression in other forms of popular culture—in radio dramas, comic books, and dime novels. By the 1930s, with tensions increasing in Europe, radio dramas like Orson Welles's *War of the Worlds* and the pulp adaptation of *The Shadow* featured bleak themes of invasion and mass chaos. The popularity of radio, comics, and new mass-market paperbacks had eroded some of the pulp and dime-novel market and even hit publications like *Black Mask* by 1940, and the rationing of paper during the war years was a severe blow to a pulp industry that had thrived earlier in the Depression years. As early as 1938, in Marvel comics pulp mysteries, publisher Martin Goodman conceived of taking stories from real life to combat fascism and demonize the Nazi menace. Marvel launched its war against the Axis powers in February 1940; then in March 1941, as the United States watched from the sidelines events abroad, superheroes the Sub-Mariner and the Human Torch teamed up to fight with the Allies in World War II. After Pearl Harbor Captain America, Miss America, and the Young Allies battled Hitler and the Japanese. Violence splashed across pages in graphic images. By June 1943 the Human Torch, simulating the fireball of aerial bombing, was destroying German super planes. Hollywood was also churning out popular serials. Batman battled the Axis in comic-book serials and on the big screen in Columbia's 1943 crime serial *Batman*, featuring the sinister enemy Doctor Daka, who kidnaps Americans, uses mind-control transmitters to "reprogram" them into zombie spies, feeds uncooperative agents to his pet alligators, and steals radium guns to develop a secret weapon to bomb U.S. cities. Pulp fiction writers similarly explored darker themes inspired by the war. Fears were even expressed in dime mystery novels like the September 1942 issue of *The Avenger* and the spring 1944 issue of *Black Book Detective*, both of which featured grisly crimes of torture and brutality.

During Production Code enforcement in the mid-1930s, censorship had intervened and delayed Hollywood's embrace of dark themes in American cinema. But the war changed film industry regulation, enabling Hollywood to target an increasingly sober home front with bolder content, which had a grittier edge and seedier visual style. The seductive world of film noir captured wartime fears and anxieties through violent action in unglamorous or disreputable working-class settings. A somber war-related zeitgeist grew out of harsh realities in America. As life on the home front became increasingly hard-boiled, so too did American film. America's involvement in the war penetrated every facet of daily life. Nearly everyone knew someone killed or wounded in combat. Pearl Harbor had stunned the nation. Everyday necessities were rationed and unavailable for the duration. Hollywood newsreels brought overseas combat to domestic audiences. These newsreels reflected a cultural perception of the war as America's morale took a hard knock. In 1989 World War II veteran Paul Fussell remembered this perception:

> For the past fifty years the Allied war has been sanitized and romanticized almost beyond recognition by the sentimental, the loony patriotic, the ignorant, and the bloodthirsty . . . Watching a newsreel or flipping through an illustrated magazine at the beginning of the American war, you were likely to encounter a memorable image: the newly invented jeep, an elegant, slim-barrelled 37-mm gun in tow, leaping over a hillock. Going very fast and looking as cute as Bambi, it flies into the air, and behind, the little gun bounces high off the ground on its springy tires . . . This graceful duo conveyed the firm impression of purposeful, resourceful intelligence going somewhere significant, and going there with speed, agility, and delicacy— almost wit.[3]

Originally countered by optimism early in the war, the grim circumstances eventually took shape in documentary images with graphic violence and an uncompromising style of realism. As the realities of combat, death, and destruction became more readily apparent, nonfiction and narrative films represented grisly actuality on theater screens. A bleak cultural terrain evolved during the war, as millions lost loved ones and casualties multiplied. The impact of this new cultural and social milieu was soon felt in the nation's film capital, affecting motion picture censorship and the industry's creative personnel. As Hollywood reacted to war, elements vital to the growth of film noir began to coalesce. Wartime Hollywood fused several *noir* influences, including cultural disillusionment, German expressionism, trends in realism, and hard-boiled fiction traditions. The Second World War created a complex array of social, economic, cultural, political, technological, and creative circumstances and was, in effect, a catalyst for film noir. Merging essential elements—such as the growth of documentary realism, studio-bound production, urban blackouts in Hollywood, filmmaking restrictions, new talent and artistic experimentation, Production Code lapses, and technological advancement—the war contributed to film noir's definitive style.

World War II influenced key aspects of Hollywood film production and shaped the unique conditions for the way film noir was created and shown to audiences. At the most practical level World War II accelerated film noir's development because essential materials such as lights, electricity, and film stock had been rationed, and other materials needed for sets and props were often in short supply. Citywide blackouts, enclosed or tarped sound stages, limits on location shooting, censorship of film content, and a severe labor shortage, as employable men departed for military duty, constrained production in unprecedented ways. At the same time, the war spurred technological advancements in lightweight camera equipment, with better lenses and high-speed light-sensitive film stock to enable night-for-night filming (often capitalizing on the expediency of wartime documentary newsreel realism conventions). World War II created opportunity for new talent in the Hollywood studio system. The film industry's wartime labor need gave greater creative (and executive) authority to talented European émigré filmmakers (for example, Michael Curtiz, Billy Wilder, Fritz Lang, and Rudolph Maté), women (for example, executives like *Phantom Lady* writer-producer Joan Harrison and *Gilda* producer Virginia Van Upp), and older men—that is, those who were over the age for combat (for example, hard-boiled writers Raymond Chandler and James M. Cain, stars Humphrey Bogart and Edward G. Robinson).

Working women in America's home front also affected how women were portrayed in film noir. Sexualized female roles targeted, and were influenced by, working wartime women, capitalizing on strong gender models while appealing to combat-hardened military men via a tough psyche and realistic violence toward the opposite sex. In the era of a bold "Rosie the Riveter" wartime female, Hollywood images such as the introductory close-up of Rita Hayworth's fabulous flip of the hair in *Gilda* and Lana Turner's entrance as blonde siren in a halter, hot pants, and high heels in *The Postman Always Rings Twice* exploited female sexuality to target a viewing audience of overseas GIs, returning veterans, often exposed to combat, and independent working women who had toughened up as the end of World War II drew near.

Less benign than Rosie the Riveter—but perhaps no less inspirational—

an iconic female arose with the war and the burgeoning *noir* series: the femme fatale. French critics Raymonde Borde and Etienne Chaumeton observed the stylized images that combined sensational violence with "a man who's already middle-aged, old almost, and not particularly handsome" and the bold emergence of a new type of woman, "masterminding crime, tough as the milieu surrounding her, as expert in blackmail and vice as in the use of firearms—and probably frigid—has left her mark on a noir eroticism that is at times an eroticization of violence." The femme fatale was deviant, a spider woman, "frustrated and guilty, half man-eater, half man-eaten, blasé and cornered, she falls victim to her own wiles."[4] Despite her strength, independence, and irreverence, however, the *noir* femme fatale was defined by the needs of the central male character. She was typically either a sexual threat or an innocent redeemer, the embodiment of male fears and fantasy. Often brutally treated, she still exuded sexuality and looked fully capable of emerging on a dark street to destroy the ill-fated protagonist. Stylish, loose, and unpredictable, this beautiful woman was, as Janey Place explains, "comfortable in the world of cheap dives, shadowy doorways and mysterious settings."[5]

The wartime American sociocultural and Hollywood filmmaking climate also allowed more latitude in film content—endorsing more crime and violence, particularly sexual violence, in these motion pictures. The cultural, production, and censorship climate in the United States changed as the war progressed. Eventually, newsreels and other propaganda openly depicted combat violence, war crimes, and atrocities, undermining Hollywood's moral patrol of the screen. It was no coincidence that studios adapted stories of domestic murder, illicit affairs, and crime. The sex, violence, sensational crime topics, and tabloid-style cinematic realism of wartime *noir* films benefited from changing patterns of censorship—and, indeed, helped cause those changes. Since 1934 Joseph Breen, chief censor for the Production Code Administration (PCA), presided over a complicated give-and-take with studio producers in the complex process of negotiation and compromise inherent in the film industry's self-regulation. Efforts to regulate onscreen sex, crime, cleavage, and violence were somewhat inconsistent owing to an overriding concern about a film's moral stance. Breen often negotiated with filmmakers, allowing some latitude on violence, for example, if conventional morality triumphed in the end. (Filmmakers craftily padded scripts with outrageously salacious material so that they could bargain for what they absolutely wanted Breen to approve in the final cut.) Violent crime films certainly were being produced by the 1930s, but their content was constrained by Production Code censorship. By the mid-1930s the PCA wielded considerable power, banning sordid screen adaptations of hard-boiled fiction such as James M. Cain's *Double Indemnity* and *The Postman Always Rings Twice.* Yet film noir flourished by the 1940s, particularly during and just after World War II, when PCA enforcement was still in place but was neither as draconian as it had been in the mid-1930s nor as liberal as it would be in the 1950s and 1960s. One reason for this development was wartime federal censorship, which complicated and often contradicted the conventional strictures of the Production Code. Midway through the war, by 1943 to early 1944, the government's patriotic political agenda motivated the federal Office of Censorship to lift its ban on depicting atrocities and war-related crimes in newsreels, in effect endorsing and promoting screen violence for propaganda purposes and establishing a precedent for narrative films, despite the film industry's PCA censorship of crime, violence, and political content.[6] Such complex industrial circumstances during World War II effectively compromised Production Code enforcement, enabling the screen adaptation and production of wartime *noir* films. The government's Office of War Information (OWI) and Office of Censorship banned Hollywood gangsters as un-American and regulated screen stories depicting the combat front or domestic home front to promote the war effort. The complexity of this wartime censorship environment led to hard-boiled film adaptations that initially depicted reformed gangsters and permitted—even promoted—patriotic crime, then avoided mentioning the war altogether to evade government regulation during World War II and anticipate postwar industry reconversion with nonwar narrative strategies. This complex, competing censorship environment throughout World War II was an important factor contributing to a rich 1940s film noir style. Censorship mediated the production process and influenced how these films were made. Ironically, the national effort to promote uplifting World War II propaganda did not preempt film noir. Instead, federal censorship regulation ultimately contributed to the growth of the dark trend. The drive for patriotic films actually paved the way for an increasing tolerance of violence and heralded a new type of Hollywood film.

The idea that film noir was a wartime phenomenon, however, has been largely dismissed or ignored by critics and scholars who have debated its nature and origins in American filmmaking. Since the 1946 inception of the term in France, scholarship on film noir has proliferated, but most studies emphasize its postwar development—possibly because the term *film noir* was coined after the war, when this dark trend was clearly apparent in Hollywood films. A long-standing critical debate has evolved over the nature of film noir as a postwar phenomenon or "period style." In his influential

"Notes on Film Noir," for example, Schrader has argued that America's entry into World War II interrupted the development of film noir that had begun with the definitive *Maltese Falcon* (1941) but was then stalled by the conflict, that upbeat wartime censorship regulation preempted the trend, and that film noir was essentially a postwar movement growing out of a "delayed reaction to the thirties." He explained:

> In 1946 French critics, seeing the American films they had missed
> during the war, noticed the new mood of cynicism, pessimism, and
> darkness that had crept into the American cinema . . . Hollywood
> lighting grew darker, characters more corrupt, themes more fatalistic,
> and the tone more hopeless. By 1949 American movies were in the
> throes of their deepest and most creative funk. Never before had films
> dared to take such a harsh uncompromising look at American life,
> and they would not dare to do so again for twenty years.

Schrader defined the *noir* series as "Hollywood films of the forties and early fifties that portrayed the world of dark, slick city streets, crime and corruption" in wartime (1941–46), postwar realistic (1945–49), and psychotic action and suicidal impulse (1949–53) films, followed by Robert Aldrich's *Kiss Me Deadly* (1955) and Orson Welles's *Touch of Evil* (1958), which rounded out the last of the classic *noir* cycle.[7] Although Robert Sklar and Thomas Schatz note the influence of the war on *noir*, many scholars—including Borde and Chaumeton, Robert Porfirio, Alain Silver and Elizabeth Ward, David Cook, Robert Ray, Frank Krutnik, Brian Neve, and James Naremore—refer, like Schrader, to *noir* as a decidedly postwar phenomenon.[8]

James Naremore, for instance, examines film noir as a distinctively French cultural construct of the literary and intellectual climate in Paris immediately following World War II, noting that "indigo moods, smoky jazz clubs, American fiction, [and] romantic isolation" were particularly relevant to the French critical conception of *noir*. He contextualizes film noir in relation to issues of French cultural reception. "In one sense, the French invented *film noir*, and they did so because local conditions predisposed them to view Hollywood in certain ways." Naremore references the sophisticated cine-club art culture pervading the pivotal "years between the postwar arrival of Hollywood movies in Paris and the beginnings of the French New Wave." He links *noir* to European avant-garde modernism, crime, "blood melodrama," and Gothic romance narratives.[9] Frank Krutnik provides a psychoanalytic framework, examining how masculinity and cultural issues influenced the postwar development of film noir. He suggests that film noir grew out of postwar realism and a decidedly postwar male psyche destabilized by shifting gender roles, by changing notions of masculinity, and by new rules of sexuality after World War II.[10]

In their benchmark 1955 study, *Panorama du film noir Américain, 1941–1953*, Borde and Chaumeton consider why American audiences had "become sensitized to films of violence and murder" and explain that by 1941 to 1942 "war affects the nation. Instantly, the documentary in all its forms (propaganda films or newsreels) assumes much greater importance in cinema programming, and the public acquires a taste for them. In the United States and England, as in the USSR, and later in Italy and France, the hostilities trigger the prodigious rise of cinematic realism. In the case of America, this realism engenders three new genres: the war film, the police documentary, and from a certain angle at least, film noir." Yet they argue that from 1941 to 1945 "the series is not yet a constituted genre" and consider 1946 to 1948 the glory days of film noir. They suggest that the war and the "discrepancy with official ideology" delayed the development of *noir*, which "lay dormant for five years," and that "the real advent of the series" did not occur until 1946. Borde and Chaumeton were keenly aware of the uncanny realism of American film noir. They noted the stylistic and narrative elements of violence and erotic metaphor in relation to psychoanalysis and sexual repression and referred to the *noir* cycle as a "series," with a definitive style, atmosphere, and subject matter, characterized by realistic settings, well-developed supporting roles, scenes of violence, and exciting pursuits. "The point of departure is realistic and, taken on its own, each scene could pass for a fragment of documentary," they observe. "It's the accumulation of these realistic shots on a bizarre theme that creates a nightmarish atmosphere" in a forbidden, complex underworld of blackmail, bribery, and organized crime depicting an ambiguous, confusing, criminal milieu where corrupt police inhabit a web of intrigue among a "whole host of angelic killers, neurotic gangsters, megalomaniac gang bosses, and disturbing or depraved stooges." Whereas the "documentary considers the murder from without, from the official police viewpoint," however, the distinctive cinematography and innovative narrative design in *noir* films are "from within, from the criminals'" point of view, employing a "different angle of vision."[11]

The French critics who first identified the *noir* series in 1946 were certainly aware that these pictures were products of the war years. Nino Frank wrote "Un Nouveau genre 'policier': L'Aventure criminelle" (A New Kind of "Police" Drama: The Criminal Adventure) in *L'Ecran Français*. Jean-Pierre Chartier penned "Les Américains aussi font des films noirs" (Americans Also Make *Noir* Films) in *Revue du cinéma,* a precursor to *Cahiers du cinéma.* Viewing these American films in France following the Occupation, Frank noted their distinctive visual style, complex narration, and psychological characters. He called films like *Double Indemnity* "harsh," "misogynistic," and "true to life," observing the "criminal psychology" and "dynamism of violent death" in "dark mysteries" on the "fringe of the law" where volatile criminals die at the end of a tortured journey, reinforcing the idea that crime does not pay.[12] Chartier recognized *noir*'s "forbidden" censorable nature, "pessimistic" first-person point of view, human despair, and "monstrous" women exploiting sex as a weapon tantalizing doomed crime victims.[13]

Other scholars briefly mention the war within more general film studies. In *Movie-Made America,* for example, Robert Sklar describes films noir as the "psychological thrillers that emerged at the time of the war," noting the "claustrophobia," "psychology," "look," and "pervasive tone" in 1940s films, where a "dark and constrictive mood derives in part from the material limitations of wartime filmmaking: restrictions on travel virtually eliminated location shooting where interior sets could serve, and stringent budgets seem to have cut down on lighting as well. Yet the gloom and constriction were not merely an accommodation to forced economies; their film-makers intended them that way." Influenced by Alfred Hitchcock's thrillers like *Suspicion,* with "its fascination with guilt and the ambiguous play of identities," he observes, the "hallmark of *film noir* is its sense of people trapped—trapped in webs of paranoia and fear, unable to tell guilt from innocence, true identity from false. Its villains are attractive and sympathetic, masking greed, misanthropy, malevolence. Its heroes and heroines are weak, confused, susceptible to false impressions. The environment is murky and close, the settings vaguely oppressive. In the end, evil is exposed, though often just barely, and the survival of good remains troubled and ambiguous."[14] In *Hollywood Genres* Thomas Schatz links film noir to the hardboiled detective genre and Orson Welles's *Citizen Kane;* in *Boom and Bust* the same author suggests a connection to Hitchcock's female gothic thrillers such as *Rebecca* and *Suspicion.* He proposes that cinematic realism during World War II created "an on-screen dynamic utterly unique to the war era. Meanwhile, a stylistic countercurrent developed in what came to be termed *film noir,* which explored the 'darker' side" of America's wartime psyche and experience.[15] In *A History of Narrative Film* David Cook considers that the war may not have interrupted the development of *film noir* and mentions the possibility that its "antiheroic vision" may have been a response to the "actual horrors of the war and the multiple hypocrisies of postwar American society."[16] In *The Kings of the Bs* Tom Flinn calls film noir "an essential part of the 1940s outlook, a cinematic style forged in the fires of war, exile, and disillusion, a melodramatic reflection for a world gone mad."[17]

Indeed, the proliferation of the *noir* series began during—and, in many ways, because of—World War II, as a trend spurred by *Double Indemnity* and enabled by the distinctive wartime factors that created the brooding 1940s period style. By investigating the actual production conditions of wartime Hollywood, this book looks at film noir before the term was coined and explores the war's role in creating it. Drawing on extensive archival research, it presents case studies of individual films and takes a behind-the-scenes look at the 1940s American film industry that produced these pictures by closely examining studio records of how and why they were made, as well as the impact of the war on filmmaking, censorship, and the way films were promoted and received by audiences. These bleak films evolved from unique filmmaking conditions during World War II and were a distinct product of wartime production and reception circumstances.

Prototypes for *noir* films began appearing before America's entry into the war in December 1941. Influenced by earlier traditions, *noir* style was emerging by 1940 and 1941 in such films as RKO's low-budget *Stranger on the Third Floor* (1940), Orson Welles's *Citizen Kane* (1941), Alfred Hitchcock's *Suspicion* (1941), and John Huston's adaptation of Dashiell Hammett's *The Maltese Falcon* (1941)—preludes to Paramount's adaptation of Graham Greene's *This Gun for Hire,* which straddled the wartime transition in late 1941 and early 1942. *This Gun for Hire* was tailor-made for wartime America and benefited from conditions leading up to the war and lapses in censorship that enabled proto-*noir* crime and violence to be produced with Code approval.

In the aftermath of Pearl Harbor, *noir* elements coalesced. Hollywood felt the impact of World War II on filmmaking conditions, motion picture censorship, the studio industry, and the cultural climate by 1942–43. Wartime preludes to film noir showcased paranoia, tough guys, espionage, and patriotic crime to support the war effort in prototype films such as *This Gun for Hire, Casablanca* (1942), and *Ministry of Fear,* where filmmaking constraints, documentary realism, and graphic violence influenced cinematic style. A decreased use of lighting is readily evident in these films, and in wartime *noir* pictures like *Moontide* (1942) and *Street of Chance* (1942), culminating in a definitive, full-blown exemplar of the *noir* crime cycle's steady emergence over several years in *Double Indemnity.*

By 1943 and 1944 true film noir emerged. Filmed during the blackouts and rationing and amid the fear and anxiety of wartime Los Angeles, *Dou-*

ble Indemnity is a fascinating case study that shows how home-front culture, institutional constraints, and economic conditions affected *noir* production. The film provided an influential model for gaining PCA approval of stories dealing with taboo crime material, using wartime realism and a psychological framework. *Murder, My Sweet* and *The Postman Always Rings Twice* show how in many ways Hollywood's growing *noir* crime trend responded to the success of *Double Indemnity.*

These films also targeted a wartime audience segregated by gender via industry filmmaking strategies and distribution systems aimed at a dual, parallel domestic home-front and military combat-front market. *Phantom Lady, Mildred Pierce,* and *Gilda* illustrate how *noir* pictures included increasing female involvement in the filmmaking process. These films reveal the distinctive female "authorship" and creative control by women in the motion picture industry (such as writer-producer Joan Harrison at Universal, writer Catherine Turney at Warner Bros., and production executive Virginia Van Upp at Columbia), specifically in the production of films noir. How gender played out on Hollywood screens, and how women were represented as "transgressive" *noir* femme fatales opposite tormented male masculinity, corresponded to a wartime female labor force inside the film industry, as well as in other areas of the domestic home front.

Film noir related to American motion picture industry trends such as the move toward independent and "hyphenate" production and the increasing role of writer-producer-directors like in-house studio producer-director Howard Hawks at Warner Bros., Fritz Lang and Nunnally Johnson at RKO, and Lang with Walter Wanger and Joan Bennett at Universal. In making and publicizing many of these *noir* pictures, filmmakers capitalized by 1944 and 1945 on sensational Hollywood promotional strategies exploiting sex and violence (in the guise of so-called realism) and evaded censorship constraints. The global conflict also refined the roles of stars in these films. Humphrey Bogart is the perfect example of this—recast from gangster and hard-boiled detective to undercover counterespionage agent, from independent isolationist to reluctant patriot and conflicted combat squad leader, then back to hard-boiled *noir* antihero. Benefiting from the gritty wartime era, Bogart rose during these years from supporting player and villain to star and hero. The war also made his non–leading man looks more palatable to wartime audiences. Another World War II–era film star, Edward G. Robinson, was also far from leading-man handsome (and also moved from playing gangsters to playing home-front everymen). As independent (and quasi-independent) production rose during the war, such films as *Laura, Detour, The Woman in the Window, Scarlet Street, To Have and Have Not,* and *The Big Sleep* reinforced and perpetuated the wartime *noir* style and were prime examples of more autonomous filmmakers gaining greater creative and executive control within Hollywood's studio system.

Before the conflict concluded, as early as 1943—shortly before Paramount filmed *Double Indemnity*—through 1944 and 1945, Hollywood's *noir* crime trend also related to studios anticipating the end of the war. In an American film industry transitioning from a wartime economy, film noir flourished as a popular and visionary business strategy by studios to produce non-war-related crime pictures in the final war years. The influence and legacy of the wartime *noir* series can be seen in later productions, such as *The Blue Dahlia* (1946) and Orson Welles's *The Stranger* (1946), and in the postwar proliferation of films noir. In the aftermath of World War II, as Hollywood faced myriad challenges from competing leisure activities and government regulation of the studio system, national politics moved increasingly toward a new cold war ideology as America's political and cultural imperative shifted from fighting the Nazis and the Japanese in open combat to containing communism, both on the international stage and on the home front. Hollywood filmmakers responded by reinventing the *noir* genre. Indeed, changes in the postwar era would ultimately modify the unique wartime filmmaking environment—including motion picture censorship, creative talent, and narrative film conventions—that had produced these definitive films and contributed to their extraordinary visual style and in turn affected the evolution of this dark trend after the war years. The cycle of films forged in the hot war of the 1940s evolved to support, protest, or simply reflect the cold war of the 1950s.

The Elements of *Noir* Come Together

A shaft of white light used properly can be far more effective than all the color in the world. The extensive range of black and white with its . . . variations is capable of producing all the visual drama . . . the greatest art . . . to give life to the dead space that exists between the lens and the subject . . . Smoke, rain, fog, dust, and steam can emotionalize empty space, and so can the movement of the camera.
—Josef von Sternberg, *Fun in a Chinese Laundry,* 1965

ilm noir certainly had roots in earlier dark films, many of which involved crime. Innovative preludes—in the United States, Germany, France, and Britain—advanced its evolution, fusing expressionism with hard-hitting realism. Silent-era American gangster pictures included D. W. Griffith's *The Musketeers of Pig Alley* (1912), which was recognized for its documentary style based on newspaper accounts of real crime. The visual design of Cecil B. DeMille's adulterous melodrama *The Cheat* (1915) was applauded for its low-key chiaroscuro pools of Rembrandt or Lasky lighting. Starring Sessue Hayakawa and Fanny Ward, it featured an illicit rendezvous, an interracial love triangle involving a married woman, a branding, a graphic struggle, a near-rape, a shooting, and swapping money for sex and brutality. As in later *noir* films like *The Big Sleep,* its sexual violence and shadowy, exotic Oriental mise-en-scène visually conveyed a mysterious world of perverse evil and taboo, explicit, or scandalous subjects.

After the First World War, German filmmakers produced a series of moody psychological horror films, among them Robert Weine's *The Cabinet of Dr. Caligari* (1919); F. W. Murnau's *Nosferatu* (1922); and Fritz Lang's *Der Mude Tod* (1921), *Dr. Mabuse, The Gambler* (1922), *Metropolis* (1926), and *M* (1931). *The Cabinet of Dr. Caligari* used claustrophobic studio interiors (even for outdoor settings), distorted spatial relationships, highly stylized sets, extreme makeup and costumes, skewed camera angles, and chiaroscuro lighting to subjectively portray a deranged narrator's point of view. *Caligari* influenced later films in its expressionist visual style, which capitalized on postwar material restrictions. As in wartime Hollywood, Weimar Germany's shortages of film stock, rationing of materials and lighting, and severe economic constraints contributed greatly to its images and design. Artificial backdrops were "pragmatic as well as thematically appropriate since, in the economic recession that immediately followed the war, the film studios, like all other German industries, were allocated electric power on a quota basis."[1] Stylization could be efficient, as David Cook explains. "In a film like *Caligari* that required many dramatic lighting effects, it was cheaper and more convenient to simply paint light and shadow onto the scenery itself than to produce the effect electrically (in fact, the Decla studio had nearly expended its power ration when *Caligari* was produced in late 1919)."[2] This was "yet another instance of the way in which technological necessity can foster aesthetic innovation in the cinema"[3]—as it would in Hollywood some decades later. Germany's state-run studio, Universum Film Aktiengesellschaft (UFA), produced many expressionist pictures in the post–World War I Weimar era. Filmmakers in Berlin benefited from the creative synergy of the Bauhaus, which, like the artistic community in Paris, was a burgeoning center of modern arts in Europe.

In 1926–27 American studios Paramount and MGM infused substantial capital into UFA under the ParUfaMet international distribution agreement, providing the German film industry with financial relief and supporting film production in the economically unstable Weimar era. ParUfaMet's transatlantic alliance also enabled Hollywood to tap into Germany's vulnerable film industry and raid UFA's creative talent. By the late 1920s and early 1930s German films showed signs of change toward an increasingly realistic style. Unsavory, shadowy, and downbeat "street pictures," known as *Kammerspielfilm,* such as G. W. Pabst's *The Joyless Street* (1925) and *Pandora's Box* (1929), combined stark realism with expressionist style—an aesthetic melding that influenced film noir. As the Third Reich rose to power, the Nazis—regarding expressionism, along with depictions of sex and crime in brooding realistic films like Fritz Lang's *M,* as the unhealthy, degenerate art of the Weimar era—took control of the state-run UFA studio from 1933 to 1945. (After the Nazis banned his 1933 crime picture *The Testament of Dr. Mabuse,* Lang left Germany. Goebbels had offered him—and he rejected—an UFA position producing films for the Third Reich. As Goebbels launched a campaign to purge Jews from the German film industry, escapist musical comedy features like *Viktor Viktoria* complemented documentaries like Leni Riefenstahl's 1935 propaganda masterpiece *Triumph of the Will.*) Talented Germans and Europeans from the filmmaking environment of pre-Nazi UFA fled to other countries in Europe or to the United States. Those who sought refuge in Paris joined a large émigré community. This migration of German talent to the French film industry coincided with "poetic realism," an important influence on film noir, and an established tradition of stylistically dark French films on unsavory urban topics—as in Russian émigré director Dmitri Kirsanov's *Menilmontant* (1924), produced in Paris; Jean

Renoir's *La Chienne* (1931) and *Les Bas-fonds* (The Lower Depths) (1936); Julien Duvivier's *Pépé le Moko* (1937); and Marcel Carne's *Quai des brumes* (Port of Shadows) (1938), *Hotel du Nord* (1938), and *Le Jour se leve* (Daybreak) (1939).

By the 1930s and early 1940s Hollywood's low-budget horror cycle was benefiting from this new immigrant talent—especially at Universal and Paramount studios. Seminal American horror films included Tod Browning's *Dracula* (1931), shot by former UFA photographer Karl Freund. Browning's film initiated the cycle, which included James Whale's *Frankenstein* (1931), *The Old Dark House* (1932), *The Invisible Man* (1933), and *Bride of Frankenstein* (1935), as well as with Karl Freund's *The Mummy* (1932), Robert Florey's *Murders in the Rue Morgue* (1932, shot by Freund), Edgar Ulmer's *The Black Cat* (1934), Roland Lee's *Son of Frankenstein* (1939), Arthur Lubin's *Black Friday* (1940), George Waggner's *The Wolf Man* (1941), and Edwin Marin's horror-spy hybrid *Invisible Agent* (1942)—all produced at Universal. Rouben Mamoulian's *Dr. Jekyll and Mr. Hyde* (1932), designed by UFA-alumnus Hans Dreier, and Robert Siodmak's *Son of Dracula* (1943) were produced at Paramount. Hollywood crime films also benefited from the aesthetic cross-fertilization between Germany and the United States as a result of ParUfaMet and, later, the war in Germany. As expatriate talent flocked to Hollywood, films tackled crime and critiqued social problems.

Throughout American popular culture—radio dramas, hard-boiled crime novels, magazine serials, short stories, comic books, dime novels, and gangster films—artists and hacks alike portrayed Jazz Age crime with gritty realism that relied on tabloid and pulp fiction sensation. Cultural expressions of crime included popular radio dramas like Orson Welles's *The Shadow;* comics characters such as *Dick Tracy, Secret Agent X-9* (originally written by Dashiell Hammett), and *The Spirit;* Marvel comics and pulp mysteries; detective mystery serials in *Black Mask, Dime Detective Magazine, Detective Story, Detective Fiction Weekly,* and *Dime Mystery* (even crime stories in mainstream publications like *Liberty* magazine); and *The Avenger* and *Black Book Detective* dime mystery novels. Hard-boiled fiction proliferated in America in the grim Depression years. Hammett, James M. Cain, Raymond Chandler, and Cornell Woolrich contributed crime yarns with tough characters and graphic violence. Like pulp stories and contemporary newsreels on actual gangsters, crime films showed sadistic violence (toward women and even animals) with a distinctive fast-paced style and shadowy look to convey their seedy atmosphere of speakeasies, cabarets, jazz, and booze. Drawn from sensational tales of real street crime in 1920s and 1930s America, early crime films—often depicting the gangster as an urban Robin

Hood—coincided with Prohibition (1919–33), when the public regarded gangsters with some ambivalence. Gangster pictures enjoyed popularity during the Great Depression—a bleak era when many felt helpless to effect any economic or social change and when the system seemed on the verge of collapse. Hollywood antiheroes took action, tried to beat the system, did something with their lot in life, and seemed to articulate cultural issues intrinsically embedded in American society. Tracing the criminal's poor beginnings, profit from the rackets, rising prominence, and inevitable demise, these tough male-oriented films dealt with working-class struggles, portraying the common man or ethnic immigrant seeking success or acculturation in mainstream America. Set on the streets of a magnetic, corrupt American city, crime pictures featured visual iconography—guns, car chases, cops, crooks, nightclubs, swanky apartments, urbane clothes—documenting the gangster's wealth and power, but they marginalized women, relegating them to peripheral roles as mothers, sisters, or molls.

The Hollywood gangster genre developed an innovative visual style at Paramount and Warner Bros. At Paramount director Josef von Sternberg, a sensuous pictorialist, collaborated with designer Dreier on silent-era films like the influential gangster classic *Underworld* (1927, written by former reporter Ben Hecht), *The Drag Net* (1928, now lost), and *The Docks of New York* (1928). Sternberg's atmospheric crime pictures anticipated *noir* crime melodramas with what Rudolph Arnheim called "uncannily lewd detail" as a prostitute "lustfully strokes" a sailor's "naked arm with indecent tattoo marks all over it, as he ripples the muscles on it for her amusement . . . This woman sees nothing of the man but power, nudity, muscle."[4] In the lax censorship climate of pre-Code Hollywood, suggestive visual innuendo heightened rough, raw, working-class sex and crime in the shadows—achieved without dialogue. Stylized mise-en-scène metaphorically captured a forbidden, sordid milieu.

In the sound era, crime films gained immense sensory appeal and enormous popularity—reproducing sirens, screams, and gunfire, while relying on tough, urban dialogue. Warner Bros. became known for its gangster pictures such as Mervin LeRoy's *Little Caesar* (1930), starring Edward G. Robinson, and William Wellman's *Public Enemy* (1931), starring James Cagney, and for realistic "social problem" films like LeRoy's powerful *I Am a Fugitive from a Chain Gang* (1932). *Scarface* (1932), directed by Howard Hawks, adapted by Hecht, produced by Howard Hughes, and released through United Artists, starred Paul Muni as the quintessential gangster antihero. Its lethal finale (one of several endings shot to appease censors) shows Muni gunned down by authorities—riddled with machine-gun bullets—falling dead on a shadowy rain-soaked city street. *Scarface* was controversial for the Hays Office because it sympathetically portrayed crime and criminals and suggested an incestuous relationship between the gangster (Muni) and his sister (Ann Dvorak). Negotiations with censors delayed the 1931 production an entire year before a revised ending was finally created and the film released in 1932. Many crime films like *Public Enemy, I Am a Fugitive from a Chain Gang,* and *Heroes for Sale* (1933) depicted World War I veterans, scarred by the brutality of war, returning to a Prohibition (and, later, Depression) era America where violence, social injustice, and corruption is rampant and basic day-to-day survival is a challenge.

Like the tough moll in gangster pictures, unruly "fallen" women anticipated the *noir* femme fatale. Married Fanny Ward (*The Cheat*), salacious Jean Harlow (*Red Headed Woman,* 1932), and lethal Bette Davis (*Marked Woman,* 1937; *The Letter,* 1940) draw guns and blow their male costars away. Like dangerous enchantress Lulu (Louise Brooks) precipitating the antihero's ruin in Pabst's *Pandora's Box* or Maria's (Brigitte Helm) evil robotic alter ego stirring up mayhem in Lang's *Metropolis,* Sternberg's pictures with Marlene Dietrich—*The Blue Angel* (1930), *Morocco* (1930), *Shanghai Express* (1932), and *Blonde Venus* (1932)—provide a template for the seductive femme fatale of the 1940s. In *Blonde Venus* mother/diva Dietrich's independence, androgynous and masculine attire, cabaret career, and sexuality are such transgressive threats to her estranged husband (Herbert Marshall) that he has her hounded by police. After an adulterous affair with millionaire Cary Grant she ends up on the run, frequenting destitute dives and seducing a police detective to her bedroom while posing as a prostitute. Sternberg's stylized lighting caresses Dietrich's features, as Marshall, wearing a fedora that completely shadows his face, informs her he'll be taking away her five-year-old son (Dickie Moore).

Another pre-Code film, RKO's *What Price Hollywood?* (1932), starring Constance Bennett and Lowell Sherman, produced by Pandro S. Berman and executive producer David O. Selznick, directed by George Cukor, showed innovative pre-*noir* style in its powerful climax. An elaborate montage sequence with impressive special effects by Slavko Vorkapich and Lloyd Knechtel featured extreme skewed low angles, rapid cutting, slow motion, superimposed prison bars, and moody sound effects, depicting a self-destructive alcoholic director's suicide in the unlit bedroom of a married starlet (whom he had "discovered" and who just bailed him out of jail). In fine *noir* fashion he searches in the dark for a match to light a cigarette, finds a gun instead, and looks in the mirror. His washed-up life and career flash before him (expanding time in a dazzling series of slow-motion montage shots), revealing a nightmare hallucination of shame and guilt as he pulls the trigger and then falls to the floor.

Despite the popularity of crime in American popular culture, mid-1930s film censorship banned Hollywood from adapting hard-boiled fiction stories and diluted the sexual content and excessive violence in crime pictures, delaying *noir* film trends. While tough-guy heroes and corrupt urban settings dominated screens in early gangster films, once the Hollywood motion picture industry established the Production Code Administration and began enforcing censorship by late 1934, censors were more inclined to discourage promiscuity, brutality, and romantic portrayals of gangsters involved in unsavory or illegal activity (such as labor racketeering and prostitution). After *Public Enemy* made Cagney a star as a gangster in the pre-Code era, Warner Bros. recast him as a crime-fighting FBI enforcer in *G-Men* (1935); gangster-turned-cop Robinson went undercover to break up the mob opposite tough-guy Humphrey Bogart in *Bullets or Ballots* (1936). Shadowy social-problem "message" pictures like Lang's *Fury* (1936) and *You Only Live Once* (1937, starring Henry Fonda as an ex-con), William Wyler's *Dead End* (1937), Michael Curtiz's *Angels with Dirty Faces* (1938), and Anatole Litvak's *Confessions of a Nazi Spy* (1939, based on an actual spy case) featured crime themes. Moody visuals evolved in Robert Florey's *Daughter of Shanghai* (1938), designed by Hans Dreier and Robert Odell, starring sleuth Anna May Wong; *The Face Behind the Mask* (1941), coscripted by Paul Jarrico, starring Peter Lorre as an immigrant turned disfigured crime boss; and Sternberg's *The Shanghai Gesture* (1941), starring Gene Tierney. Pre-*noir* B crime films included German-émigré John Brahm's *Rio* (1939) and *Let Us Live* (1939), recasting Fonda as an innocent "wrong man" framed by circumstances on death row, and Charles Vidor's *Blind Alley* (1939), starring hoodlum Chester Morris, moll Dvorak, and psychology professor Ralph Bellamy. (Brahm later directed the 1944 *noir* gothic thriller *The Lodger*.) Proto-*noir* style is seen in John Ford's *Stagecoach* (1939), shot by veteran silent-era cinematographer Bert Glennon (who filmed Sternberg's *Underworld, Blonde Venus,* and *Scarlet Empress*), and in *The Grapes of Wrath* (1940) and *The Long Voyage Home* (1940), both shot by Gregg Toland. Welles studied *Stagecoach* before directing *Citizen Kane*.

World War I veterans adapted their combat skills and turned to a violent life of crime in W. S. Van Dyke's *They Gave Him a Gun* (1937) and Raoul Walsh's *The Roaring Twenties* (1939), which simulated *March of Time* newsreels, starred Cagney and real-life World War I veteran Bogart, and nostalgically critiqued Prohibition-era crime and the gangster genre itself with the film's final line, "He used to be a big shot," describing murdered veteran

Tough guys Johnny Sarto (Edward G. Robinson, *right*) and Jack Buck (Humphrey Bogart) engage in hand-to-hand combat in *Brother Orchid*.
Warner Bros., 1940.

and reformed gangster Eddie Bartlett (Cagney). Lloyd Bacon's *Brother Orchid* (1940) parodied Warners' gangster cycle; rival Bogart nearly kills off mobster Robinson, who is revived and then reformed into a monk at the serene Monastery of the Little Brothers of the Flowers. (Little Caesar's conversion from a kingpin to a divine pacifist—resembling Friar Tuck—combines gangster-comedy and social drama, seemingly paying homage to PCA piety.) Walsh's *High Sierra* (1941) featured Bogart in his first lead and fittingly wrote the epitaph for the gangster genre, initiating a new kind of crime trend and offering a new image of screen masculinity.

In this new era fresh talent with innovative and provocative ideas would gain greater creative control over the filmmaking process as the motion picture industry neared wartime. In 1939 writer-director-star Orson Welles and British producer-director Alfred Hitchcock (who had worked at UFA early in his career) came to Hollywood as John Huston was rising up the ranks from writer to writer-director. All three would exert powerful influence on 1940s films widely regarded as *noir* prototypes. Huston's *The Maltese Falcon* (1941) recast Warner Bros.' 1930s gangster-crime tradition in a more hard-boiled 1940s style with a faithful rendering of Dashiell Hammett's tough detective fiction. Alfred Hitchcock's suspense films translated British *roman noir* novels into gothic thrillers. Orson Welles's collaboration with cinematographer Gregg Toland introduced visual flourishes and narrative techniques that *noir* filmmakers would seize on later in the decade. It was, however, an unheralded director and a largely forgotten film that first anticipated film noir.

Directed by former writer and Russian émigré Boris Ingster, RKO's B picture (produced by Lee Marcus, written by Frank Partos and an uncredited Nathanael West) *Stranger on the Third Floor* fused the expressionist aesthetic of earlier horror films with a journalistic investigative murder story in a style evoking Fritz Lang's *M* and recast its psychopathic murderer, German expatriate star Peter Lorre. RKO historian Richard B. Jewell calls it a "B-unit curiosity . . . a premature *film noir,* a picture that should, by all historical rights, have been produced in 1944 or 1945—not 1940."[5] Produced in the summer of 1940, the film features baroque, low-key cinematography by Nicholas Musuraca, which captured the claustrophobic mise-en-scène of famed RKO art director Van Nest Polglase and Albert S. D'Agostino. Known for the art deco style in Fred Astaire–Ginger Rogers musicals, Polglase would design *Citizen Kane* the next year. Also of note is outstanding special effects montage work by Vernon L. Walker.

Stranger on the Third Floor producer Lee Marcus ran RKO's B unit, supervising all the studio's low-budget releases. In 1938, then corporate president Leo Spitz encouraged Marcus to "produce some 'exploitation' pictures—films dealing with subject matter of a topical and slightly sensational nature. Marcus' initial response was *Smashing the Rackets* . . . inspired by the career of New York district attorney Thomas E. Dewey," in which Chester Morris "blasted his way through a morass of skulduggery and corruption, sweeping the city clean in 80 minutes [of] . . . breathless, pugnacious entertainment, bursting with a vitality often lacking in programme pictures."[6] Writer Frank Partos, a newspaperman educated at New York University, began at MGM and Paramount, serving on the Screen Writers Guild board. He worked on Brahm's pre-*noir* B film *Rio, The Uninvited* (1944), *And Now Tomorrow* (1944, with Raymond Chandler), *The Snake Pit* (1948), and *Night without Sleep* (1952). Writer Nathanael West, whose Republic B pictures *The President's Mystery* (1936) and *It Could Happen to You* (1937) featured what Brian Neve calls "unusual political awareness," polished the script for *Stranger on the Third Floor.*[7] As B-movie historian Don Miller observes:

> Out of nowhere in 1940 came *Stranger on the Third Floor,* a highly original, brooding little gem directed by Boris Ingster, a Russian with

no ear for American speech patterns but great facility with story construction who had labored for several years as a writer. His directorial
debut was auspicious, especially for a low-budget film . . . The Partos
script, obviously a homage to Dostoyevsky . . . is narrated in stream-
of-consciousness dialogue by the reporter. It's a carefully wrought
screenplay, but it's likely that, good as it is, it would be far less effective
in the hands of an ordinary director. Ingster contributes immeasurably to its success . . . for some striking camera images, all the more
unusual to be on display in a limited budget B film.[8]

Ingster had come to America from Russia sometime after the Revolution (immigration Americanized his name from Azar). Assistant director
on *Romance sentimentale* (1930), a short film directed in Paris by Sergei
Eisenstein and Grigori Aleksandrov and considered an early surrealist
avant-garde classic, Ingster's writing credits included *The Last Days of Pom-
peii* (1935), *Dancing Pirate* (1936), *Song of Russia* (1944), which he rewrote
to tone down wartime communist themes, and Fritz Lang's *Cloak and Dagger* (1946). He also served as writer-director on *The Judge Steps Out*
(1947–49) and the B *noir* classic *Southside 1-1000* (1950), before moving to
television as a producer on *Wagon Train*, *The Roaring 20s*, and *The Man
from UNCLE*. Although not a member of the Communist Party, Ingster
sometimes served as executive officer for the Screen Writers Guild and was
involved in its battle for recognition in the late 1930s. *Stranger on the Third
Floor* cinematographer Nicholas Musuraca was a specialist in what came to
be known as *noir* style.[9]

Ingster's film presents a cynical view of justice and uses multiple flashbacks to depict the nightmares, paranoia, and psychotic impulses of its tormented antihero, rookie newspaper reporter Michael Ward (John
McGuire). Ward witnesses a murder and furthers his career by covering the
story and testifying in court. Consumed by guilt, he faces a crisis of conscience after finding he has wrongly accused an innocent cab driver, Joe
Briggs (Elisha Cook Jr.), of the crime while the real killer, "the Stranger"
(Lorre), stalks the night, slashes throats, and prowls Ward's shadowy apartment building. Ward imagines that his loathsome neighbor, whom he has
threatened to kill, is murdered and that he is framed for the crime. Pan-
icked, Ward awakens to discover that his nightmare has actually occurred,
and he is arrested. Like a female crime detective, the reporter's fiancée, Jane
(Margaret Tallichet)—a decent, working *noir* heroine rather than a sexual
temptress—investigates the murder to clear his name and save Ward from
the electric chair. She solves the case by finding—and nearly becoming vic-

tim to—the throat-slashing Stranger, who turns out to be an insane asylum escapee.

Like social proto-*noir* 1930s films *M, You Only Live Once,* and *Let Us Live, Stranger on the Third Floor* reveals a corrupt and ineffectual criminal justice system. In the courtroom jurors and even the judge doze off, seeming not to care about the testimony that will determine an innocent man's fate and send him to the electric chair. Political officials, district attorneys, and law enforcement officers are bumbling and inept. Seasoned crime reporters indict the legal process, mocking justice yet complicitly tolerating its blatant lack of accomplishing any fair or effective solutions to crimes. Framing innocent victims and letting criminals go free, the system shows that justice does not prevail and provides no hope that this miserable state of affairs will ever change. The system's futile injustice reinforces Ward's guilt. Like later classic *noir* films, *Stranger on the Third Floor* presents a bleak view of its urban environment. Shadowy and cramped, its claustrophobic city is a dangerous and ruthless place where bureaucratic law-and-order institutions have broken down and will inhumanely bring about the demise of, rather than protect, its individual inhabitants. Even the heroine's solution to the case by finding Lorre's maniac occurs by chance—as does his sudden demise when a truck swiftly skids and accidentally mows him down.

Though much discussed, violent crimes are never shown. Simulating tabloid sensation, Ingster uses the nonfiction journalistic and courtroom investigational proceedings as a "realistic" ruse to justify vividly brutal content—dialogue describes grisly murder details in graphic accounts of blood, knives, and sliced throats. On the witness stand accused murderer Briggs recalls, "It wasn't very nice. His throat was cut. Blood was still dripping into the open drawer of the cash register." Another witness notes "a great deal of violence—the head was almost severed from the body." Filmmakers haggled with PCA censors about a variety of objections—including drinking, nudity, and sexual affairs—from early May 1940 well into the summer. The most controversial aspect of Ingster's film, however, was not the gory violence of its premise or its criminal brutality but rather another matter: "the business of the voices talking to the hero, Michael, throughout a great deal of this story, and Michael's reactions hitherto, suggest that Michael is suffering from some form of insanity . . . This same point applies in a lesser degree to the Stranger who is described as having 'an almost maniacal glint in his bulging eyes.'"[10] PCA censors had issues about depicting insanity in both Lorre's criminal stranger and hero McGuire's guilt-ridden fears—worrying about his capacity to actually be the murderer or be framed for the crime by circumstantial evidence—brilliantly rendered in shadowy psychological nightmares. The fact that Ward, in his voice-over narration, actually questions his own sanity in the dreams, flashbacks, and premonition sequences only added fuel to the censors' fire.

Insanity had long been a concern for censors. For instance, although set in a pastoral lakefront country home, the pre-*noir* picture *Blind Alley* and its title referred to gangster Chester Morris's psychotic criminal mind, corrupted by the city, revealed in vivid style through reverse-exposure images of his recurring nightmares. MGM originally tried to adapt the play on which the story was based, *Smoke Screen,* in 1935, but censors nixed the project and told the studio to "dismiss it entirely from further consideration" because its gangster hero was "thoroughly unacceptable," insisting the story violated the Code "so bad . . . that it was irrevocably beyond its pale," especially "the *suicide* of the gangster, as a means of escape from the consequences of his crimes."[11] Because it depicted crime, suicide, and psychosis, *Blind Alley* was shelved for several years until Columbia filmed it in 1939, just before RKO produced *Stranger on the Third Floor,* when the PCA advised against displaying weapons or showing crime details and warned that British censors would reject "any material dealing with insane characters and the use of an asylum as a background."[12] In 1938 Selznick's effort to adapt Daphne du Maurier's novel *Rebecca*—a masterwork of infidelity, dysfunctional sexual relationships, and domestic murder, with eerie first-person narration ("Last night I dreamt I went to Manderley again . . . ")—drew fire from censors for its immoral crimes, its hero getting away with murder, and its depiction of the protagonist's psychological instability. Female hysteria, crimes of passion, and insanity, hallmarks of Alfred Hitchcock's *roman noir* thrillers, were highly censorable. Although the PCA discouraged depictions of insanity and illegal activity onscreen, the popularity of psychoanalysis encouraged psychological themes in *Blind Alley, Dark Victory, Stranger on the Third Floor, Rebecca, Suspicion, Citizen Kane, This Gun for Hire, King's Row, Street of Chance, Now Voyager, Shadow of a Doubt, Spellbound,* and many wartime *noir* pictures. Censors reiterated concern over the depiction of insanity in *Stranger on the Third Floor* for three months, from May 7 to July 24, and even added a P.S. to its PCA seal: "The British Board of Film Censors will delete scenes of Peter Lorre if they regard him as insane. Other political censor boards will probably delete the [psychological nightmare] scenes of the [imagined] death march, and of the death chamber, and Ward being strapped in the electric chair."[13]

The film's proletarian social critique is significant and even more distinctive than that in many later *noirs.* Two major themes emerge in the film—its emphasis on social injustice, money, poverty, and Depression-era anxieties, and the overwhelming feeling of guilt suffered by its protagonist. Social and cultural changes taking place in the United States between World War I and World War II influenced 1920s–30s American popular culture, including social-realist theater and working-class fiction, and dealt with the dashed hopes and meager existence that so many endured in the Great Depression. Like hard-boiled detective fiction, these working-class themes flourished during a time when many were down on their luck and survived because they were willing to do the humblest work. Championing individuals, the working-class hero—or antihero like the gangster, ex-con, tough everyman turning to crime just to survive, or the streetwise hard-boiled detective—was a man who lived by his wits and challenged corrupt institutions in a hardscrabble world. Emerging from the Depression, many ordinary people surviving the 1930s could identify with such working-class themes. Like later *noir* pictures, Ingster's film critiques the American Dream to suggest it is an unpredictable urban nightmare of gloom and futility. Ward's struggling protagonist mutters how his low-rent boardinghouse is a dive. Commenting on the very *noir* visuals that surround him in the black stairway of the apartment building, he complains: "What a gloomy dump. Why don't they put in a bigger lamp?" The film suggests that if he had more money to "move up" in the world, he'd live in a big, bright house with an abundance of light, ensuring his comfort and safety. If his landlord had, or spent, more money—and if the B picture was a more lavish A film—images would be bathed in the high-key radiance of bigger, brighter lamps.

The low-budget production constraints in *Stranger on the Third Floor* aided the film's ominously shrouded visuals in depicting a shady working-class milieu. Ingster and Musuraca created a black abyss, achieving striking film noir images on an economical budget. As material concerns and filmmaking constraints tightened by 1940, with the war ramping up overseas and the U.S. becoming more directly involved, *Stranger on the Third Floor* was a top-tiered B picture filmed on a small budget put to good effect with shooting confined mainly to contained sound stages. Drawing from expressionist horror films, Ingster and Musuraca used camerawork to portray a nightmarish world, framing characters and action from skewed angles. A series of montages conveys the disturbed state of Ward's psyche, most strikingly when out-of-kilter, oblique "Dutch" angles highlight a hallucination in which a mob encircles him and accuses him of murder in a cramped interrogation room. The walls behind Ward seem to come alive with elaborate weblike patterns to reveal his delirium, while bars of doom and crisscrossing shadows emphasize his entrapment and inner turmoil. Harsh "demon" lighting (lit from below to contort facial features, as in horror pictures) and twisted close-ups expose vicious characters indicting him for the crime. The sound track amplifies Ward's dislocation from reality. Eerie music, ominous voices, and his distraught conscience haunt Ward, providing a desperate narration as he talks to himself and signaling a spiral of hysteria closing in on him. As Tom Flinn observes:

> The dream sequence itself is so completely expressionistic in style that it resembles an animation of one of Lynd Ward's woodcut novels (*God's Man, Madman's Drum*) with strong contrasts in lighting, angular shadow patterns, and distorted, emblematic architecture; in short, a kind of total stylization that manages to be both extremely evocative and somewhat theatrical. The use of [a] tilted camera destroys the normal play of horizontals and verticals, creating a forest of oblique angles that recalls the unsettling effects of expressionist painting and cinema. The tilted camera was a favorite device of horror.[14]

On May 16, 1940, Edwin Schallert of the *Los Angeles Times* announced that "Margaret Tallichet (Mrs. William Wyler) has been signed for 'Stranger on the Third Floor,' [a] murder mystery tale by Frank Partos at RKO. Since her marriage she has seldom done screen work."[15] The next day the *Los Angeles Times* reported that "John McGuire will have the lead opposite Margaret Tallichet in 'Stranger on the Third Floor.' Boris Ingster, RKO writer will direct."[16] On May 29 the *Los Angeles Times* ran Schallert's article under the headline "RKO Signs Lorre for Two Leading Roles":

> Peter Lorre, who did such interesting work a few years ago in pictures like "M," "The Man Who Knew Too Much" and "Crime and Punishment," will again be returning to thrillers. He will play the title part in "Stranger on the Third Floor" at RKO, and has further signed a two-picture deal with the studio . . . Radio-Keith-Orpheum has hopes for restoring Lorre to his former pre-eminence in the special field in which he made such a hit several years ago. Later he was sidetracked by the "Mr. Moto" films, which were never too popular.

Schallert added, "Margaret Tallichet and John McGuire will have romantic leads, while Elisha Cook Jr., Ethel Griffies, Charles Judels and Frank Faylen are to act in the support."[17] One month later the *Los Angeles Times* wrote that "Margaret Tallichet is discussing a term contract with RKO all because she looks good in the rushes of 'Stranger on the Third Floor.'"[18] On June 30 *Los Angeles Times* columnist Philip K. Scheuer reported:

Elaborate shadows convey Ward's nightmare of the electric chair in *Stranger on the Third Floor*.
RKO, 1940.

Filming of a potentially important "different" picture has started at
RKO. Its name is "The Stranger on the Third Floor," and Frank Partos,
who wrote it (in complete continuity form) out of sheer enthusiasm
for the idea, peddled it for two years before Lee Marcus, at Radio, finally decided to take a chance on it. Partos and Boris Ingster, who is
directing, regard the technique experimental. It contains flash for-
wards as well as flash backs: and paints, to put it briefly, the ironic
predicament of a reporter who testifies against an accused murderer
and is then placed in a position where circumstantial evidence would
prove him guilty of a like crime. We've all imagined ourselves in a similar spot at one time or another—but Partos is the first to do anything
about it.[19]

It was an experimental time at RKO, when the studio was willing to take
chances many other studios wouldn't. Adopting the motto "Quality Pictures
at a Premium Price,"[20] new RKO president George Schaefer had just offered
Orson Welles, a newcomer with no filmmaking experience, a carte-blanche

contract with unprecedented creative freedom and control over his projects as a writer-director-star. Schaefer—interested in prestige A pictures—was more hands-off on Marcus's B-films unit, allowing Marcus greater creative latitude. Perhaps in an effort to enhance his own status at the studio, Marcus may have carved out extra resources (and meager funds) for a project like *Stranger on the Third Floor* because he could see it was trying to achieve something far more interesting and artistic than many conventional B movies offered at that time.[21] Shot in twenty-seven days, from June 3 to July 3, *Stranger on the Third Floor* was released on August 16, 1940.[22]

RKO's sensational ads promoted *Stranger on the Third Floor* like a bizarre B movie, combining horror, crime, and mystery thrillers. The studio also played up the psychological angle ("He DREAMS a killing then has to prove his innocence!"), hyped its tabloid realism ("Haunting nightmare turns grim reality . . . as murder witness almost dreams himself into the electric chair"), and showcased how different and shocking the film was. Taglines—seemingly straight out of the pulps—screamed: "NIGHTMARE MURDERER!" "MANIAC KILLER Stalks the Night!" "Strange! Startling! Sensational! If you like your murderers DIFFERENT . . . Meet the . . . STRANGER on the *Third Floor* with PETER LORRE*." Along with these lines was the shady, menacing face of Lorre. One ad featured Lorre shot with low-angle "demon" lighting beneath the tagline: "TRAILING A 'TIPTOE' KILLER! MURDER . . . in a nightmare that comes TRUE . . . to haunt an innocent man . . . Mystery thriller to baffle you." All of this runs above a bare-footed Tallichet revealing a length of bare legs, sans stockings. Another read: "KILLER A mystery thriller with a baffling new slant!" "FUGITIVE FROM FEAR! When damning evidence in maniac killing switches from suspect . . . to star witness!" "*Suppose* YOUR WORST DREAMS CAME TRUE*!!* Wouldn't it be awful? . . . This man's did . . . and he faces the same false murder charge he visioned! . . . *A New Slant on a Murder Story . . . With a Swell Romance to Help It Along!*" A lobby card showed Lorre about to strangle Tallichet, with McGuire looking on beneath the tagline, "NIGHTMARE OF CRIME! *Stranger* on the THIRD FLOOR."[23]

RKO's press book began: "Few murders are committed in the presence of witnesses—yet men and women die in the chair for them! The answer—circumstantial evidence! Here's an astonishing picture that deals dramatically with this problem of justice—is it justice blind or justice true-seeing? Filmed in a manner that makes it a screen novelty, this arresting story has Peter Lorre featured in one of his telling characterizations, and an engaging couple of youngsters in the romantic roles." One of the press book's promotional pieces, "Eccentric Camera Work Marks Drama," noted the film's "striking and unusual camera angles," "light-and-shadow effects never before seen" onscreen, and lighting with "reflected sets" that "transforms" everyone in "sinister, distorted guise." The piece continued: "Reflections of sets thrown on an off-white panorama are utilized as backgrounds instead of actual sets," so everything "is exaggerated, just as it is in a nightmare. Through the use of fog, an invisible paint that blends with the fog to obliterate the floors, and small pieces of scenery erected on huge, empty stages lined with hazy cycloramas, the sense of fantasy and unreality is created and preserved."

In another piece, "Makes Miniature of Movie, Then Actual," the press book publicized Ingster's working method for planning and designing the film:

> At the request of the director, Boris Ingster, each of the 243 scenes in "Stranger on the Third Floor" was sketched in detail and then built in miniature before the picture went into production at the RKO Radio studios. In addition, trick lighting effects were developed and tested and tiny figures of the principal actors were arranged and moved about to determine the most effective positions and camera angles to be used. When everything was completed, the miniature sets were photographed, and any necessary changes made before the first scene was shot.

Ingster explained that "this advance work saves time when the actual shooting begins" and "leaves the director's mind free from most of the mechanical problems and permits him to devote his attention and energy to his players."

RKO called the film a "crime drama novelty," "out of the ordinary," an "unusual romance" that "flourishes in the somber shadow of a maniac's terror campaign . . . Drama, suspense and exceptional realism . . . in a web of circumstantial evidence over a murder case." In "Screen Drama Has Girl Steno-Detective" the press book promoted the female sleuth: "A pretty secretary who turns amateur detective and thus saves her reporter sweetheart from the electric chair, pursues a danger-filled course in RKO Radio's 'Stranger on the Third Floor.' Margaret Tallichet is seen as the courageous heroine, while John McGuire plays her boy friend. Peter Lorre tops the cast as an unbalanced man of mystery whose crimes involve the reporter on a murder charge until the girl exposes him." Adding a bit of sexual violence, beneath a photo of Lorre grabbing the starlet (titled "It's the Menace!") a caption read, "Margaret Tallichet dares not express the fear she feels when Peter Lorre's fingers fasten, talon-like, on her shoulders." The press book also promoted Lorre's "European photodrama 'M' in which he won world-wide recognition" and called Lorre an "eerie stranger" and "menace in the mystery," whose "presence mysteriously coincides with two sensational crimes for which innocent men are condemned."[24] Although the film's remarkable dream sequences, special effects depicting Ward's guilt-obsessed nightmares, haunting voice-over, and brooding antihero flirting with insanity are truly unforgettable and influential to *noir,* it is curious that Lorre wasn't given more screen time—especially since he received top billing, was a known international star, and featured so prominently in RKO's publicity. The romantic leads were fine for B-player performances, and Elisha Cook Jr. is wonderful as the taxi driver framed for the crime, but Ingster's low-budget picture—lacking a star—could only have benefited from more fully utilizing Lorre's spine-tingling talent. In was certainly clear which actors shined (Lorre, Cook) to reappear in later *noir* features.

By August 30 the *Hollywood Reporter* called *Stranger on the Third Floor* "interesting on a number of counts. It misses being an outstanding picture through almost total absence of comedy relief and a weak ending. It is notable for the intense mood it builds up, for some striking montage effects and for providing a showcase for the talent of its male lead, John McGuire. The story is heavy psychological drama all through." It praised Musuraca's photography and lighting as "a major contender for honors," along with Polglase's atmospheric design, Walker's special-effects montage work, and Marcus's courage in producing such an experimental film. "A good third of the picture shows the psychosis of the reporter as he broods over his actions, while his thoughts are spoken aloud. A large portion is also told through flashbacks. In spite of these involved story-telling methods, Boris Ingster has successfully built his suspense, ofttimes gripping."[25] Philip K. Scheuer of the *Los Angeles Times* loved the film. In "Ingenious Film Shown" he called *Stranger on the Third Floor* "impressionistic" and wrote that "Lorre Scores," explaining that Ingster's film develops an "ingenious premise":

> Adapted by Frank Partos from his own original story, the picture makes free use of thoughts both spoken and pictured, as well as a dream. These scenes are photographed impressionistically, with a fair amount of imagination. They recall the halcyon era of German films and the New York Theater Guild. The production rates as a novelty and should exert a spell above that of the routine program effort. With it, Boris Ingster accomplishes a promising directorial debut, although he has been inclined to exaggerate the "real life" sequences to the proportions of the fantastic . . .

As the child-like paranoiac, Peter Lorre contributes his simplest and most effective sketch of a killer since "M." It is the same role, of course, but one that stands repeating. Elisha Cook Jr. is swell as the convicted man. John McGuire makes Michael just a typical "guy" and beauteous Margaret Tallichet takes a decisive step forward as an actress . . . Roy Webb's score is characteristically spooky.[26]

By September *Los Angeles Times* columnist Jimmie Fidler called *Stranger on the Third Floor* "a whodunit sure to produce enough chills to offset early autumn heat."[27]

Other critics were not as enthusiastic. *New York Times* critic Bosley Crowther chided the film's first-time director:

Mr. Ingster, a former script-writer, obviously is a fellow who wants to make pictures which are "different." But from the evidence at hand, it looks as though his inspiration has been derived from a couple of heavy French and Russian films, a radio drama or two and an under-done Welsh rarebit, all taken in quick succession . . . In every . . . respect, including Peter Lorre's brief role as the whack, it is utterly wild. The notion seems to have been that the way to put a psychological melodrama across is to pile on the sound effects and trick up the photography.[28]

A few days later *Harrison's Reports* wrote, "This melodrama is strictly limited in its appeal: as far as the masses are concerned, the story is too harrowing—at its conclusion, one feels as if one had gone through a nightmare . . . The closing scenes, in which the heroine traps the lunatic murderer, are a bit terrifying."[29] *Variety* liked how Peter Lorre put "over another of his studies in film mania as the escaped lunatic, his very appearance on the screen paving way for the darkest doings," and commended the film's effective "premonition" dream sequences. Even so, *Variety* called the modest film "too arty for average audiences" and complained that it "doubtlessly cost more than necessary for fancy camera effects, lighting and trick dubbing . . . The street sets scream their artificiality," and Peter Lorre is wasted as a "maniacal murderer." Many reviewers compared the film to *The Cabinet of Dr. Caligari* in combining stylized "techniques of suspense and thrill" with realistic accounts of two New York City murders.[30] Yet the dark vision and wild aesthetics in *Stranger on the Third Floor* were not immediately accessible to critics or filmgoers. Viewers, it seemed, were not quite ready for film noir.

Stranger on the Third Floor failed to generate a full-blown film noir trend in the early 1940s, not only because the film was too wild but also because of basic studio economics that may have actually preempted the cycle's development. Emerging from receivership in 1940, RKO backed an artsy experimental project offering more than the usual programmer in a "premium" B picture—the top-budgeted "inexpensive" B film in its 1939–40 box-office season. By 1940 RKO's inexpensive B films cost $50,000 to $171,000 to produce—modest numbers compared to the studio's $300,000 to $350,000 average, MGM's $777,000 average, or the industry-wide average of $400,000 for a feature film.[31] The creative, industrious constraints of low-budget film production contributed to the development of a 1940s *noir* aesthetic. Offering higher-quality economy, many *noir* films were "in-betweeners"—modest or "near"-A pictures that were more expensive than conventional B pictures yet less extravagant than the higher tier of top-budgeted prestige pictures. RKO, the leanest-budgeted of the Big Five, had a history of executive turmoil, changes in personnel, and bouts with receivership that encouraged the studio to economize; like Warner Bros., it had a reputation for running a tight ship, producing modestly budgeted pictures—fewer and less-lavish A films than MGM—in an effort to cut costs compared to the other Big Five studios. (B films at the larger major studios had more resources to work with, resulting in a more polished style than the rock-bottom economy and no-nonsense production values of the "Poverty Row" minors like Republic, Monogram, and PRC, which churned out much cheaper pictures.) Ingster's top-flight B *noir* achieved near-A production values with $129,486 in direct costs and a final cost totaling $171,192—just $72 over budget. Its domestic North American earnings, however, were a mere $112,000; and, as the global conflict had already curtailed international markets and reduced revenue possibilities, foreign earnings for *Stranger on the Third Floor* totaled only $74,000. The premature film noir, far from generating a lucrative Hollywood trend, spelled a $56,000 loss for RKO studio.[32] Ingster's unconventional film may have done better with a wider market abroad. By 1940, Jewell explains,

> World War II continued to have an impact on the motion picture business. During the year, Denmark, Norway, Holland, Belgium and France fell to the Germans and heavy aerial bombardment closed many theatres in Great Britain. Since RKO was now increasingly dependent on domestic earnings, it focused on films that had always fared well with American audiences: comedies, musicals, escapist melodramas and more pictures highlighting "Americanism." In accor-

dance with the general industry trend, RKO eschewed any stories based on contemporary world problems. Thus, even though the European conflict was wreaking havoc on company commerce, the production philosophy was to pretend that World War II did not exist.[33]

RKO's 1940 films did poorly at the box office, and the studio replaced Lee Marcus as B-unit head in 1941.

Regardless of its limited popularity, *Stranger on the Third Floor* is certainly noteworthy and a significant prelude for the *noir* series. Its low-budget innovation was a forerunner to other *noir* preludes the next year, films such as Paramount's *Among the Living* (1941, also promoted like a horror picture) and 20th Century–Fox's *I Wake Up Screaming* (shot in 1941, released in early 1942). The extraordinary photography in *Stranger on the Third Floor* anticipates the definitive *noir* style of such films as *Phantom Lady, Double Indemnity,* and *Murder, My Sweet.* Its visual style influenced later RKO pictures such as producer Val Lewton's low-budget psychological horror cycle in films like Jacques Tourneur's *I Walked with a Zombie* (1943) and *The Leopard Man* (1943). *Stranger on the Third Floor* cinematographer Musuraca's moody *noir* style is seen in other Lewton pictures such as Tourneur's *Cat People* (1943); Mark Robson's *The Seventh Victim* (1943) and *The Ghost Ship* (1943); Robert Wise's *Curse of the Cat People* (1944); and later *noir* films like Robert Siodmak's *The Spiral Staircase* (1946), John Brahm's *The Locket* (1946), and Tourneur's classic *Out of the Past* (1947). Peter Lorre's "Stranger," like his infamous child killer in *M,* is unable to control his own actions. Lorre made a career playing flawed or disreputable characters in later *noir* preludes like *The Face behind the Mask, The Maltese Falcon, Invisible Agent, Casablanca,* and *noir* films *The Mask of Dimitrios* and *Black Angel.* While *Stranger on the Third Floor* portrays a tame woman rather than a bold, sexualized *noir* femme fatale, its female detective anticipated *Phantom Lady* and *The Dark Corner* (1946). Ward's guilt-ridden psyche and nightmare flashbacks with distraught voice-over narration was the stuff *noir* was made of. The film's wild psychological montages anticipate the experimental *noir* subjectivity in *Blues in the Night, Moontide, Murder, My Sweet, Spellbound,* and *Black Angel.* RKO house composer Roy Webb reused themes from his haunting *Stranger on the Third Floor* score in *Murder, My Sweet.*

A year later Orson Welles and cinematographer Gregg Toland achieved remarkable deep-focus composition-in-depth cinematography, technical innovation, and a sophisticated flashback narrative featuring multiple points of view. *Citizen Kane* centered on a self-destructive antihero. Like a *noir* crime film, as in Ward's *Stranger on the Third Floor* reporter-detective cracking a case, it revolved around a reporter's endeavor to solve a mystery. It simulated *March of Time* newsreels, nonfiction realism, and tabloid journalism as an anonymous newsreel reporter investigates an infamous deceased mogul, Charles Foster Kane (Welles, in a role based on press tycoon William Randolph Hearst), to decipher his dying word, "Rosebud." The reporter-detective tries to uncover the threads of Kane's tragic albeit famous life of money and lonely alienation. The cynical fact-finding reporter, like the flawed antihero, is ultimately unsuccessful, however, oblivious to Kane's quest for love and happiness as the film progresses to a bitter, existential *noir* finale. Like the social critique in *Stranger on the Third Floor,* the American Dream is exposed as a nightmare; wealth, power, and upward mobility are revealed to corrupt, trap, and doom individuals to personal despair and futility. Oppressive cluttered sets visually impose on vulnerable characters shot at extreme angles to reveal their entrapment beneath caged ceilings. Its brooding tone and deep shadow silhouetting reporters backlit by *Time on the March* dailies in a dark projection room certainly anticipated film noir. In contrast to Ingster's B film, *Citizen Kane* was an A picture, budgeted at $740,000, with final costs totaling $840,000. Despite its brilliance, Hearst launched a negative publicity campaign, limiting the film's domestic earnings to $990,000 (with $300,000 in foreign rentals), ultimately contributing to a $160,000 loss for RKO.[34] As Welles worked on *The Magnificent Ambersons* the following year, the studio was again on the verge of receivership, and top brass ousted corporate president George Schaefer, who had hired Welles. (His successor, Charles Koerner, adopted a more modest, commercial-oriented motto for the studio: "Showmanship instead of Genius.") In a wartime effort to economize RKO saved the sets from *Citizen Kane* and reused them—disguised by low-key lighting and oblique angles—in *The Magnificent Ambersons* and *Cat People.* Although film noir in early 1940s Hollywood was not yet a profitable or popular venture, World War II would eventually accelerate its evolution.

Preludes came together in stylish "gothic" suspense thrillers. As bombs ravaged London, British National's gothic thriller *Gaslight* (1940), called *Angel Street* in the United States, was a precursor to George Cukor's 1944 version. Directed by Thorold Dickinson, produced by John Corfield, and bathed in shadow, it starred Anton Walbrook (Austrian Adolf Anton Wilhelm Wohlbruck, a German/Austrian film-stage veteran famous for his performance in Powell and Pressburger's *The Red Shoes,* 1948) as a murderous thief and polygamist driving his wife insane. Like hard-boiled *série noir,* the term *film noir* derived from *roman noir,* or "black novel," which was what eighteenth- and nineteenth-century French critics called the British gothic novel. As Thomas Schatz has noted, gothic thrillers developed dark stylistics relating to "gender difference, sexual identity, and the 'gender distress' which accompanied the social and cultural disruption of the war and postwar eras." Schatz compares hard-boiled detective narratives to gothic *roman noir*, centering on an "essentially good though flawed and vulnerable protagonist at odds with a mysterious and menacing sexual other."[35] Alfred Hitchcock's British thrillers *The Lodger* (1926), *Blackmail* (1929), *The Man Who Knew Too Much* (1934), *The 39 Steps* (1935), and *Young and Innocent* (1937) were notable preludes to film noir. David O. Selznick hired Hitchcock following *The Lady Vanishes* (1938) and produced his Hollywood debut. Hitchcock's *Rebecca* and *Suspicion* (1941) initiated Hollywood's gothic thriller cycle—which continued with *Shadow of a Doubt* (1943), *Spellbound* (1945), and *Notorious* (1946)—a dark hybrid of the female gothic and espionage thriller that is linked to film noir. Like film noir, gothic thrillers dealt with gender distress and psychic trauma. Distinctive and unique in their own right, Hitchcock's *Shadow of a Doubt, Spellbound,* and *Notorious* ventured closely to the *noir* series. Although the sunny atmosphere of *Shadow of a Doubt* was flooded with bright daylight in a small northern California town—purposely shot, for the most part, on location outside Hollywood rather than on a dark, claustrophobic sound stage—the paranoia, gender distress, and brooding downbeat finale of *Suspicion* provided a prelude to *noir* as warfare escalated abroad. French critic Nino Frank compared *Suspicion* to film noir when defining the term in August 1946, as did Borde and Chaumeton in 1955, calling it "criminal psychology."[36]

Paranoid "good girl" redeemers and "working girl" career women countered sexual femme fatale temptresses in many *noir* pictures. Creative executives in Hollywood's motion picture production system often manufactured these images. Joan Fontaine embodied the gothic redeemer-victim in Hitchcock's *Rebecca* and *Suspicion*. By 1941 Selznick, after winning Best-Picture Oscars for *Gone with the Wind* (1939) and *Rebecca,* was a shrewd Hollywood talent broker, employing the likes of Hitchcock, Joan Fontaine, Ingrid Bergman, and Vivian Leigh, then profitably loaning his director and stars to various Hollywood studios. RKO borrowed Hitchcock and Fontaine for *Suspicion*. In this classic gothic thriller, young and innocent Lina (Fontaine) meets, has an affair with, and marries a suave enigmatic stranger named Johnny (Cary Grant). Her charming and mysterious older husband, with a dubious and secretive past, becomes an alluring but potentially predatory sexual presence who, she suspects, is plotting to kill her. RKO publicity promoted a moody Grant as "a reckless gambling adventurer who introduces Fontaine to a life of debts, excuses, evasions and fears in one of the most ominous roles of his career."[37] Drawing on earlier horror cycles, Hitchcock's gothic picture uses a progressively *noir* style. *Suspicion* begins as a light, romantic comedy and moves into more disturbing drama—visually shifting from bright, high-key lighting to a low-key, shadowy design.

Suspicion was originally intended as a 1935 low-budget adaptation of Frances Iles's (a pseudonym for Anthony Berkeley Cox) gothic novel *Before the Fact*. After shelving the project for six years, RKO upgraded it to a more substantial A budget when Hitchcock showed interest in the story. Although the picture's crew included Vernon L. Walker, Van Nest Polglase, and cinematographer Harry Stradling (who won an Oscar for *The Picture of Dorian Gray* in 1945 and shot Elia Kazan's *A Streetcar Named Desire* in 1951), the glossy, high-production values and amply budgeted expense of *Suspicion* would lead to a visually brighter film than RKO's earlier, more modest, proto-*noir* pictures. Outgoing RKO vice president and production chief Harry Edington, a former agent whose clients included Grant, was a casualty of a power play on the part of RKO president George Schaefer, who desired hands-on supervision of studio production and did not like Edington. Schaefer stripped Edington of his duties, gave him *Suspicion* to produce, then refused to give him screen credit to get him to leave the company. So there is a phantom producer on this film—promoting Hitchcock's prominent image as auteur. Just months before Pearl Harbor, chief censor Joseph Breen changed jobs, leaving the PCA to become new RKO production chief (a kind of puppet vice president under Schaefer)—no longer censoring *Suspicion* but publicizing multiple endings prior to its release.[38]

Hitchcock adapted the novel, casting former comedy star Grant as a dubious English ne'er-do-well plotting to murder his wife—emphasizing her questionable sanity, making the villain a perception in her mind, creating an exploration of paranoia. Hitchcock even suggested RKO brass change its title to *Johnny*, showcasing Grant.[39] An independent artist with his choice of roles at different studios, Grant enjoyed more control over his career than stars who were under contract to various Hollywood studios. Fontaine claimed he even had leading-lady approval of costars. She recalled that halfway through filming *Suspicion,* Grant realized the "whole picture was being told through the eyes of the woman, which gave him quite a shock."[40] Male executive authority and gender dynamics of the production process underscored the narrative gender distress central to proto-*noir* gothic thrillers. Men had power, made decisions, and determined how women were represented onscreen—which is all the more ironic in *Suspicion* because two women, Joan Harrison (Hitchcock's former assistant) and Alma

Reville (Hitchcock's wife), collaborated with writer Sam Raphaelson on the screenplay. An example of how male industry executives called the shots, *Ladies' Home Journal* traced the "manufacturing process" of female stars in "Star Factory," with photos of Fontaine being trained, groomed, and refined by RKO as a "finished product, a masterpiece created and sold by Hollywood's master craftsmen."[41] Fontaine, in an effort to assert more control over her star persona and select roles, begged Hitchcock for the lead, Lina, in *Suspicion*. In a handwritten card on her personal stationary the actress pleaded:

> Dear Hitch: I'm returning "Before the Fact" which I have read with avid interest and find my life completely changed: *I must do that picture*. Oh, please dear, darling Hitch—I'm convinced it will be another "Rebecca" and if anything, I find my enthusiasm even greater for Mrs. Hygarth than for Mrs. de Winter. I am even willing to play the part for no salary, *if necessary!* Really, Hitch, my gratitude for letting me read the book—this is the first urge I've felt to go back to work since "Rebecca"—and I'm sure with you at the helm, I would not regret it. Please pull for me—I shall be eternally grateful. My love, Joan. P.S. I'm trying to be most restrained![42]

Selznick reprimanded Fontaine in a nine-page letter on August 15, 1940, to a "very dear, very young Joan . . . After all . . . I have gone through to get you out of the frustrated bitplayer-and-second-lead-in-Republic-Westerns status in which you had found yourself," which, regrettably, most studios felt was her "maximum due. Too many people in Hollywood . . . know of your work before 'Rebecca' " and the "unprecedented and expensive steps which I took."[43] Selznick certainly launched Fontaine's career, yet his remonstrance was rather severe. Selznick substantiated his "expensive investment" in Fontaine as a star commodity "developed as a result of a risk and a gamble that I took . . . against the unanimous opinion of everyone inside and outside our company, including Hitch"[44]—implying this opposition to her was held by all of Hollywood. RKO had miscast Fontaine in minor B roles for years and then dropped her contract after *Gunga Din* (1939). George Cukor's *The Women* (1939) was a stepping stone for the actress before Selznick and Hitchcock developed her persona in *Rebecca*. Fontaine encountered considerable hassles from Selznick for lobbying Hitchcock for *Suspicion* (she was put on suspension after refusing to do *Back Street* at Universal following *Rebecca*). RKO paid a lucrative $116,750 to Selznick to cast Fontaine in *Suspicion*. Selznick paid her a mere $17,833 salary and then noted, "I don't care . . . so much about how much she makes as I do about making sure we keep her in line." His nearly $100,000 profit indicates he cared about power and money.[45]

Hitchcock's *romans noir* embedded gender distress into the filmmaking process. On the set Fontaine received an icy reception; intimidation tactics made it clear she was expendable. The verisimilitude of Fontaine's shy, naive—progressively emotive—performance on camera and off contributed to the narrative excess and female hysteria in Hitchcock's gothic thrillers. Hitchcock groomed and refined Fontaine's apprehensive ingenue image. Like *Stranger on the Third Floor, Citizen Kane, Rebecca,* and later wartime *noir* films, *Suspicion* cleverly used psychology and a paranoid, imagined point of view to gain endorsement from Hollywood's Production Code censors and critical Academy Award acclaim, despite a gothic premise portraying husbands or lovers committing crime—in apparently trying to murder the women they love. Thomas Elsaesser observes in these suspense pictures of twisted, dysfunctional relationships an "oblique intimation of female frigidity producing strange fantasies of persecution, rape and death—masochistic reveries and nightmares, which cast the husband into the role of sadistic murderer."[46] Grant's menacing performance in *Suspicion* personifies this masculine threat—temperamental Johnny dominates his submissive wife. By the finale his dark side and unpredictably dangerous masculine charisma typifies a mysterious, potentially malignant gothic male, culminating in a strikingly *noir* ascent up a shrouded spiral staircase with a deadly glass of poisoned milk to murder his young wife. Hitchcock casts long, spiderweb shadows spreading out from a backlit doorway. A somber Johnny climbs the stairs in a pitch-black room, bringing the lethal drink (lit from inside the glass so it glows in the dark) to Lina's bedside. The darkness shadows Grant's face, almost in complete silhouette, lit from below to demonize his features.

Most prewar 1940s American film viewers were not ready for a proto-*noir* lover-turned-murderer in Grant. Based on preview audience survey cards from 1941, filmgoer reception was decidedly downbeat toward *Suspicion*'s portraying the actor in a sinister role: "You violated the first big principle of every human—preservation of life at any cost . . . Why ruin Cary Grant on such a long drawn out picture as this? Please put him in more comedies with Irene Dunne." Viewers complained, "I don't think RKO will make any money out of it and it won't do Cary Grant any good." As the United States edged closer to entering World War II, however, American audiences were toughening up. A few viewers actually protested: "Up to the last scene everyone thought Cary Grant was the murderer so why confuse the entire audience by changing the impression. He should admit to trying to murder her, then after confessing, attempt to murder her."

Although Fontaine's distraught ingenue did not correspond to the classic hard-boiled gender roles of lethal femme fatales—where in a full-blown *noir* narrative an erotic woman would be a sexual predator, killing off her male counterpart—her gothic victim can be seen as a psychological prototype for the *noir* good-girl redeemer who often loses her man to a more sexual and deadly temptress. While many were at a "loss to conceive any possible ending short of an asylum for the heroine," several viewers thought Fontaine should have a stronger role: "She should . . . kill him in self-defense or escape and be killed during the pursuit." Another called her an "immature, driveling sentimentalist with no conception of real love—just a sex-starved intellectualist grabbing the first man who showed any interest in her," willingly drinking the "supposed poison her husband offers, proclaiming love for her would-be murderer. What sane woman would act that way?" Others complained, "It was a great mistake to put two such actors in a picture that was ridiculous from start to finish . . . difficult to understand . . . especially after Joan Fontaine drinks what she thinks is death potion. And how the audience laughed! Did you think Cary Grant's promise to reform at all convincing? I don't think it fooled anyone but the wishy-washy Joan Fontaine. Just scrap the picture and give Joan and Cary another lease on life." They added, "She should pull a gun out" when she goes to the cliffs at the film's finale "for the purpose of killing him." Brandishing a weapon certainly suggests crime and combat. Stronger screen images of women would soon coincide with "Rosie the Riveter" and working females in America's wartime home front.

After filming from February 1941 through the summer, *Suspicion* was previewed in June 1941, its ending reshot in late July, postproduction sound and editing completed in August, and the film was released at the end of the year—just before Pearl Harbor—in November 1941. Hitchcock's atmospheric visual design in its climax, like RKO's low-budget *Stranger on the Third Floor* and Welles's *Citizen Kane,* is as dark as film noir. The film was difficult to categorize— "You started out with a light love story well-flavored with humor and in the middle it becomes a mystery story"—described by one viewer as: "*The* finest pseudo-mystery picture I have ever seen."[47] December 1941 ads exclaimed, "You would remember this picture . . . for its great *love story.* You would praise it . . . for its thrilling Hitchcock *suspense.* You would see it . . . [for] its two brilliant *stars . . . And here . . . all three* of these exciting features . . . bring you the most thrilling hours . . . ever spent before a picture screen." Featuring an ominous image of Grant, "charming enough to make any woman love him . . . desperate enough to ruin the life of the woman he loved," publicity noted the *"terror"* that Grant, "at his dramatic best," inspired in heroine Fontaine in a *noir*-inflected reversal paralleling a growing serious concern among Americans regarding the war abroad.[48] A trade clipping read, "Grant Changes Type in Picture" in a "drastic change from the lighthearted comedy of his recent films" and "goes in for romantic drama in a big way in 'Suspicion.'"[49] The film was a huge critical and box-office hit, winning Fontaine a Best Actress Oscar. By November 24, 1941, Schaefer wired Hitchcock: "DEAR ALFRED: ORCHIDS TO YOU AGAIN. REVIEWS EXCELLENT AND PICTURE DOING OUTSTANDING BUSINESS. WE ARE ALL VERY HAPPY AND KNOW YOU MUST BE TOO. REGARDS."[50] Hitchcock's proto-*noir* prestige picture, which cost $1,102,000, was not only the most expensive film but also the most financially successful production released in RKO's 1941–42 box-office season, grossing a generous $2,225,000 and—unlike *Stranger on the Third Floor* or *Citizen Kane*—netting a $440,000 profit for the studio.[51] The increasing film noir style seen in Hollywood's gothic thrillers accelerated as the country neared wartime, yet these early proto-*noir* RKO films lacked a truly hard-boiled hero or femme fatale. *Noir*'s tough, conflicted spirit, narrative corruption, and hard-bitten psyche grew out of anxieties, paranoia, and harsher realities in America's home front and the rough-and-tumble world of pulp fiction detectives that Hollywood could finally adapt with a darker nuanced style during the 1940s.

Another piece of the *noir* puzzle—the hard-boiled detective—appeared on screens in Dashiell Hammett's *The Maltese Falcon*. Hammett's detective stories provided a *série noir* alternative to *roman noir* films like *Suspicion*. While the gothic narrative—and even the dramatic subplot of childhood and marital discord in *Citizen Kane*—revolved around domestic melodrama, showcasing gender distress, female hysteria, unhappy home life, and dysfunctional sexual relations, the domestic realm of the family and home are conspicuously absent in the hard-boiled detective narrative. Unlike Hitchcock's British setting in gothic thrillers, Hammett's world is distinctively male-centered, urban, and American. Action takes place not in the pastoral English countryside (as in gothic novels) but on U.S. city streets at night. Hammett's characters, predominantly male, are tough, shady, often detectives interacting with criminals. In *The Maltese Falcon* detective Sam Spade is sleeping with his partner's wife, comfortable with and complicit in the world of crime around him. Such a premise was highly censorable to the Production Code and was a prototype of Raymond Chandler's moody detectives and James M. Cain's protagonists who were actually criminals. These stories were presented according to their central masculine point of view.

2

In 1948 Chandler wrote, "I did not invent the hard boiled murder story and I have never made any secret of my opinion that Hammett deserves most or all of the credit. Everybody imitates in the beginning . . . Since Hammett has not written for publication since 1932 I have been picked out by some people as a leading representative of the school." In a revealing statement he explained, "This is very likely due to the fact that *The Maltese Falcon* did not start the high budget mystery picture trend, although it ought to have. *Double Indemnity* and *Murder, My Sweet* did, and I was associated with both of them."[52] Hard-boiled themes, as in Hammett's fiction, complemented the work-oriented culture of the American home front and combat front as defense production was prioritized and American family life was disrupted, suspended out of necessity "for the duration."

Hammett drew on his real-life experience in his detective fiction. A private eye and veteran of World War I, Hammett was permanently scarred by his military service, which ultimately destroyed his health and ended his detective career, leading him to pursue crime writing. Published by Alfred Knopf and appearing in *Black Mask* by late 1929–early 1930, *The Maltese Falcon* was purchased for $8,500 by Warner Bros. in June 1930. It centers on detective Sam Spade, who investigates the murder of his partner after taking on a mysterious female client. The plot grows more complex when Spade encounters a series of murders and shady characters who are all after the prized Maltese Falcon and are conning each other, and killing, to get it. Spade's alluring client, with whom he has an affair, turns out to be the criminal who murdered his partner and whom the authorities take to jail. Produced for $278,000 in 1931, racy pre-Code era *The Maltese Falcon* (later retitled *Dangerous Female*), directed by Roy Del Ruth and starring Ricardo Cortez (as Spade), Thelma Todd (as his conniving client, Miss Wonderly), and Bebe Daniels (as Spade's secretary), earned $330,000 and was compared to another Warners picture that year, *Public Enemy.* Warner Bros. production chief, Darryl Zanuck, championed hard-edged social realism and in January 1931 explained, "Prohibition did not cause crime, gang violence, or a corrupt environment, but rather Prohibition merely served to bring crime before the public eye."[53] Referring to *Public Enemy* and linking Warners' successful gangster cycle to Hammett's hard-boiled detective narrative, Zanuck considered *The Maltese Falcon* an exemplary social critique of a growing urban American problem that did not therefore violate the Production Code—despite the fact that while violence was toned down, illicit sex saturates the film and surrounds Cortez's cavalier playboy private dick. Although Spade, like a real detective, searches a room very thoroughly, revealing the "playboy" to be a hardworking sleuth, the wild pre-Code 1931 version of *The Maltese Falcon* almost resembles a variation on a *Thin Man* movie rather than a tough, gritty, brooding film noir.

Although the picture lacked the shadowy cinematography and ambience of 1940s *noir* films, as well as the hard-boiled style of Hammett's novel, in early 1931 censors called *The Maltese Falcon* "very interesting" and "satisfactory" for the Production Code, stating that women staying all night with Spade were not objectionable but that the details were merely too suggestive. They requested the couple sleep in different beds and rooms—Warners made a mockery of this restriction, with sarcastic dialogue, rumpled satin bedsheets, tousled hair, and intimacy with lingerie, making it clear that the onscreen couple had slept together. Censors also expressed concern that "the girl stopping for Spade in the bathroom" was objectionable; the "sexy shot of girl bathing in tub" and shots of murders violated the Code; drinking was "not very offensive" but a violation of the Code because it did not provide sufficient characterization. By April censors objected to "revealing" nude shots of Todd in Spade's bathroom, to Cortez forcing her to undress in front of him to search for stolen money, and to mistress Iva Archer's line, "Who is that dame wearing my kimono?" on discovering Todd in his bedroom. Censors also protested that police were not held in a good light and that justice should have criminals arrested. Censor Jason Joy told Motion Picture Producers and Distributors of America (MPPDA) president Will Hays they needed "some help cleaning up Warner Bros.' *Maltese Falcon*." Hays suspected Jack Warner was "trying to get *The Maltese Falcon* out without complying" with the Code.[54] Warner Bros. left much of the suggestive material in the 1931 version of *The Maltese Falcon*, although murder is not shown. Law and order triumph in the end, though, as Cortez visits Todd in jail following her arrest. Like many gangster heroes she is depicted sympathetically once her crime has caught up with her. Locked up behind bars and lying face down, she bursts into tears in the cramped confines of her cell; her arrest has also benefited Spade, who has been promoted to chief detective for the district attorney. After the PCA blocked the re-release of *The Maltese Falcon* in 1934, and after Zanuck left to head 20th Century–Fox, Warner Bros. remade it with a new title, *Satan Met a Lady* (1936), directed by William Dieterle and disguised as a bright, sanitized, and comparatively upbeat Bette Davis vehicle that also lacked the *noir* ambience of *The Maltese Falcon* novel.

Five years later, John Huston adapted and directed what has become the definitive version of Hammett's detective yarn, effectively capturing the novel's hard-bitten milieu. Huston's *The Maltese Falcon* (1941)—like *Double Indemnity, Laura,* and *Murder, My Sweet*—not shown in France until

1946, was recognized by critics Frank, Chartier, and Borde and Chaumeton as a hard-boiled *série noir* prelude. As in many *Black Mask* stories, its detective protagonist worked alone in a harsh, unforgiving urban milieu; the story ends on a downbeat note, although the lone detective survives his rough and shady circumstances, similar to the gothic heroine's enduring despite her unsettling romantic predicament. Gothic gender roles are reversed, however, in the hard-boiled detective narrative. The male antihero's sexual threat is the femme fatale who initiates his case and structures the story. When the dangerous female client-turned-seductress in *The Maltese Falcon* lies—and admits to lying—to Sam Spade, the cynical private eye replies, "We didn't exactly believe your story. We believed your two hundred dollars." He blandly explains, "You paid us more than if you'd been telling the truth, and enough more to make it alright." Like the gothic ingenue entrapped in her remote domestic environment and in the psychological prisms of her perceived distress, the independent hard-boiled male protagonist is a liminal figure, usually isolated by his own choosing. Like the lone western gunman navigating an unfriendly terrain, he is a solo professional, often a former cop who now works outside the law, in lieu of the police— rejecting the values of both his unsavory surroundings and the conventional law enforcement institution. If he has a partner, his partner is inevitably killed. As Spade searches on his own for Archer's murderer in *The Maltese Falcon,* Chandler's Philip Marlowe works alone in *The Big Sleep* and *Farewell My Lovely,* and Bogart's partner is killed in *Dead Reckoning,* as is Mitchum's in *Out of the Past.* The hard-boiled detective lives by his own personal code of honor and seeks his own brand of justice. Recognizing the legal system's inbred corruption and incompetence, police and the courts are often as dubious as the criminals. A "self-styled existentialist" and "cultural middleman," Schatz explains, the private eye's "street-wise savvy and penchant for violence enable him to operate within the urban jungle, while his moral sensibilities and innate idealism align him with the forces of social order." In a malignant universe where crime and the black market pay, however, the hard-boiled detective's idealism ultimately guarantees that he will fail in his effort to reform the world around him, which he "accepts with a shrug, lights another cigarette, and returns to his seedy office to await another case."[55]

Writer and first-time director Huston wanted to capture the tough feel, atmosphere, and style of Hammett onscreen. "I decided to follow the book rather than depart from it," he explained. "I attempted to transpose Dashiell Hammett's highly individual prose style into camera terms: i.e., sharp photography, geographically correct camera movements; striking if not shocking set-ups."[56] Low angles captured the ceiling of sets as in Welles's *Citizen Kane*. Jack Warner approved the project after seeing Huston's scene-by-scene breakdown of Hammett's novel that the screenplay followed closely. After years of PCA bans and censorship restrictions on hard-boiled fiction, changes at Hollywood's Production Code office in 1941 enabled a few *noir* preludes like Huston's faithful rendering of Hammett's *Maltese Falcon* to be adapted with more of their censorable glory. Joseph Breen became an "industry man" and briefly abstained from his role as censor, taking a job as RKO's executive vice president in charge of production by mid-1941 through spring 1942. Breen's departure from his position as PCA chief created a timely lapse in PCA censorship for nearly a year. He resigned from the PCA in March 1941, just after Roosevelt signed the Lend-Lease Act to aid the war effort. Evidently Breen was exhausted, joining RKO after heated battles with Howard Hughes over *The Outlaw*. A *Variety* headline read: "Hays Purity Coder Adamant on Resigning."[57] *The Outlaw* was a major challenge to PCA authority when it received a Code seal of approval in June 1941. Breen left on June 15. Breen's running of operations at RKO ended as an exercise in futility, but it did provide him a respite from the Hays Office. It also gave Hollywood a taste of a PCA without Breen. His exposure to production executive ranks and absence from the PCA dovetailed with Huston's *Maltese Falcon*, Hitchcock's *Suspicion* finale, Welles's *Citizen Kane* and *The Magnificent Ambersons*, and *noir* preludes *This Gun for Hire*, *Moontide*, and *Street of Chance*.

Production Code correspondence for Huston's version of *The Maltese Falcon* begins and ends rather abruptly. On May 22, 1941, after Lend-Lease and Breen's resignation from the Hays Office, Warner Bros. producer Henry Blanke sent a "temporary" script to the PCA's more liberal-minded Geoffrey Shurlock. Given the history of the salacious project, it is not surprising that, even on the way out, Breen fired back a series of missives to Warner Bros. studio chief Jack Warner—the very next day, followed by letters on May 27 and June 6—objecting to the story's drinking, sex, and profanity. On May 31 Breen sent a letter to MPPDA president Will Hays summarizing a "resume of our actions since April 30, 1941" regarding *The Maltese Falcon* property, which he categorized as a "crime-horror" picture. After a lapse in correspondence, and after Breen's departure, by August the PCA called Huston's film a "melodrama-detective mystery" and granted it a seal of approval. For good measure censors sent Jack Warner a letter on September 10 confirming that *The Maltese Falcon* met the Code.[58]

Production for *The Maltese Falcon* had, of course, already begun on June 9, 1941—shot chronologically in continuity with the novel, as cinematographer Arthur Edeson lit the "Spade and Archer" window in Sam Spade's office. Although much pre-Code sex and nudity were purged, illicit affairs and violence remained. The harsh atmosphere of Archer's murder and the burning of the freighter *La Paloma* were aided by Warners' newly installed fog machine and huge water tank on the back lot. The studio was proud of these atmospheric devices and wanted to show them off. (They certainly added a smoky milieu to films like *The Sea Hawk* in 1941.) *Maltese Falcon* associate producer Henry Blanke (an UFA alumnus who worked as production manager on Lang's *Metropolis*) cultivated even darker proto-*noir* visuals in Anatole Litvak's 1941 pictures *Out of the Fog* (a moody racketeer yarn with glistening water, black nights, and abundant fog shot by James Wong Howe, starring hoodlum John Garfield—after Bogart was rejected—with Ida Lupino) and *Blues in the Night* (a shadowy rain-drenched "gangster musical" jazz *noir* filmed by Ernest Haller, starring heavies Lloyd Nolan and Howard da Silva, Richard Whorf, Priscilla Lane, Betty Field, Jack Carson, "Dead End" kid Billy Hallop, and a young Elia Kazan).

Huston's version of *The Maltese Falcon* was more pensive, brooding, murky, and mysterious than Warners' earlier 1930s efforts at capturing Hammett's seedy masculine milieu. Now danger and menace lurked in the shadows. The enemy is omnipresent. Unexpectedly, private dick Sam Spade is slipped a Mickey and sprawled out cold on the floor. Amid the cramped corridors and venetian blinds, friendly strangers are often ruthless foes. Spade is human, a tough, grizzled man of action who is suddenly violent and unpredictable. He has demons of his own that he battles, suffers torment and psychological conflict, and is less than invincible. While *The Maltese Falcon* is not quite as visually dark as *Stranger on the Third Floor, Citizen Kane,* or the low-lit climax of *Suspicion,* its hard-boiled detective framework is narratively closer to film noir—certainly, at least, more so than *Citizen Kane* or *Suspicion.* Its elevated status as a *noir* prototype owes much to its handling of story, characterization, star, and genre. After George Raft declined the lead, Blanke and Huston assembled a superb ensemble cast—including Humphrey Bogart (as Sam Spade), Mary Astor (Spade's lying femme fatale client Brigid O'Shaughnessy), Peter Lorre (conniving, effeminate Joel Cairo), Sydney Greenstreet (his screen debut as dangerous "Fat Man" Kasper Gutman), Elisha Cook Jr. (young hothead Wilmer Cook), and Ward Bond (Spade's police detective friend Tom Polhaus). Bogart personified Sam Spade. Huston admitted, *The Maltese Falcon* starred Bogart "playing the right part," where "something happened . . . lights and shadows composed themselves."[59] Known for supporting roles as gangster heavies in 1930s B films, Bogart's big break was sympathetic crime hero Roy Earle

Casualty Sam Spade (Humphrey Bogart) sprawled out cold after *(left to right)* Wilmer Cook (Elisha Cook Jr.), Joel Cairo (Peter Lorre), and Kasper Gutman (Sydney Green-street) slip him a Mickey in *The Maltese Falcon.* Warner Bros., 1941.

in *High Sierra*. A true hard-boiled hero, his tough but often conflicted male image captured film noir's hard-bitten spirit.

The Maltese Falcon was quite a modest and economical film—shot in six weeks, principal photography wrapped on July 18. After executive producer Hal Wallis instructed Huston and Blanke to pick up the narrative pace, complaining it was "too leisurely" ("it must be fast, there must be action in the picture") and requesting a "punchy, driving" tempo, Bogart fired up staccato crime-style action. Brigid wasn't a typical tough-talking dame or street moll; Wallis thought Astor "too coy and ladylike." Huston sped up production, eliminated the original ending in Spade's office, and completed the picture two days ahead of schedule. Unit manager Al Alleborn reported to Warner production manager T. C. "Tenny" Wright that costs through July 17 totaled $327,182—$54,000 under the film's June 2 budget of $381,000.[60] After retakes on August 8 and September 10 the film's final cost totaled a mere $375,000, more than RKO's *Stranger on the Third Floor* the year before but less than half the cost of *Citizen Kane* and nearly a third the cost of *Suspicion*.[61] Released in October 1941, *The Maltese Falcon* was enormously popular by the time of the Pearl Harbor attack. After very little advance publicity, and as the United States entered the war, Huston's film was a surprise hit—reinforcing Bogart's box-office appeal and eventually grossing $952,000 in North American earnings and another $409,000 overseas, despite the greatly curtailed wartime foreign market, totaling $1,361,000 by 1943.[62] (Warners scrambled to move Bogart's name from below the title and costar Astor's name to larger type above the title.) Studio publicity played up gun-toting Bogart's tough *High Sierra* gangster image, sexualized Astor in a slinky, tight, bare-waisted gown with plunging neckline (not shown in the film), and mentioned Hammett. Taglines—suggesting crime and combat—clamored: "*A STORY AS EXPLOSIVE AS HIS BLAZING AUTOMATICS!*" Warner Bros. promoted how Huston, who had an art background, designed the film in advance as a first-time director—much like RKO's promotion of Ingster on *Stranger on the Third Floor.*[63] Bosley Crowther of the *New York Times* called *The Maltese Falcon* "the best mystery thriller of the year . . . brisk and supremely hardboiled." Earlier versions weren't "half as tough . . . a combination of American ruggedness with the suavity of the English crime school—a blend of mind and muscle—plus a slight touch of pathos." He called Bogart "a shrewd, tough detective with a mind that cuts like a blade, a temperament that sometimes betrays him, and a code of morals which is coolly cynical."[64]

The independence, isolation, and irreverence of hard-boiled antiheroes were ideal prewar qualities readily adaptable to more politically charged protagonists in topical espionage pictures. Political propaganda potboilers and espionage thrillers by émigrés such as Alfred Hitchcock, Anatole Litvak, and Fritz Lang were influential prototypes for the violent, paranoid *noir* trend—particularly vis-à-vis psychological crime films, federal censorship, and reformed gangsters. Bogart's tormented tough guy, a model of 1940s *noir* masculinity, related not only to hard-boiled source material like *The Maltese Falcon* but also to reworkings of the gangster cycle as wartime neared. Screen gangsters and their unethical, often illegal, activity were considered "un-American," banned as unpatriotic, and censored by the government's Office of Censorship in the war years.[65] Previously the industry's self-regulation by PCA censors discouraged crime, violence, sex, adultery, and political content in Hollywood films. The federal Office of Censorship, however, encouraged political content showing war-related crimes and violence to stiffen patriotic resolve. This shift in regulatory principles produced an odd pairing of espionage themes and disguised gangster heroes; crime films supporting the war (and evading PCA censorship with realistic war-related crime material) appeared even before America entered the conflict. As the war broke out in Europe, Warners "declared war" on Germany in its own way, recasting gangster Robinson as an FBI G-man ferreting out Nazi spies in America in Litvak's topical *Confessions of a Nazi Spy*. Espionage narratives established graphic patriotic crime, gratuitous violence, often sexual violence, gaining censorship approval while ushering in paranoid criminal psychology and unstable antiheroes (as in gangster cycles) in a corrupt setting. Overseas, impressive *noir* preludes included Hitchcock's British espionage thrillers *The Man Who Knew Too Much, The 39 Steps, Secret Agent* (1936), *Sabotage* (1936), and *The Lady Vanishes;* Graham Greene's hard-bitten British spy fiction *A Gun for Sale / This Gun for Hire* and *Ministry of Fear;* and British National's shadowy espionage picture *Contraband* (1940), retitled *Blackout* in the United States, shot as blackouts cloaked Great Britain under aerial assault, directed by Michael Powell, written by Powell and UFA-alumnus Emeric Pressburger, produced by John Corfield. Set in blacked-out war-torn London, it featured a city so dark that street vendors sell flashlights to get around. Nazi spies knock out Danish former-navy captain—and *Caligari* star—Conrad Veidt, triggering a wild moody psychological montage reminiscent of *Stranger on the Third Floor,* anticipating *Moontide* and *Murder, My Sweet.*

In retooling to support America's war effort, as censors tolerated growing screen violence but viewed gangsters as anti-American and potential fodder for Nazi propaganda, Hollywood transformed criminals into more patriotic, guilt-ridden, unstable, and self-destructive proto-*noir* protagonists—a variation on mobsters—combating espionage, sabotage, and fifth columnists; in doing so studios succeeded in evading censorship.[66] Filmmakers repackaged gangster-crime conventions to conform with regulatory restrictions. Political potboiler and espionage pictures like *Foreign Correspondent* (1940), *Saboteur* (1942), *This Gun for Hire, Across the Pacific, Hitler's Children,* and *Ministry of Fear* grew popular as America was drawn into warfare. Personal sacrifice, sense of duty, and love of America redeemed criminals, adapted as "disguised" gangsters, reformed for the national good to support the cause. Many espionage preludes with "patriotic" crime, paranoid psychology, and subjective *noir* point of view include a tough masculine psyche simulating combat.[67] Spy crime thrillers included mysterious undercover female operatives—multifaceted counterespionage career women—who, like paranoid redeemers and hard-boiled femme fatales, inhabited a world of intrigue with brooding visual style, such as that in Hitchcock's *39 Steps* and Powell and Pressburger's *Contraband/Blackout.* Hollywood's psychological antiheroes conveyed a crisis of masculinity, with strong, independent—often working—femme "threats" to patriotic male crime figures. An early *noir* film incorporated these antiheroes into the cynical espionage genre.

This Gun for Hire depicts psychologically volatile criminal antihero Philip Raven (Alan Ladd), who spurns women and relishes cold-blooded murder and illegal activities, in a film that straddled Hollywood's wartime transition. Paramount purchased Graham Greene's 1936 crime novel *A Gun for Sale* (retitled *This Gun for Hire* in the United States) for $12,000 in 1941.[68] While Greene's book was set during the interwar 1930s in Britain, the studio changed its setting to wartime 1940s California and then redirected its unsavory plot in order to support America's Allied war effort by adding topical themes about Japanese chemical bombs against the United States. Raven is transformed from a hit man being hunted by police into an unlikely patriotic martyr battling the enemy. W. R. Burnett (who wrote *Little Caesar, High Sierra,* and *Asphalt Jungle* and coscripted *Scarface*) and Albert Maltz adapted the investigative thriller that centered on an assassin's violent quest for revenge, murdering criminals—even slapping and shooting women—after being double-crossed. Raven meets a beautiful woman, Ellen Graham (Veronica Lake), recruited by a senator to serve as an undercover agent and kidnapped by a lewd crime operative, Bates (Laird Cregar). Bates is a subversive fifth columnist conspiring to sell poison gas and chemical weapons formulas to the Axis enemy in Japan, which would enable the Japanese to bomb American cities. Tough-guy Raven foils the plot and saves the alluring agent but is still gunned down by authorities (and her police detective fiancé, Robert Preston). Greene was not thrilled by the film's topical subplot involving a "female conjurer working for the FBI," which had nothing to do with his novel, yet on the brink of World War II Paramount was sold on the premise of Greene's book—where protagonist Raven murders a government minister and instigates a war.[69] In the novel Raven was scarred by a harelip, which fueled his sociopathic impulses. The topicality of *This Gun for Hire* successfully won over the PCA as the United States entered the global conflict. By late 1941 the temporary lapse in PCA enforcement with Breen's departure and the attack on Pearl Harbor enabled Paramount to justify a violent story and patriotic criminal with a war-related sabotage plot to attack America.

Several factors shaped the production of *This Gun for Hire.* Not only did the war enable patriotic violence to be adapted and approved by PCA censors, but it also influenced the film's actual production with material constraints that affected how *This Gun for Hire* was shot. War-related filmmaking restrictions affected Hollywood as early as 1940, with significant

Disguised gangster Philip Raven (Alan Ladd) goes undercover to infiltrate the chemical factory and foil the Axis plot to bomb U.S. cities in *This Gun for Hire*. Paramount, 1942.

constraints by fall 1941, when *This Gun for Hire* began filming. The *New York Times* reported frequent studio recycling of sets just before Pearl Harbor. Archival correspondence indicates tremendous cost-cutting measures in studio production practices by 1941–42.[70] Many of these material limitations accentuated attributes that would later be considered so characteristic of film noir style: rain, fog, smoke, mirrors (rather than ornate sets), resourceful angles, night locations, and tented or tarped back-lot shooting (which enabled filming at minimized expense in the economically tight environment ramping up to the war).

In the tradition of efficient B-unit filming, Paramount art director and German expatriate UFA-alumnus Hans Dreier, working with cinematographer John Seitz, had definite ideas about how to design and shoot *This Gun for Hire*. Originally educated as an architect, Dreier began working as a designer for the Paramount subsidiary UFA-EFA in Berlin in 1919, with such influential German designers as Paul Leni, who later joined Universal in Hollywood (establishing a prototype for the studio's pronounced horror aesthetic and dark visual style). Dreier's expressionism followed the lines set down by Walter Rohrig, Herman Warm, and Walter Reimann (who designed *The Cabinet of Dr. Caligari*) and soon surpassed even *Caligari* in technical sophistication. Dreier also worked with G. W. Pabst's outstanding designer Erno Metzner, benefiting from his art direction skills and ability to manipulate decor for dramatic effect.[71] With thirty-four films to his credit in four years, Dreier had joined Paramount in the United States as a designer in 1923; he rose to supervising art director of the studio by 1932 and remained in that position until his retirement in 1950. Dreier's art department, known as the "Dreier College," provided rigorous training for apprentice designers on the German expatriate's visual aesthetic style (seen in the dark urban atmosphere of city streets and working-class waterfronts in Josef von Sternberg's early crime films influential to *noir*) and trained protégé Hal Pereira (with whom he designed *noir* films *This Gun for Hire, Double Indemnity, Ministry of Fear,* and *Sunset Boulevard*). Not surprisingly, Dreier is credited with significantly influencing Paramount's "European" visual style.

As budget constraints and the studio's effort to reduce costs became more apparent, Paramount preproduction and budget meetings began in August 1941 regarding how to cast and shoot *This Gun for Hire.* Dreier planned on using modest studio sets for the project, combining them with transparencies and second-unit location shooting of gasworks, junkyards, and freight yards at night. By late October Dreier outlined details for cutting production costs at a Paramount budget meeting and hired contract production designer Lynd Ward from New York. Dreier adopted measures to reduce location filming, noting that Seitz could get "any effect" with backgrounds and effects such as using rain and a "straight on shot" to obscure the length of a back-lot street. Costumes were simplified; sets were pared down, using mirrors to add depth. Second-unit shooting of locations was done at night or in early morning "to catch fog" and obscure star Veronica Lake's double. These factors intensified a murky *noir* rail yard as Raven eludes police. Adding a psychological dimension to the picture highlighting a destabilized criminal psyche, a dream sequence of Raven's nightmare was planned. The sequence was determined to be "50% too large," however, so that director Frank Tuttle would have to "make it in cuts," with producer Richard Blumenthal specifying these cuts be shot from "exaggerated angles." Given these restrictions in planning and designing the film, building an expensive skull set was rejected in favor of dissolving from Raven to the dream. At the end of November Blumenthal informed Pereira in the art department that $8,000 was approved for the dream sequence and to prepare a miniature set—adding that the sequence would be shot after the picture had completed shooting with star Alan Ladd. In line with fiscal restraints, the cast were not big-name stars but minor players. The original casting budget had called for $103,000, which included a $40,000 salary for Raven's role (even Peter Lorre was considered for the part) and $10,000 for Lake's role (intended for Betty Fields). Consistent with efforts to reduce expenses, however, the studio cast newcomer Ladd as Raven for a mere $4,216 (well below Lake's top billing and salary of $6,900 and even less than supporting player Robert Preston's $6,500 salary).[72] The picture was rushed into production to showcase sultry blonde star Lake.

Noir images in *This Gun for Hire* related directly to the war and accentuated tracking the domestic sabotage and chemical warfare by a foreign enemy; it gets darker and darker as events progress to unravel more insidious details about the conflict and espionage, visually conveying fifth-columnist anxiety via its shrouded mise-en-scène. The film's imagery becomes blacker as the narrative unfolds to reveal domestic corruption aiding the evil Axis powers and subverting the American way. In fact, the most compelling *noir* style coincides with the film's narrative shift from isolationism to greater involvement in the war effort and the risky domestic consequences of ignoring such a call to military action. A fine example is the nearly pitch-black scene in an abandoned shack where Raven hides out overnight from the authorities. Paranoid and on the run, the film's criminal protagonist, despite his disturbed psychology, criminal acts, and brutality, is ultimately not the perceived threat. Guilt and remorse haunt him, authorities punish him, and he patriotically aids the country. Completely hidden in the dark, his voluptuous (undercover FBI agent) hostage cajoles him to battle the enemy as she reveals Japanese operatives are developing poison gas to attack U.S. cities. At the scene's claustrophobic *noir* climax, the dark face and fedora of Raven and the shapely silhouette of his beautiful captive, Ellen, are visually enveloped in such deep, ominous shadow that they are barely visible as they discuss sabotage, subversion, the threat of enemy bombs, chemical warfare, and the democratic imperative of the United States. Raven's tormented killer remains a study in contradictions. The war effort redeems him—in fact, most of the material that drew the PCA's objections actually remained in the film despite repeated requests from censors to comply with their requests for changes.

Paramount adopted a savvy strategy to gain Production Code endorsement of the project. On October 10, 1941, Luigi Luraschi of Paramount's censorship department submitted the reformulated crime script with two patriotic war films, *True to the Army* and *The Fleet's In*, to the PCA's Geoffrey Shurlock for consideration. Three days later the PCA—in the absence of Breen—stated the basic story for *This Gun for Hire* met the requirements of the Production Code, yet a two-page list of objectionable details needing correction was appended to the letter. Items included indecent displays of nudity, violence, homosexuality, juvenile delinquency, inappropriate language, and behavior suggesting illicit sex or disrespect toward figures of authority in law enforcement. The PCA requested that the film's opening, where Raven brutally hits his maid, be masked or offscreen (stating it would be deleted by political censor boards). Before Raven executes a traitorous old man's lover—firing through a door—for witnessing his murder, censors wanted the woman's attire changed from a negligee to a dress to reduce the suggestion of illicit sex. (Paramount instead dressed her in a satiny black dress to suggest a gangster's moll.) Censors also wanted to minimize the suggestive delivery of the old man's line "my—er, wife" when introducing his mistress. The Hays Office preferred that two killings be "handled carefully" to "avoid gruesomeness" and called for deleting of some dialogue ("I'd buy myself a farm, get a couple of chickens and lay my own eggs") and images ("no hanging figure in the dream sequence"). Discouraging juvenile delinquency and censoring homosexuality, censors pointed out that it was illegal for thirteen-year-olds to operate pinball machines and that it was "unacceptable" to "portray the male dressmaker as effeminate." Suggestive fondling by the opposite sex was also a cause for concern: lascivious criminal Bates's pat on Ellen's knee must be "handled inoffensively." The PCA objected to showing any grisly "details of committing crime," like "sack weights and cat gut" murder weapons.

In the tradition of padding scripts with salacious material—or simply to make the movie more interesting and sell tickets—Paramount added sexualized violence to the film. The attractive young woman in a slinky black dress whom Raven murders was originally an old lady in Greene's novel. The studio also added a character not in the book. The saboteur's tough-guy assistant, Tommy (played by Marc Lawrence, who was frequently called on to play hoodlums, as in *Blind Alley* and *Dillinger*), is a fairly obvious gangster figure—"disguised" to comply with political pro-American censorship. Though dressed as a chauffeur, bellboy, or manservant wearing a prim uniform, Tommy talks like a gangster, using recognizable slang with violent behavior—especially toward women. Tommy's job is to kill kidnapped Ellen and dump her body into the reservoir. Relishing his task, Tommy praises his own scheme as "a work of art—up she'll bob without a mark on her . . . a suicide. Beautiful!" The PCA was concerned about the inclusion of this character, suggesting omitting his dialogue referring to the "sack weight and cat gut" murder. The PCA was more generally disturbed by the film's violence. Censors suggested that the "business" of Raven "kicking Tommy in the stomach and Tommy crashing down the dark stairway" must be "handled carefully" to "avoid any unnecessary brutality." The PCA also stipulated that Raven not commit "cold blooded murder" for "revenge" and that the film "avoid undue sympathy for the murderer." And it cited "special regulations" regarding crime that "prohibit the showing of police dying at the hands of criminals" and that it was "unacceptable" for Raven to kill any cops. While the Hays Office allowed Raven to murder his criminal opponent, censors expressed concern over any "undue gruesomeness" and requested that Raven not deliberately shoot him a second time.[73] The PCA's lenient approach in this instance contrasted with Breen's, which was initially more cautious and condemning of proposals—outlining censorship objections that, if rectified, might enable PCA endorsement—and withheld final approval of the project until these items were changed.

Principal photography for *This Gun for Hire* ran from October 27 to December 6, 1941, with two extra days of filming on December 15 and 16. By November the PCA was "happy to report" that the script "meets the requirements" of the Code. Ultimately, it was the timing of the project that gained swift PCA endorsement of the violent patriotic film. As Pearl Harbor put the nation and the Hollywood filmmaking community on high alert, filming was interrupted not only by the real-life attack that disrupted its production but also by Ladd's week-long hospitalization for pneumonia just days before. As Roosevelt addressed the nation on December 8, Paramount finally sent a revised script to Shurlock at the PCA. The Hays Office approved *This Gun for Hire* the very next day, although most of the PCA's requested revisions had not been made.[74] In the aftermath of the attack, as the United States entered the war, severe war-related restrictions precluded the crew from shooting additional sequences because of sound-stage and material shortages. A few days after principal photography was completed, sound stages for Raven's dream sequence became unavailable until January 3, 1942.[75] Despite the absence of the dream sequence in available versions of the film, Ladd's performance as tormented criminal Raven infused a psychological dynamic into Paramount's wartime story, implying the antihero's nightmare psyche. Joseph Breen returned to the Production Code office in May 1942, months after the PCA granted a seal of approval to *This Gun for Hire* in late January.

Even with cost-cutting measures, the film's $500,000 price tag exceeded its $449,000 budget.[76] The film was a success, however, with both critics and audiences. *Variety Weekly* reported *This Gun for Hire* made $1 million.[77] Its March–June 1942 publicity and release capitalized on the war in a big way. Paramount promoted patriotic crime with a distinctively masculine, psychological ethos and "combat mentality" that vicariously tapped into the

Dynamite with a girl or gun, will he kiss or kill her?—Pistol in hand, Raven (Alan Ladd) rescues Ellen Graham (Veronica Lake) from enemy fifth columnists and carries her off as a hostage on the run from police in *This Gun for Hire*. Paramount, 1942.

war effort. Publicity referred to Alan Ladd as "Trigger Man," "Wary with a woman . . . Tender with a kitten . . . But a terror with a trigger! He's the 'KISS and KILL' Ladd they're all talking about!" Ads read: "A Lone Wolf . . . dynamite with a girl or a gun!" "Killer without a Conscience! Lover without a Heart?" "Kiss Her . . . or Kill Her! Which will he do?" The press book exclaimed Lake "Finds a Guy too Tough to Take!" and "Dons Boy's Garb for Role . . . quite fashionable in Hollywood these days."[78] *Motion Picture Herald* called *This Gun for Hire* a "gangster film with [a] patriotic twist," noting that the story's topical "interest" added a sense of wartime immediacy. Three months into the war, America's mobilization effort was in full throttle. *Motion Picture Daily* outlined Paramount's formula for success: "Director Frank Tuttle skillfully blended a blood-and-thunder spy melodrama with psychopathic overtones" and Lake and Ladd to produce "taut action and suspense." Ladd's unstable mercenary antihero is described as a "psychopathic killer," hiring out his "services to the highest bidder," yet "tormented by nightmares of a killing which he committed as a youth, he derives satisfaction during the day from the sheer lust of murder."[79] *Look*'s

April 1942 review of *This Gun for Hire* plays up the military angle, calling Ladd a "professional killer" hired by "enemy agents" to retrieve the secret formula for producing "poison gas" in a California factory and murder treasonous informants. It exploited the film's "Japanese plot to shower deadly chemical bombs on American cities" with a "cold-blooded lone gunman" who aids a nightclub singer working for the government to combat a saboteur. On May 29 Philip Hartung of *Commonwealth* noted that the story's "cold violence" was "natural cinema material." Espionage was at the heart of *Life*'s June 22, 1942, feature on *This Gun for Hire*. Primed for action, Ladd's Raven is repeatedly called "the killer" who (alluding to the draft for military combat) "receives orders by mail to do a little job of murder and tests out his only friend: his automatic." Tapping into home-front anxieties and paranoia about espionage, sabotage, and chemical warfare, the piece even shows killer Ladd disguised in a gas mask to pull off his ultimate coup against subversives in the chemical plant. Lake's photo is surprisingly androgynous. Like female factory workers, she is cloaked in masculine garb and "hides her hair under a man's hat."[80] Reflecting shifting gender roles during the war, both male and female characters in *This Gun for Hire* are complex and unpredictable, even duplicitous, defying stereotypes. *This Gun for Hire* solidified stardom for Ladd and Lake and spun off sequel pairings of the couple in adaptations of Dashiell Hammett's *The Glass Key* (1942) and Raymond Chandler's *The Blue Dahlia* (1946) at Paramount.

At Warner Bros. Bogart became a rising star, gaining fame as private detective Sam Spade following *The Maltese Falcon*. After Pearl Harbor Warners wanted another *Maltese Falcon* but, like Paramount, preferred patriotic themes, as in espionage crime films like *This Gun for Hire,* with more topical narrative propaganda. Bogart's hard-boiled screen persona was adapted, becoming an anti-Nazi gambler opposite Peter Lorre and Conrad Veidt in *All through the Night* (1942), followed by *Across the Pacific* and *Casablanca.* Warners publicity called Bogart "the male star that says excitement" and capitalized on the film's hard-boiled patriotism: "the brand newest twist in big-time action—gangsters vs. Gestapo—*and it is welcome now!*"[81] In fact, *All through the Night* was even more successful than *The Maltese Falcon,* earning $1,002,000 domestically and a total gross of $1,510,000, and became a model for Bogart's next role as a trench coat–clad military counterespionage agent—coincidentally named "Rick"—thwarting Japanese subversives in *Across the Pacific.* By 1942 Bogart crystallized his screen image and confirmed his A-film star status as rugged-individualist-turned-romantic-patriot Rick Blaine in *Casablanca.* As America became more heavily involved in World War II, hard-boiled *série noir* crime fiction made exemplary screen material. Its stark vision, minimal style, fast pace, graphic sex, life-like violence, and cynical edge suited the bleaker experience, raw realities, and lean, no-nonsense filmmaking climate of wartime Hollywood. Inspired by the tough hard-boiled detective of *The Maltese Falcon,* the brooding horror-crime-psychological-social critique of *Stranger on the Third Floor,* the tabloid cynicism and technical perfection of *Citizen Kane,* the gothic thriller suspense and gender distress of *Suspicion,* and the sociopathic reformed gangster of *This Gun for Hire,* this wartime climate would integrate many *noir* preludes in the industry's process of mobilization. In the wake of the attack, as the shock of Pearl Harbor resonated—affecting many productions (like Paramount's filming of *This Gun for Hire* and *Street of Chance* and Fox's *Moontide*) and encouraging patriotic crime pictures like Warners' *All through the Night, Across the Pacific, Casablanca,* and Paramount's *Ministry of Fear*—grave fears about another possible attack on the West Coast grew. Facing the grim anxieties and tough consequences of potential invasion, sabotage, and a mad world at war as the conflict progressed, widespread blackouts and bomb scares began in Los Angeles as the nation's movie capital went on heightened alert and Hollywood adapted to a new, unique network of conditions for the duration as "West Coast Lights Dimmed."[82]

Hollywood in the Aftermath of Pearl Harbor

On December 7, 1941, Pearl Harbor brought the global conflict home. The Associated Press noted, "Peace had exploded into the terror of war . . . a bedlam of noise and smoke . . . whistling bombs fell from the sky." In his firsthand account of the attack, veteran James Anderson recalled, "I could see flames, fire and smoke . . . I saw two men flying through the air and the fire, screaming as they went. Where they ended-up I'll never know."[1] Another World War II veteran, Paul Fussell, wrote, "The damage the war visited upon bodies and buildings, planes and tanks and ships, is obvious. Less obvious is the damage it did to intellect, discrimination, honesty, individuality, complexity, ambiguity, and irony, not to mention privacy and wit."[2] This dark cultural transformation is evocative of what French critics found to be so uncanny about American film noir. Despite censorship that promoted "morally uplifting" screen material, a jaded psyche—crucial to film noir—informed films produced during the Second World War that reflected many grave concerns. The uncertain fear, violence, and agonizing hardship of everyday life in wartime America coincided with rationing of basic daily items, war-related shortages and nonmaterial deprivations. This speaks of the profound variance between condoned, regulated, censored, and sanitized propaganda representations of the war and the realities of wartime culture.

World War II's influence on America was far reaching and multifaceted—culturally, politically, ideologically, economically, socially, industrially, technologically, and aesthetically. The global conflict and military mobilization in the United States affected myriad wartime considerations and Hollywood filmmaking practices. War-related circumstances, constraints, incentives, and the government's role in the media—and the film industry's effort to mobilize the war effort—culminated in a distinctly American national cinema. Wartime social, economic, and political concerns redefined and transformed the face of American culture. Abroad, many Europeans fleeing the war emigrated to the United States as the Nazis gained power in the mid-1930s and advanced through Europe by late 1939–41. As early as 1940 Roosevelt had committed U.S. economic support to militarily aid Allies in Britain. This commitment coincided with a massive U.S. military buildup as the federal government became increasingly involved in American industry in moving toward a war economy. Meanwhile, Japan was gaining significant power in the Pacific. With the Japanese bombing of Pearl Harbor, the United States officially declared war on Japan and joined Allied forces against Nazi Germany. Millions of American men went off to war, while millions of American women went off to work in factories to aid wartime industrial production. The military effort and America's surging war machine became an increasing social and economic domestic priority.

At the height of the conflict active military personnel totaled 12,123,455; of these, nearly 300,000 Americans would die in battle, and more than twice as many would be wounded.[3] The conflict deeply affected people and ordinary experience. Novelist William Styron noted, "The class just ahead of me in college was virtually wiped out. Beautiful fellows who had won basketball championships and Phi Beta Kappa keys died like ants in the Normandy invasion. Others only slightly older than I . . . stormed ashore at Tarawa and Iwo Jima and met ugly and horrible deaths on the hot coral and sands."[4] Raymond Chandler, who lived in Los Angeles from 1934 through the end of World War II, wrote to Mrs. Alfred Knopf (his publisher) as he worked on *Farewell, My Lovely:* "The effort to keep my mind off the war has reduced me to the mental age of seven. The things by which we live are the distant flashes of insect wings in a clouded sunlight." He described life in Los Angeles: "There is a touch of the desert about everything in California, and about the minds of the people who live here. During the years when I hated the place I couldn't get away, and now that I have grown to need the harsh smell of the sage I still feel rather out of place here."[5]

The Lights Go Out in Hollywood

Pacific coastlines were gripped by "plain, simple, mass hysteria" following the bombing of Hawaii.[6] In the aftermath of Pearl Harbor the lights went dark in Hollywood. A major military center throughout the duration, Los Angeles enforced blackouts, dimouts, and civil defense air-raid drills in the wake of growing fear and anxiety that Japanese forces might attack America's West Coast. City lights blacked out, sirens wailed, rumors spread, and antiaircraft guns fired. Los Angeles cop and future mayor Tom Bradley recalled, "It was panic. Here we are in the middle of the night, there was no enemy in sight, but someone thought they saw the enemy. They were shooting at random."[7] On December 11, 1941, the *Los Angeles Times* front page read: "LOS ANGELES BLACKED OUT: BOMBS FIRE JAP BATTLESHIP. Planes Search Skies for Foes: Southland Plunged into Darkness as Army Reports Presence of Unidentified Aircraft; Searchlights Seen and Gunfire Reported." Beneath the bold headline a nearly pitch-black photo dominated the page. Taken the previous night, it could easily be an image from a classic 1940s Hollywood film noir. Its title reads, "DOWNTOWN LOS ANGELES GROPES IN ITS FIRST BLACK-OUT." Below, a caption reads: "BROADWAY IN DARKNESS ... the news camera pictures a black cavern, broken here and there by shop signs which merchants were slow in turning out. Cars made light streaks." The article began: "A gigantic black-out, covering the area from Bakersfield south to San Diego and eastward to Boulder City and Las Vegas, Nev., went into effect shortly after 8 o'clock last night on orders from the Army 4th Interceptor Command. It continued until 11:03 p.m. As Los Angeles went dark amidst considerable confusion and uncertainty, the Interceptor Command announced: 'This is not a practice black out.'"[8] What originated as false reports of Japanese bombing attacks on the West Coast in the week following Pearl Harbor became real when Japanese submarines were actually spotted patrolling just two miles off the coast up and down California. (Though there was never an invasion of, or any major damage to, the U.S. West Coast from Japanese submarines, they fired at fishing boats and an oil refinery off Santa Barbara, sunk a freighter up the coast, and floated bombs, starting forest fires.) Panic and alarm swept the city. Xenophobia ran rampant. Soon the government was organizing the internment of Japanese Americans and Japanese resident aliens. Widespread fears of German spies and Japanese subs amplified home-front anxieties.

Xenophobic racial and ethnic prejudice throughout American society during the Second World War was evident in the treatment of ethnic minority groups at home, including Germans, Italian Americans, Japanese Americans, and Japanese resident aliens, and in the media's portrayal of powerfully distorted stereotypes, particularly in Hollywood films. In an environment steeped in wartime anxiety and potential sabotage, the Federal Bureau of Investigation began requiring foreign alien registration to facilitate investigating and monitoring "enemy aliens" residing in America during World War II. The pervasive scope of such a comprehensive nationwide home-front operation added a frightening bit of surveillance and paranoia to everyday life. Resident aliens having citizenship in countries with which America was currently at war, such as Nazi-occupied European states, included many creative individuals in the Hollywood filmmaking community (for example, Michael Curtiz, Peter Lorre, and Max Steiner, among

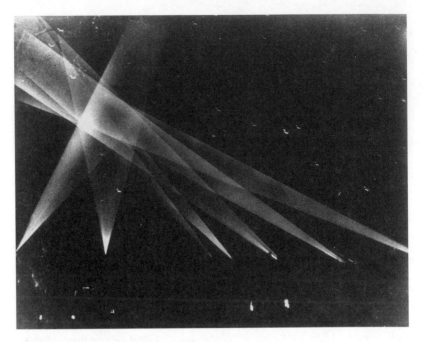

Searchlights and antiaircraft fire fill a blacked-out Los Angeles sky.
USC Special Collections Regional History Center.

other European expatriates). By December 1941 the FBI, charged with watching aliens, had "acquired dossiers on virtually every alien in the country," identifying potential security risks. Congress had passed Alien Registration Act legislation in 1940, requiring them to provide substantial information to the FBI and to periodically report to the federal government agency to facilitate "classification" and surveillance of aliens.[9]

As America mobilized for the war and workers moved from rural areas to city factories, film noir's onscreen urban milieu became more familiar than even a decade earlier. As military production required twenty-four-hour shifts, after-hours settings also became familiar. Blacked-out wartime cities at night resembled the black surroundings and shadowy abysses in film noir. James Cain and Cecil B. DeMille served as air-raid wardens, enforcing the blackouts in Hollywood. "They would drive up and down the steep roads in the dark, making sure everyone in the hills had their lights out or their curtains drawn during those nervous blackouts when Southern California was certain Japanese planes were on the way to do a Pearl Harbor on Grauman's Chinese Theatre." Cain noted, "The war is rotten and stands me on my head."[10] At the heart of *noir*, wartime fears and anxiety were expressed in pictures that explored crimes of brutality with tough characters and—as censorship permitted—graphic violence. Early war-related films like *This Gun for Hire, Across the Pacific, Casablanca,* and *Ministry of Fear* cloaked their crime, violence (even sexual violence), and paranoia in patriotism to slip past censorship. These *noir* prototypes tapped into the growing fears of many Americans, including filmmakers in Hollywood.

Indeed, Los Angeles was classified as a "theater of war" and potential battleground by the U.S. Army. Adding to wartime anxiety was rationing. At motion picture studios film stock, equipment, and electricity were rationed, and lights were used more sparingly on sets shrouded in blackout curtains. Such constraints contributed to the development of a darker trend of American crime dramas. Suddenly Hollywood studios were restricted from shooting at off-studio locations in Los Angeles during the day (for security reasons and because of various war-related rationings [gasoline, rubber tires, autos] and material shortages) and prevented from photographing planes, trains, railroads, bridges, and manufacturing and transportation facilities, all of which were deemed vital to the war effort. Studios, however, could film locations in Los Angeles at night—but fear of sudden blackouts, dimouts, and noise from patrolling planes affected Hollywood productions in the basin's war zone.

Wartime material limitations extended into every sector of the nation's manufacturing industry. The government launched a litany of new federal organizations designed to coordinate economy and propaganda. The War Manpower Commission determined the necessary workers required for military, industry, agriculture, and civilian needs. The War Labor Board (WLB) dealt with labor-management disputes in defense-related industries. The War Production Board (WPB), a civilian agency, regulated America's wartime economy and production of military goods. The Office of Price Administration (OPA) rationed availability and production of civilian goods and set rents and prices.[11] Many Americans accustomed to abundant natural resources and a ready supply of manufactured consumer goods—with a "frontier aura" of freedom and a "milieu of easy excess" affecting "imaginative and psychological relations with their peers"—experienced a "distinct shock" given the shortages and deprivations of the war years.[12] In 1943 Chandler described wartime meat rationing in his "one-store town" near Los Angeles:

The meat situation would make you scream. On Wednesday morning the guy opens at 7 A.M. and all the desert rats are there waiting for him to give out numbered tickets. Anybody who delays long enough to

Lights dim in a Los Angeles blackout.
USC Special Collections Regional History Center.

wash his face is automatically classed as parasitic and gets a high number, if he gets one at all. On Thursday at 10 the inhabitants bring their
bronchitis and halitosis into the store and park in front of the meat
counter and the numbers are coonshouted. When we, having a very
late number, kick our way up to the collapsed hunk of hamburger we
are greeted with a nervous smile that suggests a deacon caught with
his hand in the collection plate, and we leave bearing off enough meat
for the cat. This happens once a week and that is all that happens in
the way of meat . . . I should be out in the desert trying to dig up a

dead gopher. We happened on a rib roast a couple of weeks back, just walked in and said hello, and there the damn thing was. We ate for six nights running, behind drawn curtains, chewing quietly, so the neighbors wouldn't hear.[13]

As the conflict wore on into the summer of 1943,

the nation was ready to abandon the save-and-sacrifice ethic of 1942. Weary of shortages and rationing, of long hours in dingy factories, of curfews, car pools, and Victory Gardens, Americans pursued diversion to relieve the oppression of war . . .

The war years also bared the flesh. The War Production Board ordered cutbacks in the use of all fabrics . . . Dubbed "patriotic chic" by Manhattan designers, the new styles included backless dresses, bare shoulders, short skirts, plunging necklines, and daring two-piece swimwear. The change had been spurred by more than the attempt to conserve cloth or to assert femininity at a time when so many women had adopted male roles. Female fashions suggested the war-inspired weakening of traditional moral values. The consequences of a war that had eroded the moorings of family, church, and community were frightening. In just four years, truancy and juvenile crime had increased by more than twenty percent, the divorce rate by more than sixty percent . . .

[Cultural changes during the war] unleashed forces that Hollywood could not ignore. The 1930 proscriptions against violence and murder, and especially adultery and illicit sex, now seemed outmoded; the endless stream of movies about fearless warriors and faithful wives old-fashioned. Just beyond the door of the Production Code Administration on Hollywood Boulevard, sex was in the ozone.[14]

Wartime conditions would have a tremendous impact on the development of film noir in particular. Despite rationing restrictions, Hollywood did terrific business and "boomed" over the course of the duration. Breaking records and maximizing the financial return of each picture, top-budget A films played longer—and made more money—in theaters during the war. Films that previously played for a week now often played for a month— MGM's popular *Mrs. Miniver,* showcasing strong home-front women and patriotic sacrifice, played several months in the summer of 1942. The trend of showing a smaller number of quality pictures for a more extended period of time meant that fewer films were needed to actually bring in more lucrative profits at the box office. The motion picture industry capitalized on a growing demand for A-class product, which accompanied America's wartime market. Although there was actually a decline in the overall number of pictures released industry-wide, Hollywood focused on making a greater number of top-billed A pictures—including high-quality in-betweeners, near-A, and top-budgeted *noir* pictures. Home-front audiences reinforced the industry's growing appetite for A fare with longer runs in theaters drawing larger crowds at the box office. With many cost-cutting measures, war-related material shortages, and constraints affecting filmmaking—as concern grew over war restrictions such as its ration of film stock (as materials like silver nitrate used to make film were vital to manufacture bombs) and even fears of possible shutdown to conserve vital resources for the combat effort—studios also stockpiled pictures, releasing fewer of the films they made and saving some for later release, as seen in the delayed release of many wartime *noir* pictures like *Ministry of Fear, Mildred Pierce, Conflict, The Postman Always Rings Twice,* and *The Big Sleep.* Wartime conditions made color film less practical and often unavailable. By late 1942 *Variety* reported, "In a race against the time when wartime exigencies are expected to circumscribe activities via further inroads on talent, technicians, material and equipment, Hollywood studios are steaming ahead at the speediest production clip in history in order to build up their picture stocks."[15] In a flurry of burgeoning *noir* activity Paramount adapted Cornell Woolrich's *The Black Curtain* (as B *noir Street of Chance*) on the heels of *This Gun for Hire,* followed by *Ministry of Fear* and *Double Indemnity;* 20th Century–Fox released *I Wake Up Screaming* and shot *Moontide;* Val Lewton's RKO B unit filmed Woolrich's *Black Alibi* (as *The Leopard Man*) and proto-*noir* psychological-horror classics *Cat People, The Seventh Victim, The Ghost Ship, I Walked with a Zombie,* and *Curse of the Cat People,* followed by Chandler's *Farewell, My Lovely;* Warners completed *Conflict;* Universal shot Woolrich's *Phantom Lady* and *Christmas Holiday;* Monogram produced *When Strangers Marry;* and hard-boiled writers like Chandler penned tough screenplays.

Among the chief effects of the war was a manpower shortage Hollywood experienced as top stars, writers, directors, technical personnel, and production executives joined the war effort. In 1942 twenty-seven hundred studio employees left Hollywood for active military duty, and by 1944 more than six thousand had entered the service. Male stars such as James Stewart, Clark Gable, Mickey Rooney, Henry Fonda, Tyrone Power, Robert Taylor, Robert Montgomery, Douglas Fairbanks Jr., Red Skelton, Alan Ladd, and Glenn Ford; directors John Huston, Frank Capra, John Ford, William

Wyler, and George Stevens; even studio executives Darryl Zanuck and Jack Warner enlisted. Hollywood's labor need provided wartime opportunity for actors like Fred MacMurray, John Wayne, Ronald Reagan, and older men unable to serve, such as Humphrey Bogart and Edward G. Robinson; for cinematographers Arthur Edeson, John Seitz, and Henry Sharp; and for writer Raymond Chandler.

In November 1943 *Variety* noted: "Shortage of story materials and writers now has film companies seriously ogling the pulp mag scripts and scriptors. It marks the first time that Hollywood has initiated a concerted drive to replenish its dwindling library supplies and its scripter ranks from the 20 cent-a-word authors of the weird-snappy-breezy-argosy-spy-crime-detective mag school."[16] An influx of new talent ably filled creative positions—including actors Gregory Peck, Van Johnson, and Ray Milland; directors Mark Robson, Robert Wise, Edward Dmytryk, and Jacques Tourneur; and the many émigrés from Europe. Hollywood's expanding émigré community included Fritz Lang, Robert Siodmak, Edgar Ulmer, Billy Wilder, Fred Zinnemann, Anatole Litvak, Peter Lorre, Conrad Veidt, Henry Blanke, Paul Henreid, Ingrid Bergman, Marcel Dalio, Alfred Hitchcock, Jean Gabin, Michael Curtiz, Max Steiner, Boris Ingster, Douglas Sirk, and Joan Harrison. Other new faces gained their first shot at filmmaking as an increasing number of women became involved in the production process. Despite the rise in female creative positions (writing, editing, even producing), women often had to function and write as men within a studio system environment dominated and controlled by a male power structure. Female talent, however, did enjoy success during the war. Studios targeted a wartime audience segregated by gender and initiated a massive wartime distribution network aimed at a male combat audience at international military fronts and a domestic (or Allied) female home-front audience.

As support for the war ramped up, federal income tax brackets rose to 90 percent to finance the defense buildup. This tax rate affected the majority of Hollywood's top-salaried talent. To avoid the wartime 90 percent income tax bracket, much of Hollywood's highest paid (often creative, executive, or "above-the-line") talent sought independent production deals as combination writer-producer-directors, or "hyphenates," so income would be taxed at a mere 25 percent, as capital gains rather than as salaried income. These increasingly powerful hyphenate writer-directors, writer-producers, and producer-directors also enjoyed greater (often unprecedented) creative control during the 1940s. As basic materials became scarce, film industry production costs rose. Studio executives initiated across-the-board pay cuts for personnel to support the war effort. Extravagant production and travel plans were pared down unless they could be justified as promoting the war effort. As the war continued, wartime conditions and material limitations significantly influenced filmmaking practices as Hollywood coped with severe production restrictions by 1941 (escalating in 1942 and 1943). Such constraints necessitated stringent rationing of supplies and film stock, decreased use of lighting and electricity, war-related bans on filming transportation and military facilities, elimination of daytime location shooting in Los Angeles (for security and rationing purposes), air-raid and civil defense drills, dimout and blackout regulations at night, careful use of sound-stage production space and construction supplies, tarping over studio back-lot "exteriors," and recycling of sets and costumes.

In Hollywood the government's war efforts extended beyond rationing. Like other U.S. industries, the motion picture industry experienced increased federal involvement throughout the war years. Domestic political policy and national debate, antitrust legislation, social and economic concerns, wartime business and consumption following the Depression, and mobilization of propaganda in other media significantly influenced film production and Hollywood's motion picture industry in relation to overall American popular and political culture during World War II. Washington's House Un-American Activities Committee (HUAC), the Paramount antitrust case, and television research and development—factors contributing to "dis-integration" of the Hollywood studio system after the war—were initiated during the late 1930s as wartime events in Europe escalated. The government conveniently stalled federal antitrust action against the vertically integrated studio system oligopoly as motion picture production was redirected toward supporting and promoting the war effort.

The Office of War Information (OWI) was the government's official propaganda agency. It served as liaison between Washington, the national press, and media and disseminated news releases and information about the war to radio, press, and motion picture news media.[17] The OWI's mission was to formulate and carry out, "by means of the press, radio and motion pictures, programs designed to facilitate an understanding in the United States and abroad of the progress of the war effort and of the policies, activities, and aims of the government."[18] Through its Hollywood office, the Bureau of Motion Pictures (BMP), the OWI infused political propaganda into Hollywood films to highlight the war effort with domestic social, political, and economic issues crucial to wartime American culture. Thus Clayton Koppes and Gregory Black point out that although wartime films reflected American culture, censorship and external forces such as government mediation significantly "refracted" wartime representations through "multiple mirrors" that often affected images. These myriad factors culminating in the final release of film "products" and affecting the wartime production of American films are especially important as they relate to America's wartime experience and pressures placed on the industry during the early to mid-1940s. As Koppes and Black suggest, Office of War Information regulation in Hollywood represented the "most comprehensive and sustained government attempt to change the content of a mass medium in American history . . . Wartime censorship told the mass media what not to make known" and what "should, in fact, be included . . . Labor and capital buried their differences for a greater cause; class, ethnic, and racial divisions evaporated in the foxholes and on the assembly line; even estranged family members were reconciled through the agency of war."[19] The wartime propaganda experience is fascinating not only for the messages generated by this unique film industry liaison with Washington but also for how changes in policy influenced Hollywood films and popular culture. Shallow and simplistic messages translated into a skewed "New Deal / One World" vision on the screen, including Hollywood's racially stereotypical representations of the enemy or unity in combat squads reflecting a cross section of society, despite the fact that, in reality, ethnic minorities such as African Americans remained segregated during the conflict. In June 1942 the federal government established the OWI, influenced by its liberal vice president Henry Wallace (later attacked by HUAC as "soft on communism" in the conservative cold war era).

By early July the OWI focused on the film industry by consolidating operations that had been headed by Lowell Mellett since December 1941. The Bureau of Motion Pictures created a list of six "acceptable" themes: (1) issues—why we fight, (2) the enemy—whom we fight, (3) united nations and allied peoples, (4) work and production, (5) the home front, and (6) the fighting forces. Dissension among different organizations—including the Office of War Information and its West Coast Bureau of Motion Pictures, Office of Censorship, competing branches of the military, Hollywood studios, the industry's existing mechanism of self-censorship through the Production Code Administration, and the relationship between key individuals at those organizations such as Elmer Davis, Lowell Mellett, Nelson Poynter, Byron Price, Ulric Bell, and Joseph Breen—created a complicated censorship environment where regulatory bodies often contradicted each other. Many factors affected Washington's efforts to streamline and consolidate regulation, control the dissemination of propaganda, and convey a unified message to mobilize the American public: win the war.

The government increasingly regulated film content by 1942–43 as the

film industry faced external federal regulation through the OWI's Bureau
of Motion Pictures. Midway in the war, however, the federal Office of Censorship sanctioned prowar propaganda and violent depictions of
(racial/Japanese atrocity) crime for war-related propaganda purposes.[20]
This policy regarding crime conflicted with the studio system's Production
Code censorship. Federal regulation coincided with a decrease in the industry's internal self-censorship regulation by the Production Code Administration during World War II. Warner Bros.' *Confessions of a Nazi Spy* undermined the PCA's effort to prevent the depiction of propaganda in
Hollywood films and contributed to what Richard Jewell calls the "slow
process of PCA liberalization," which continued throughout the war. Six
months after America's entry into World War II the political agenda of the
Bureau of Motion Pictures discouraged "any cinematic moment that might
compromise the vision of an all powerful, utopian United States, from realistically gruesome battle scenes abroad to black market activity at home."[21]

The OWI political agenda (and racial polemics) in wartime newsreels
condoned and promoted screen violence for propaganda purposes—establishing a precedent for narrative films, despite PCA censorship. This regulatory shift would ultimately enable increasing war-related and *noir* crime
violence to be depicted onscreen. As in many Hollywood propaganda narratives, political potboilers like RKO's 1943 low-budget yarns *Hitler's Children* and *Behind the Rising Sun* in Val Lewton's unit—directed by Edward
Dmytryk just before *Murder, My Sweet* and *Cornered*—capitalized on patriotic crime and violence, converting gangsters into the enemy, especially
Nazis.

Fritz Lang's potboiler *Hangmen Also Die* (1943) conveyed propagandis-
tic brutality—and a litany of Code violations—based on real events. The
film was shot in newsreel style and incorporated documentary newsreel
footage. Simulating an investigative thriller, it tackled actual wartime atrocities, corruption, and murder in a Nazi-occupied city. Publicity for this film
revealed Hollywood's growing propensity for violence as a result of the war.
Ads read: "KILL . . . KILL . . . KILL . . . KILL . . . " *Motion Picture Daily* called
Hangmen Also Die "authentic." Noting its "Nazi reign of terror," "blood-
bath," "implacable reality," and "brutishness" beyond "customary Hollywood studio manner," *Variety* called it "grim and shocking," "hideous reality," a "forceful document . . . almost documentary cinema," and "the most
effective piece of propaganda to emerge from Hollywood," where "guns and
cruelty of the occupation police" and "hostage murders" have the "dreadful fascination" of "good war pictures." The publication also commended
James Wong Howe's stark photography as "magnificent," opining that

"propaganda can be art." James Agee wrote, "They have chosen to use brutality, American gangster idiom, and middle high German cinematic style to get it across, and it is rich with clever melodrama," with "over-*maestoso* directional touches, and the sort of Querschnitt sophistication for detail which Lang always has." A girl is shown in silhouette, imprisoned with a ragged, beaten woman. Howe's low-key proto-*noir* backlighting casts long, barred shadows across the claustrophobic cell—anticipating the shadowy jail scene in *Phantom Lady*. Like *noir*'s gangsters and corrupt cops, Lang's Nazis sip coffee, eat sausage, crack knuckles, and pop pimples while torturing prisoners and ordering executions—"a fat repulsive figure of energetic horror," a "gross, shrewd [Gestapo] detective, painstakingly piecing together his case with the aid of torture and treachery . . . punctuated by orgies with women and beer."[22]

Politically topical and censorable content was justified by the urgency of World War II, and realism drew on true stories of events often resulting from the war. Dramatization of atrocities was allowed because they actually happened. (Lang's film was an independent production released through United Artists, which also released co-owner Charlie Chaplin's *The Great Dictator* in 1940 and, like Warner Bros., was willing to take more risks with regard to PCA censure of topical violence and political subjects in support of the war.) As the government condoned the graphic depiction of political war-related violence for propaganda purposes in newsreels, filmgoers were exposed to increasingly stark documentary images onscreen by mid-1943. This exposure coincided with a "sudden willingness" by the PCA to endorse projects based on material that had formerly been banned. In terms of censorship, for example, *Double Indemnity* was a "watershed" picture. It enabled a plethora of *noir* films to be produced and approved by the PCA during and after the war.[23]

Responding to extensive wartime cost-cutting measures, creative economizing affected Hollywood *noir* film style. Hard-boiled icon Robert Mitchum once jested, "Hell, we didn't know what *film noir* was in those days. We were just making movies. Cary Grant and all the big stars got all the lights. We lit our sets with cigarette butts."[24] Director Mark Robson recalled that in shooting *The Seventh Victim* (1943) on a studio sound stage with recycled sets and back-lot streets "the less light we put on them the better they looked."[25] In fact, war-related international market closures, reduced revenue, necessary cost-cutting, and material shortages began to be a concern in Hollywood as early as 1940, coinciding with RKO's production of *Stranger on the Third Floor*. By August *American Cinematographer* was already addressing the issue in "Cinematographers Show How to Achieve

Production Economies." *This Gun for Hire* is a fine example of filmmaking constraints affecting how pictures were shot even before Pearl Harbor. In the early 1940s, as America became more directly and heavily involved in the international conflict, production concerns escalated. In 1941 Harry Warner spoke to a group of cameramen, writers, directors, and actors with passionate patriotic resolve: "The thoughtless waste of one hundred feet of film may cost the life of an American soldier who may be your son or your brother." In March 1942 Warner stated, "Waste more deadly than sabotage." Jack Warner chastised actor Peter Lorre for blowing a series of takes: "There is a war on, and we are trying to save film."[26] It was a severe concern by late 1942 and even more sorely felt by 1943.

Tremendous material restrictions hit the film industry by 1942–43. War-related rationing; government-mandated $5,000 set-construction limits; and constraints on lighting, electricity, gas, tires, rubber, cars, and location shooting became a reality as blackouts, dimouts, and air-raid drills prepared for possible West Coast attack. Alfred Hitchcock and cinematographer Joseph Valentine circumvented wartime set-construction limits by leaving Hollywood and shooting *Shadow of a Doubt* (produced in 1942, released in 1943) on location in Newark, New Jersey, and Santa Rosa, in northern California, but still had to film around dimout restrictions on lighting for night scenes. Macabre gothic crime thriller *Shadow of a Doubt* starred Joseph Cotten as the "Merry Widow" murderer and Teresa Wright as his niece and namesake. Gordon McDonell's *Uncle Charlie*—adapted by Thornton Wilder, Sally Benson, and Alma Reville—originally included a "John Garfield type" and a "Fontaine type." Hitchcock wired Fontaine in June 1942: "DO YOU WANT TO PLAY THE LEAD IN MY NEXT CONFIDENTIALLY BECAUSE S[ELZNICK] DOES NOT KNOW I'VE TELEGRAPHED YOU LOVE."[27] In January 1943 *Life* magazine announced, "$5,000 Production: Hitchcock makes thriller under WPA order on new sets":

> Alfred Hitchcock has already proved himself ingenious in creating suspense-filled melodramas. As a director of one of the first movies to be produced under the Government restriction placing a $5,000 ceiling on new materials used for sets, he has shown he has more than one trick up his sleeve. Accustomed to spending more than $100,000 on sets alone for one picture, Hitchcock made *Shadow of a Doubt* by reverting to the "location shooting" of early movie days. Instead of elaborate sets he used the real thing. To shoot scenes supposed to take place in New Jersey, he traveled cross-country and shot them in New Jersey. Instead of building a studio version of a typical American city,

his main setting, he searched for a ready-made one. Selecting Santa Rosa, Calif. (pop. 13,000), Hitchcock with his cast and crew took over the entire city for four weeks, converted it into a complete motion-picture studio. The result is an exciting and highly realistic film whose new set cost, mainly for studio replicas, was well under the imposed limit.[28]

In June 1942 cinematographer James Wong Howe addressed the issue of Hollywood's war-related rationing and industrial production restrictions in *American Cinematographer,* proposing that "visual suggestion can enhance 'rationed' sets."[29] As rationed filmmaking materials became more limited by 1943, Howe argued that realistic techniques could effectively and expediently render high production values, suggesting "newsreel style" as a means to aesthetically achieve production economy in the lean filmmaking environment of wartime Hollywood. "Unaware of the documentary method before the war began . . . audience[s] saw newsreels, 'March of Time' . . . but real awareness grew only when nations began to record on film the history of their countries at war. We began to see documentaries from England and Russia and . . . Germany. Magazines like *Life* and *Look* acquainted us with the documentary 'still' . . . Film taught us what war looked like."[30] Hollywood's realism trend added a nonfiction look to patriotic crime pictures and combat films. *Noir* visual style benefited from World War II documentary trends and what 1940s cinematographers Howe and John Seitz and director Billy Wilder called newsreel style. *Noir* preludes like *This Gun for Hire* fused topical realism and expatriate expressionism as cameramen composed *noir* mise-en-scène to create a stark aesthetic in these dark pictures.[31]

Advances in news coverage to report combat overseas contributed to a surge in war-related documentaries and newsreels during this time. (In fact, newsreels and documentaries related to the war were quite heavy before Pearl Harbor.) Between 1942 and 1943 newsreel companies transformed their headline-focused production into more timely, graphic depictions of military action from the front; 80 percent of all newsreels in 1942 included coverage of the war, and this rose to 90 percent in 1943. By late 1942 FDR eased military restrictions on filming actual combat, while technological and combat reporting logistics improvements aided news coverage. Documentary film coverage improved as Hollywood filmmakers joined the military and as war-related British documentaries were released in the United States. John Ford's short film *The Battle of Midway* (1942) and the British nonfiction feature *Desert Victory* (1943) both won Oscars, as widespread documentary film coverage of the war and combat dramas, such as *Wake Island* (1942) and *Sahara* (1943), more accurately dramatized combat. Based on actual events in Africa, the stark cinematography in *Sahara* simulated the gritty filming limitations of front-line news coverage: available lighting producing darker high-contrast images and using faster light-sensitive film stock and portable lightweight cameras to capture military action. Director of photography Rudolph Maté, who later shot *Gilda*, was nominated for an Academy Award for his camerawork on *Sahara*. James Agee acknowledged the film's influential visual style: "It borrows chiefly from the English, a sort of light-alloy modification of realism which makes the traditional Hollywood idiom seem as obsolete as a minuet."[32]

Newsreel visual style complemented the graphic content of combat films, becoming more brutal and violent, aided in part by the federal government's condoning the depiction of war-related atrocities for propaganda purposes by 1943–44—a precedent for narrative film content in direct collision with the Production Code.[33] Wartime films noir produced in 1943 and 1944, such as *Double Indemnity,* keenly illustrate this trend toward more graphic content enabled by the easing of PCA enforcement. Documentary screen accounts of the conflict grew uncompromisingly realistic and grim, as in John Huston's graphic news report *The Battle of San Pietro* (filmed in 1944, released in May 1945), as the war continued and Washington became more permissive with federal censorship.[34] Many wartime narrative films included newsreel footage for heightened authenticity, and this appropriation of realism and real-life violence refined proto-*noir* cinematography.

Howe had been particularly impressed with wartime documentary. He recalled the darker shadows in combat documentaries filmed with available light, showing stark graphic content and a tattered, deglamorized setting to newsreel audiences. "In a fairly recent Russian documentary there is a remarkable shot. In the foreground is the narrow slit of a cellar window. Silhouetted against the window is the helmet of a Russian sniper. The background is the street outside—a jumble of battle-shattered buildings." The camera, just a few feet behind the dark shadow of the sniper's head, films the action. As a "German soldier emerges cautiously from the cover of a wall," the sniper shoots and the Nazi soldier "crumbles under the impact of the bullet . . . The face of the Russian sniper is never seen. Nor does the half-light of the cellar provide any convenient high lights on his helmet," only natural source light. "Despite the hundreds of thousands of feet of battle shots being shown," Howe explains, "we are not accustomed to seeing such an intimate picture of a man's death." It is real. "Equipment now in use by the Army and Navy, developed from the necessity of wartime expediency, offers a new and vital opportunity to the motion picture industry, a new and much-needed mechanical flexibility and simplicity." He adds that using small cameras developed to facilitate wartime shooting will also "solve staggering production problems," liberating the camera from previous filming limitations. Howe noted it was no longer necessary to "knock an automobile or a plane apart to let a camera in . . . Many cameramen now in the armed forces will return to Hollywood with a finer appreciation of equipment and its use, along with experience in the making of documentary films." After filming Lang's propaganda film *Hangmen Also Die*, Howe asserted that "good photography is always documentary."[35]

Independent producer Samuel Goldwyn noted the importance of documentary pictures beyond newsreels and combat films. Industry trades cited the increasing trend toward realism in Hollywood and the American public's avid interest in the war. Audiences preferred "factual material as against synthetic screen war drama," and the trades forecast an increase in this trend "even after peace, when the dramatic and tragic happenings of war can better be appreciated in retrospect."[36] Realistic wartime coverage was hitting American screens, and even during the war filmmakers were returning from combat. The *New York Times* actually cited the wartime David O. Selznick–Alfred Hitchcock psychological *noir* thriller *Spellbound* (originally titled *The House of Dr. Edwardes*) as an exemplar of this industry trend toward realism. It referred to the film as Hitchcock's first Hollywood project after returning from military service directing documentary films for the British Ministry of Information:

> The suspenseful murder-mystery plot is laid in and about a sanitarium. To provide an explanation of psychiatry and the treatment of mental diseases necessary to a better understanding of the story, the beginning of the picture is to be strictly documentary . . . The film will open on the private asylum and, as the camera takes in the various departments and elements of the institution, a narrator, in typical factual style, will describe the place and the scientific treatment accorded the patients. Then, to use Mr. Hitchcock's expression, the camera will "drift" into the unfolding of the fictional story.

Hitchcock explained that the "utilization of the documentation method solves a problem in the telling of this unique scientific-background story that could not have been adequately handled otherwise." Interestingly, this is not how Hitchcock's finished film begins. Hitchcock fuses the original conceit for *Spellbound*—simulating nonfiction technique—with his trademark psychological suspense conventions to create a wartime *noir* thriller that plays with subjective point of view, memory, and amnesia and creates sexual tension. Hitchcock even convinced producer Selznick to hire famed surrealist Salvador Dalí to design a wild dream sequence—shot by William Cameron Menzies—that was cut and shortened in the final release. *Spellbound* stars Ingrid Bergman as a psychologist flirting with danger by becoming romantically involved with a criminally unstable coworker (Gregory Peck), who she knows is an impostor and possibly a murderer. The lucrative World War II–era *noir* film earned nearly $5 million.[37]

Technological advancements in film production precipitated by the war—producing lightweight production equipment, better "coated" camera lenses, and faster light-sensitive film stock—made actual night-for-night shooting possible in deep focus with significantly less light. Cinematically, the complex circumstances of the war contributed to starker visual style and narrative content in wartime Hollywood film productions. The combination of war-related material limitations (conserving sets, lights, electricity, film stock), blackout and dimout regulations—informed by anxieties over wartime bombing—advanced the development of *noir* films. Newsreel style capitalized on wartime production constraints, technological possibility, blackouts, and decreased lighting to facilitate a darker style of Hollywood cinematography. What emerged during the war was a stark graphic, hard-hitting style of realism that also sought to emulate war-related front-line news coverage shot with available lighting and visually translate it to the bigger Hollywood narrative screen. War-related material limitations—especially shortages of film stock—and a new emphasis on combat realism contributed to a trend toward comparatively inexpensive, economical, black-and-white films, which ultimately outnumbered more lavish Technicolor pictures (with the exception of 20th Century–Fox Betty Grable musicals). These World War II narrative filmmaking trends coincided with the massive production of documentary newsreels that successfully promoted a prowar American national agenda and established cinematic precedents in the depiction of onscreen violence, death, crime, and racial representations (echoed in stark footage of photojournalism magazines such as *Life*). Studios sought projects that could be shot under efficient cost-cutting production constraints—shadows, rain, fog, low-key lighting, and reflective surfaces (mirrors, water), as well as disguised, recycled, or sparse sets—while capitalizing on racy depictions of crime, violence, and sexual topics that were now possible because of lapses in PCA enforcement during the war.

Adapting to Wartime

With America's entry into World War II, and with Breen still away from the PCA, Hollywood seized the opportunity to gain PCA endorsement on screen material with censorable content. The period immediately following U.S. involvement in the war provided a golden window for studios to get the jump on potentially censorable productions before the Bureau of Motion Pictures' effort to regulate film content commenced six months later. Like *This Gun for Hire*, 20th Century–Fox's *Moontide*, Paramount's *Street of Chance*, and Warner Bros.' *Across the Pacific* and *Casablanca* were produced during this permissive period. Just days after Pearl Harbor, Warner producer Hal Wallis purchased the *Saturday Evening Post* serial "Aloha Means Goodbye" at the behest of writer Richard Macauley, and Bogart was given the lead undercover ex-naval officer role "combining acid and comedy" to exploit his success in *The Maltese Falcon*. Eventually, studio head Jack Warner retitled the dark, racist, anti-Japanese espionage action film *Across the Pacific*. Warner's paranoid post–Pearl Harbor *Maltese Falcon* follow-up features proto-*noir* cinematic style, where a mirror reflects the menacing face of a Japanese voyeur in Bogart's black bedroom. *Across the Pacific* reunited Bogart with *Maltese Falcon* costars Mary Astor and Sydney Greenstreet—and even included a walk-on role by Peter Lorre—as well as director John Huston, who had to leave during production to serve in World War II (as *All through the Night* director Vincent Sherman completed the picture). *Across the Pacific* earned critical accolades and handsomely recovered its $576,000 cost, grossing $1.3 million for Warners.[38] In fact, after seeing the public's enthusiastic response to *Across the Pacific*, Jack Warner called Bogart the studio's Clark Gable.[39] Promoting American victory, posters for the film showed the star clobbering a Japanese soldier; the posters were available in two versions—one read, "SNAPSHOT OF A GUY WHO LOVES HIS WORK"; the other exclaimed, "FOLKS, I'VE BEEN SAYING THIS SINCE DECEMBER 7!"[40]

One film in particular captures the spirit of the anxieties at Warner Bros. studio and provides fascinating insight into wartime filmmaking conditions in the nation's motion picture industry. As a kind of microcosm for wartime Hollywood, *Casablanca* illustrates the important actual wartime life and daily constraints in the filmmaking home front leading to *noir* during this time. While not usually associated with film noir, the film's uncanny, uncertain violent wartime environment—and destabilized crime psyche so crucial to *noir*—was a patriotic prelude to the emergence of the *noir* series in this social, political, and ideological terrain. Blackouts and wartime conditions certainly affected the film's production—it was as if someone had drawn the blinds as it captured wartime fears and anxieties. Much of the cinematography in *Casablanca,* though not quite film noir, was even darker than *The Maltese Falcon.* Despite the sentimental nature of its tragic romance—and the nationalism of its patriotic imperative—its underlying illicit love triangle and adulterous protagonists, crime, corruption, intrigue, and black market operations created an atmosphere that was an interesting, albeit unlikely, wartime prototype for film noir. Hollywood's *noir* trend began to proliferate a year later—after young Austrian expatriate Billy Wilder directed his third film, *Double Indemnity,* at Paramount and as *Casablanca* won the Best Picture Oscar for 1943. Like *The Maltese Falcon* and *Double Indemnity,* the corrupt setting, shady characters, shadowy visuals, and barbed witty dialogue in *Casablanca* anticipate film noir.

Casablanca revolved around the illegal activity in a smoky bar in the shady, exotic setting of French Morocco and its cynical, mysterious American-exile owner. Like film noir's ambiguous and duplicitous urban jungle, Casablanca is a cramped, crowded, claustrophobic city where an underworld climate and abundant dubious nocturnal activity proliferate. A microworld of fog, blackouts, late-night curfews, payoffs, scanning searchlights, and Rick's neon sign, the narrative is populated by gangsters, gamblers, con artists, and corrupt cops, along with Nazis and desperate refugees willing to sell their souls to get to America. Rick is a jaded war veteran who sticks his neck out for nobody, much like private dick Sam Spade in *The Maltese Falcon.* Although he has a past and has had affairs with women, he is callously unaffected by romantic pursuits until the reappearance of ex-flame Ilsa (Ingrid Bergman), which triggers an alcoholic binge, a tumultuous flashback of their war-torn love affair, his self-destructive rage, and a heated, bitter exchange in his shadowy bar after hours. The story becomes a love triangle when she turns out to be married, resumes her affair with Rick, and persuades him to give her letters of transit to help get her resistance leader husband safely out of the country. All through *Casablanca* Ilsa's eyes glisten in the dark, especially when she stands in the doorway of the blackened abyss of Rick's bar or is poised to shoot her lover (Bogart) in his bedroom surrounded by barred shadows. In the end, despite the unsavory and dangerous criminal setting, like Spade in *The Maltese Falcon,* Bogart's conflicted antihero does the right thing—in this case gunning down the Nazi commander, sending his love off (with her husband), and leaving with his buddy Renault (Claude Rains) to join the war effort.

Murray Burnett and Joan Alison's play *Everybody Comes to Rick's* arrived at Warner Bros. studio the day after Pearl Harbor. Story department head

Irene Lee approved it just days after the attack, as lights went out in Hollywood and Los Angeles went on heightened alert. Hal Wallis, in charge of A pictures, purchased the screen rights for $20,000 on December 27, 1941. By February 1942 Wallis, no longer supervising all of Warners' top productions, had negotiated a new contract, giving him greater creative control over a few individual projects. Now an in-house independent producer, Wallis personally had his eye on a prestige picture for Bogart. When Jack Warner suggested George Raft for the lead, Wallis insisted Rick was ideally written for Bogart. In the first draft of the script Rick's lover, Ilsa, was Lois Meredith—tough, single, seductive, duplicitous—more of a loose femme fatale, two-timing and dumping Rick, returning as another man's mistress, pulling a gun, and having sex with him. Writer Julius Epstein called her "hard-boiled, sophisticated. She was a cosmopolitan woman who slept around a lot . . . Well, who was going to believe that about *Ingrid Bergman?*"[41]

Wallis wanted to borrow émigré actress Bergman from Selznick as Bogart's costar. It was a perfect choice to satisfy the Hays Office. On his return to the PCA in May 1942 Joseph Breen haggled to sanitize Lois and clean up the taint of illicit sex and moral impropriety. (One wonders if *Casablanca* would have been more of a *proto-noir* if "hard-boiled" Lois hadn't been tamed and racy material purged.) Wallis sent writers Julius and Philip Epstein to pitch the project. Julius recalled, "I start to tell the story. 'Uh, it's about Casablanca, and the *refugees* are there, and they're trying to get out, and there's letters of *transit,* and a fella has them and the cops come and get him'—And I realize I'm talking about twenty minutes and I haven't even *mentioned* the character of Bergman. So I say, 'Oh, what the hell! It's going to be a lot of shit like *Algiers.*'" *Algiers* had been a smash hit for Hedy Lamarr and Charles Boyer, and almost a shot-for-shot rip-off of *Pépé le Moko* (which in turn was loosely based on Hawks's gangster picture *Scarface*). Wallis considered casting Lamarr as Lois, but MGM chief Louis B. Mayer nixed the idea. Wallis even changed the title from *Everybody Comes to Rick's* to *Casablanca* in an effort to copy *Algiers.* The ambience of *Pépé le Moko* and its Hollywood incarnation, *Algiers,* is palpable in *Casablanca.* Sanitized Ilsa "deceives and betrays both men." She had "an element of danger about her . . . part lover, part destroyer, and enchantress whose innocence could both beguile a man and lure him to his destruction. Or at the very least, leave him in a railroad station in Paris with his guts kicked in." Wallis had his choice of the best Warner Bros. talent, including Hungarian-born Austrian émigré director Michael Curtiz, whom he assigned to direct the picture. Curtiz contributed a distinctly European style, tight pace, and realistic action to *Casablanca.* The film recast romantic melodrama with dark political hues, verbal wit, espionage themes, and Nazi occupation; like *This Gun for Hire* it redeemed unsavory and criminal deeds with patriotic sacrifice. The PCA described its plot as "an American nightclub owner in Morocco who helps an anti-Nazi couple escape to America via Lisbon."[42]

The property was well suited to the studio's political stance. Warner Bros., headed by Harry and Jack Warner, was the most topical, prowar, pro-FDR, anti-Nazi, economically frugal, and systematically rigid of Hollywood's major studios—especially during the war. Originally from Poland, Harry had faced anti-Semitism firsthand and was fervently against the rise of Hitler and Nazi fascism spreading throughout Europe. The most politically and ideologically progressive of the majors, Warners took political risks: it was the first Hollywood studio to speak out against the Nazis—in the early 1930s, well before its colleagues. Warners was also the first to close its German facilities (in July 1934), regardless of international revenue considerations. Moreover, Warner Bros. was willing to take chances with provocative, topical films such as *Confessions of a Nazi Spy*. After leaping from minor to major in the late 1920s by capitalizing on the conversion to sound films, the studio prided itself on Depression-era efficiency, in expediently churning out tightly paced pictures cheap and fast. By the early 1940s Warners, like other Hollywood studios, produced fewer films a year, with an increasing number of higher-budgeted A pictures. In the constrained production environment of Warner Bros. the war heightened concerns about saving film, paper, and electricity and avoiding wastefulness. In March 1942 the internal studio publication *Warner Club News* emphatically stated the importance of turning lights off and saving nails (the first item to disappear from hardware supplies during the war)—not only to cut costs but to aid in the war effort. Economic compulsion fueled a kind of war-driven institutional fervor. "Colonel" Jack Warner exclaimed: "Without them [nails] we cannot build sets, without sets it would be almost impossible to make pictures. When we can't make pictures there are no jobs for any of us."[43]

In the growing fear of a Japanese attack on the West Coast by late December 1941 (as negotiations to purchase *Everybody Comes to Rick's* progressed), studio paranoia ensued as to whether Warners' twenty-one sound stages should be camouflaged by the art department because they resembled Lockheed's airplane hangers nearby. (Rumor had it Colonel Warner considered painting a huge arrow atop their largest sound stage stating: "Lockheed, That Way ⇒" to discourage enemy planes from targeting the film studio with bombs.) Warner Bros. was the most expedient studio to mobilize for the war effort—from its corporate institutional policy donat-

ing trucks and transport equipment to mobilizing individual volunteer employees and Warner "Warvets" ex-servicemen in operating searchlights,
firearm training, and patrolling the coastline against possible enemy aircraft attack. War-related constraints and paranoia certainly influenced production on *Casablanca*. Claude Rains's corrupt prefect of police, Captain
Renault, refers to evening curfews, gasoline rationing, even rationing
women. The PCA objected to Renault's remarking how "extravagant" Rick
is "throwing women away" and adding, "Someday they may be *rationed!*"
(The line was changed to "scarce.")[44] Wartime filming for *Casablanca* ended
daily at 6:30 p.m. to allow production cast and crew to get home before
dark. The lead story in the *Los Angeles Times* the day *Casablanca* began
shooting stated "unidentified airplanes" had "caused Los Angeles to be
blacked out the night before. The planes had turned out to be friendly, but,
two days later, a nightly dimout began in some parts of the city, in order to
reduce the danger of American freighters' being spotlighted by Japanese
submarines."[45]

The progressively dark visuals in *Casablanca* correspond directly to the
war: the darkened exterior neon sign and searchlights outside Rick's implying blackouts and air raids; the pitch-black interior of the bar as Rick hits
the bottle and remembers Paris—triggering a wartime flashback of his earlier romance, the Nazis invading Paris, and rain pelting his fedora, trench
coat, and letter from Ilsa at the train station after her mysterious disappear-
ance; recurrent low-key interiors as Ilsa appears in a shard of light in Rick's
blackened bar and later in his private office or peers through venetian blind
shadows in Victor's (Paul Henreid) hotel room. Rick's self-destructive binge
and tormented masculinity in an unlit room evoke the self-destructive male
antihero in film noir. Ilsa's recurrent, mysterious reappearance in the dark—
even holding a gun pointed at Rick as she surprises him in his private office—also suggests a *noir* femme fatale. Wartime material limitations affected filming and cultivated the film's proto-*noir* images. The Paris
flashback was the first sequence shot when production began in May 1942.
The train station was a recycled set from *Now Voyager*. (Warners was recycling by late 1940–41, disguising sets made for its patriotic wartime money-
maker *Sergeant York* with rain, mist, shadow, and low-key lighting so that
they could be used in the gritty musical gangster *noir Blues in the Night*.)[46]
The famous finale for *Casablanca* used murky fog, dim lighting, and a distant long shot of props with dwarf extras in the background to create the
illusion of larger sets. A phony cutout plane and Warners' sound stage #1
doubled for an airport. Such techniques, devised to trick the eye, would be
applied to the imagery and aesthetics of film noir.

Producer Hal Wallis had wanted cinematographer James Wong Howe to film the picture, but the talented cameraman was committed to another Warners production. Instead, silent film veteran Arthur Edeson, cinematographer on classic horror films such as *Frankenstein, The Old Dark House, The Invisible Man,* and *The Maltese Falcon,* shot *Casablanca* and lit director Michael Curtiz's beautiful close-ups of Ingrid Bergman. Wallis, however, was not satisfied with the overall look of the film or the slow pace of shooting. In fact, he criticized Edeson so much that assistant director Lee Katz and sound man Francis Scheid recall that the cameraman broke into tears.[47] On May 26, 1942, after Edeson had taken an hour and a half to light one scene the day before, Wallis emphasized, "I, too, want a beautiful photographic job on this picture, which offers a great deal of background and color for a cameraman, but you were present at all the meetings we had about all the war emergencies and the necessity of conserving money and material, and I must ask you to sacrifice a little on quality, if necessary, in order not to take these long periods of time for [lighting] setups." Wallis repeatedly insisted that Edeson use darker low-key lighting with greater contrast to film scenes of Rick's Cafe. In a June 2, 1942, memo to Edeson he wrote: "I am anxious to get real blacks and whites, with the walls and the backgrounds in shadow, and dim, sketchy lighting." Days later, Wallis was still complaining that Rick's Cafe—and the film—was not dark enough. Out of this creative tension the shady wartime atmosphere in *Casablanca* was palpable in its dark, moody effects lighting and proto-*noir* visual style.[48]

Casablanca was a classic cultural product of wartime Hollywood, influenced by myriad external factors—from conditions in a 1940s American home front to filmmaking in the Los Angeles "theater of war," along with industry and studio politics, production circumstances, individual players, and their interacting personalities and conflicts. It reflected the economic, aesthetic, and ideological concerns of studio heads Jack and Harry Warner, producer Hal Wallis, director Michael Curtiz, writers Howard Koch and Julius and Philip Epstein (and an uncredited Albert Maltz, who had co-scripted *This Gun for Hire,* and Casey Robinson), and the cast and crew. Alongside such concerns were the obvious demands of Hollywood's studio system mode of mass production, PCA censorship by Joseph Breen, financial restrictions of the government's War Production Board, and the overall political climate of the war. *Casablanca* had an international cast with creative personnel that included some of the best talent in Europe, in many cases a result of the war abroad. Famous émigrés included not only Curtiz and music director Max Steiner but also the murderous sleepwalker of *The Cabinet of Dr. Caligari,* Conrad Veidt (Major Strasser); the psychotic murderer in Fritz Lang's German horror film *M*, *Stranger on the Third Floor*, and *The Maltese Falcon*, Peter Lorre (Ugarte); the star of French poetic realist Julien Duvivier's *Pépé le Moko* and Jean Renoir's *Grand Illusion* and *Rules of the Game*, Marcel Dalio (Croupier), who had seen his picture on World War II posters depicting "the typical Jew"; Dalio's wife, Madeleine Le Beau (Yvonne); *Now Voyager* star Paul Henreid (Victor Laszlo); *Intermezzo* star Ingrid Bergman (Ilsa); *Invisible Man* and *Mr. Smith Goes to Washington* star Claude Rains (Captain Renault); *Maltese Falcon* star Sydney Greenstreet (Senor Farrari); character actor S. Z. Sakall (Carl); Leonid Kinsky (Sasha); Helmut Dantine (Jan Brandel); Curt Bois (Pickpocket); Ludwig Stossel and Ilka Gruning (Mr. and Mrs. Leuchtag).

Fortunately, production on *Casablanca* began the month before the Office of War Information was created (in June 1942) and well before the wheels of its propaganda apparatus were fully under way in regulating screen content in Hollywood. The film would certainly not have been made in the same way—or at all—if the OWI had regulated its content. The termination of OWI's funding in June 1943 illustrates how, in the end, OWI missed the point that Hollywood was already savvy to: propaganda in a story is more powerful and palatable when its message is unobtrusive to the viewer.[49] Wartime topicality was central to *Casablanca*. Newsreel realism conventions were incorporated in an effort to simulate documentary headline news, such as opening the film with a spinning globe and map as in news shorts of the war. Capitalizing on the Allied offensive Operation Torch in North Africa and the real Casablanca appearing in papers, Warners' publicity heralded: "Never before have you had a picture so newsworthy . . . so hot-out-of-the-headlines!" Ads read, "CASABLANCA: CAPTURED BY THE ALLIES . . . BUT HOLLYWOOD GOT THERE FIRST! Only days before the North African invasion, Warner Bros. put the finishing touches on their film story of the fight for Africa . . . Prophetically titled 'Casablanca.'" Taglines read, "THEY HAD A DATE WITH FATE." Publicity cited French commentators commending "how realistic" the film's scenes of the actual city were. The Warner Bros. press book even promoted ample "red meat" in *Casablanca*—referring to the crime-and-passion "illicit-romance" angle so controversial to the PCA and so integral to the development of film noir—generating provocative controversy for editorial discussion. Publicity even hinted at an evocative femme fatale promotion searching for the "Mystery Woman of Casablanca."[50]

Rick's shift from independent loner to patriot paralleled U.S. policy in aiding the Allies. The film allegorically depicts America's move away from isolationism to involvement in the war. Given heated U.S. Senate hearings between conservatives and New Dealers debating this issue by the late 1930s (conservatives accusing Warners and the motion picture industry of liberal prowar propaganda), FDR's interventionist change in national military policy was indeed controversial prior to Pearl Harbor. Wartime censorship was significant in suppressing representation of gangsters and black-market activity as un-American;[51] on film, crime and corruption were less overt, more duplicitous and insidious—especially authority figures aligned with the Nazis. (In *Casablanca* everyone is double-dealing everyone else!) In a sense the cinematic depiction of corruption, the black market, and illegal activity was a metaphor of the wartime American home front. The war years actually saw a marked increase in crime, with rising gangster, black-market, and other illegal activities. Because of wartime rationing and the scarcity of consumer material goods as the Office of Price Administration (OPA) allocated items in the tremendous push toward military production, illicit activities in the home front rose to the highest level since Prohibition.[52] Filmed in the summer of 1942, *Casablanca* was completed in November for $1,039,000, premiered Thanksgiving, and released in January 1943. It was a hit for Warners—earning $3.4 million domestically, another $3.4 million overseas, critical acclaim, Academy Awards for direction and screenwriting, as well as picture of the year—all growing out of a unique wartime cultural and filmmaking climate in Hollywood.[53] (The next year Warners reunited Bogart, Rains, Greenstreet, and Lorre in Curtiz's patriotic *Passage to Marseille,* noted for its *noir* shadow and flashbacks within flashbacks within flashbacks.)

Another transitional film straddled the wartime production climate in Hollywood in the wake of the Pearl Harbor attack. Early preludes came together on a moody, atmospheric picture with extraordinary black images, *Moontide,* a fascinating, underappreciated early film noir. Based on Willard Robertson's novel, a hot-tempered, alcoholic dockworker, Bobo (Jean Gabin), carouses with dubious characters (Thomas Mitchell, Claude Rains), suffers a blackout, with no memory of his after-hour revelry, and fears he has strangled an old sailor (Arthur Aylesworth) who turns up murdered. He has an affair with, lives with, and marries a scrappy waitress (Ida Lupino) after she tries to commit suicide. When his blackmailing murderous friend Tiny (Mitchell) frames him and then attempts to rape his new bride, beating and nearly killing her, Bobo hunts him down in a rage. *Motion Picture Herald* cautioned, "Because of its strong nature, the picture is aimed exclusively at adult audiences."[54]

At 20th Century–Fox, studio chief Darryl Zanuck had worked with producer Mark Hellinger, screenwriter John O'Hara, and writer Nunnally

Johnson to adapt the story. Hellinger had produced Warner Bros. crime films *They Drive by Night* (1940), *High Sierra,* and *Brother Orchid* and would go on to produce *noir* films *The Killers* (1946), *Brute Force* (1947), and *Naked City* (1948). German expatriate director Fritz Lang and cinematographer Lucien Ballard (known for his brooding black-and-white interior photography and lighting in *Morocco, Let Us Live, Blind Alley,* and *The Lodger,* and who later shot *The Killing, The Wild Bunch,* and initial work on *Laura*) began shooting *Moontide.*

It was Jean Gabin's first Hollywood film after fleeing Nazi-occupied France. Star of Julien Duvivier's *Pépé le Moko,* Jean Renoir's *Les Bas-fonds* (The Lower Depths), *Grand Illusion, La Bete humaine* (The Human Beast), and Marcel Carne's *Quai des brumes* (Port of Shadows) and *Le Jour se leve* (Daybreak), Gabin played a tough working-class loner and drifter, not unlike Bogart's hard-boiled detective, who exuded strong, steamy masculinity and a charismatic screen presence ideally suited for proto-*noir* crime films. (Bogart even starred in Gabin's role in Lux Radio Theatre's version of *Moontide* in April 1945.) Bosley Crowther of the *New York Times* compared the film to *Quai des brumes* and described *Moontide* as "misty, moisty," "ponderously moody," and essentially a "picture of moods and atmosphere." He called Gabin "strapping," the "Spencer Tracy of French pictures," and "Charles Boyer from the other side of the railroad tracks." "You might almost think the lights and camera were working on a glamorous female star from the way they are concentrated on Mr. Gabin's roughly handsome phiz. You might suspect his drowsy eyes, his tight lips and his thatch of grizzled hair were more important to the picture than the usual conventions of a plot."[55] Along with Gabin's sex appeal aimed at home-front women, Bobo's casual camaraderie with his buddies, like the male bonding collegiality in *Casablanca* and combat pictures, no doubt appealed to men in military units. Like *Stranger on the Third Floor* and *Murder, My Sweet, Moontide* featured a wonderfully bizarre psychological montage of its inebriated antihero's altered state of mind. Surrealist painter Salvador Dalí—who collaborated on Luis Buñuel's French avant-garde pictures *Un Chien Andalou* (1929) and *L'Age d'or* (1930) and created the haunting dream sequence for Hitchcock's *Spellbound*—designed sketches and paintings for the seaman's drunken nightmare. In detailed and lengthy memos to Zanuck, Gabin also offered a great deal of input on the script and his character.

Production on *Moontide* was interrupted by the departure of director Lang, cinematographer Ballard, and the Day of Infamy that shook the entire country. While Lang insisted he worked only briefly on the picture prior to leaving the studio, he and Ballard shot *Moontide* from late November 1941 for several weeks into December, when director Archie Mayo—who directed *Bordertown* (1935), *The Black Legion* (1936), and *The Petrified Forest* (1936) at Warner Bros.—and veteran cinematographer Charles Clarke took over. Most of *Moontide* was filmed after Pearl Harbor. Mayo and Clarke shot the picture from mid-December through mid-February 1942. War regulations prevented shooting the picture on location in San Pedro, near the Los Angeles harbor. Instead *Moontide* was mainly photographed in a big tank on an enclosed interior set with an artificial indoor quay on Fox's lot enveloped in deep shadows, fog, and glistening with water. Mayo complained about the noise from patrolling planes overhead during the shooting.[56]

At Paramount, following *This Gun for Hire*—as *Moontide* was being shot at Fox—producer Sol C. Siegel, director Jack Hively, cinematographer Theodor Sparkuhl, and art directors Hans Dreier and Haldane Douglas were filming another definitive, little-known yet impressive World War II–era film noir. *Street of Chance,* scripted by Garrett Fort and Philip MacDonald and based on Cornell Woolrich's 1941 crime novel *The Black Curtain,* was an exceptional B picture. Packed into seventy-four minutes, with A-class production values, it was Hollywood's first *noir* adaptation of Woolrich's fiction. It stars Burgess Meredith as Frank Thompson a.k.a. Danny Nearing, a regular married-working-guy turned disturbed-amnesiac framed for murder and sought by police as he tries to uncover his past. Claire Trevor stars as Ruth Dillion, his mistress, a "working girl" housekeeper and nursemaid on a corrupt wealthy suburban estate (and an unlikely murderess), adding a love triangle to the story. Filmed on contained sound stages and studio back lots just as the war broke out, *Moontide* and *Street of Chance* are much darker visually and more completely rendered in shadow than earlier proto-*noir* pictures—even *This Gun for Hire* and *Stranger on the Third Floor.* Like *Moontide, Street of Chance* is shrouded throughout, yet unlike *Moontide,* it includes a femme fatale. Whereas most of *Moontide* filming straddled events at Pearl Harbor, *Street of Chance* was filmed entirely in the aftermath of the attack. Shot on a brisk schedule and efficient budget, its lean $227,752 production ran from January 22 to February 19, 1942, amid the chaos, frenzy, and constraints of wartime Los Angeles.[57] The Paramount picture remarkably captures the anxiety of the time, which is viscerally palpable in the film's disturbing milieu. It begins with the everyday goings-on in a city, when, in a freak accident, scaffolding from atop a building that is under construction collapses and knocks Thompson/Nearing (Meredith) out cold. He is soon chased by thugs who appear to be gangsters and who run down his cab and smash the window in with the butt of a gun. These hoodlum pursuers turn out to be police detectives, headed by swarthy and

Amnesiac Frank Thompson (Burgess Meredith, *right*) hides from police pursuing him for murder in *Street of Chance.*
Paramount, 1942.

relentless tough-guy cop Joe Marucci (Sheldon Leonard) tracking him down like a killer.

Paramount's October 5, 1942, press book featured Meredith holding a gun upside down casting a shadow with translucent hands pointing fingers at him. "THEY TELL ME I KILLED A MAN! TWO WOMEN SAY THEY LOVE ME ... *I can't remember!* Did I commit murder ... did I betray my love? What strange secrets are buried in my past? I've got to find out! Come to the 'STREET OF CHANCE' where women come to forget ... one man came to remember!" An ad showed a double image of Meredith wearing a fedora with a cigarette dangling from his mouth with the taglines, "THE MAN WHO LIVED TWICE!" and "A MAN WITH 2 PASTS ... 2 LOVES! *To which does he belong?*" Publicity featured a headshot of Meredith in a missing persons flyer with the banner, "*Why Am I Wanted For* MURDER? Who am I? Am I in love? What is my name? Where have I been for the last three years? *I CAN'T REMEMBER!*" It showed a figure of a tough man clad in a fedora and suit holding a smoking gun standing over a corpse sprawled on the ground below. Taglines clamored: "*Shocking! Unusual! Unforgettable!*" "AM I A MURDERER?"

"WHAT STRANGE SECRETS ARE BURIED IN MY PAST? I'VE GOT TO FIND OUT!"
It promoted the film as a *"Strange . . . haunting drama!"*[58]

On the film's Los Angeles release, in October, the *Hollywood Reporter* wrote, "Cornell Woolrich's 'Black Curtain' was a murder mystery novel with considerably more than average meat on its bones. It told of a man struck on the head, who upon regaining consciousness learns he has been missing from home for a year and . . . becomes aware that a stranger is shadowing him, a fellow revealed to be a police officer . . . Without being certain of his guilt or innocence, he is forced to investigate a cold case that is filled with dramatic surprises." *Variety* observed:

> The fairly commonplace idea of an amnesia case provides the basis for a taut, compelling picture in "Street of Chance." It's obviously a modest-budget effort, yet so adroitly written and deftly presented that it grips attention and . . . should get excellent reviews . . . [The w]rinkle that makes "Street of Chance" such an enthralling picture is that the story is told entirely through the eyes of a central character, the amnesia victim played by Meredith. Thus, the spectator is never tipped off, but finds the slowly unfolding story as baffling and as terrifying as it is to the hero. In this way, when a sinister-looking stranger begins shadowing him, the hero is mystified and frightened, and the spectator is just as much in the dark. Same is true of the hero's midnight flight from his apartment, with his wife, and of his bewildering reception by a strange girl in a dingy boarding house.

Harrison's Reports also praised the film:

> This picture is, by far, one of the best mystery melodramas to have come out of Hollywood in a long time, and it could certainly hold its own as the top half of a double-bill. The story is given a novel twist in that at the start the hero comes out of a state of amnesia to find that the police are hunting him for a murder he does not remember having committed. Owing to the clever screen play, the expert direction, and the good performances, one's interest never lags, for the spectator is as mystified as the hero while he attempts to unravel both the crime and the circumstances under which he became involved.

Motion Picture Herald reviewed the film positively as well:

> Few pictures to come out of Hollywood in a year can compare in sustained suspense with this. It is a thrill-packed drama of a man sud-

denly awakened to the fact that he has been the victim of amnesia for
a year and that he is wanted for a murder of which he remembers
nothing . . . The suspense is built up with unerring skill. The audience
is left to grope its way through the maze of plot and get its clues along
with the chief character—the amnesia victim—as he backtracks . . .
in his memory . . . It is an unusual and interesting picture and right
in the groove for those who like their melodrama straight and their
mystery just that. The fact that it demands more than is usual of its
audience may restrict its appeal but will intensify the enthusiasm of its
admirers.[59]

A few weeks later, however, Bosley Crowther of the *New York Times* dismissed the innovative B *noir* film as merely

Burgess Meredith groping fearfully about in an effort to prove that he
is innocent of a murder pinned on him while he was suffering from
amnesia. Considering that embarrassing dilemma, it is understandable that Mr. Meredith should behave as though he were still in a state
of oblivion and take a lot of time to reconstruct his past. But the effort
is generally tedious, the details a little far-fetched, and the solution of
the crime not very convincing nor even poetically just . . . Jack Hively
has directed in a deep-shadowed, brooding-mystery style. But "Street
of Chance" doesn't really go anyplace; it is just a byway across an old
familiar field.[60]

Yet as an early example of low-budget film noir it was uncanny. The dangerous random accidents in *Street of Chance* occurred suddenly and out of
nowhere (much like how Americans felt about the Pearl Harbor attack)
with lethal consequences and a labyrinth of chaos spiraling out of control.
The film's confusing outside world that entraps a paranoid antihero in a
convoluted, elaborate, and unlikely psychological crime plot was just the
stuff *noir* was made of. As soon as the picture was finished, Hively joined
the military.

Ministry of Fear is another fascinating transitional work shot during the
conflict. Based on Graham Greene's 1943 supernatural mystery novel and
visually cloaked in deep shadow, it grew out of espionage thrillers like
Greene's *This Gun for Hire*, Powell and Pressburger's *Contraband/Blackout*,
and Hitchcock's *The Man Who Knew Too Much, The 39 Steps, Secret Agent,
Sabotage, The Lady Vanishes, Foreign Correspondent,* and *Saboteur*. Directed
by Fritz Lang and scripted by associate producer Seton I. Miller, *Ministry of*

Fear fused mental instability, crime, paranoia, hard-boiled patriotism, and a detective narrative. Like *This Gun for Hire*, it combined espionage, a disturbed protagonist's tormented psyche, and the critical necessity to commit patriotic crime in the national interest—to aid the Allies and evade capture by the authorities or termination by the Axis. Paramount acquired *Ministry of Fear* for Alan Ladd, but he enlisted in the military, so Ray Milland was cast to play conflicted murderer-turned-patriot Stephen Neale, who leaves an insane asylum and journeys across battlefronts to hide out in wartime London (or Hollywood's incarnation of it). He then pursues and dismantles a Nazi spy ring. *Ministry of Fear* opens in a blackened sanitarium as Neale is distraught and about to be released after doing time for the mercy killing of his wife. Lang's moody *noir* showcases Neale's psychology and distorted subjective point of view—suspect, his criminal tendencies remain ambiguous and his innocence is not certain. In a classic *noir* twist we later learn Neale was falsely arrested and nearly went crazy in the asylum after being accused of murdering his wife, who had actually committed suicide.

Heralded for its striking visual style, *Ministry of Fear* adeptly transfers combat mentality to a duplicitous, lethal home-front environment. The atmospheric setting becomes a nightmarish, labyrinthine universe that makes no sense—the milieu is surreal, existential, and claustrophobic as Neale is caught in a trap, framed while trying to solve a case, fighting a covert operation in a *noir* mesh of lies and secrecy. He stumbles into an eerie carnival—a deceptive front raising money for the enemy's war effort—where a fortune-teller beckons him into a shadowy tent for a psychic reading. Uncertain of his own sanity, Neale is surrounded by shady characters and chance occurrences and is pursued by an elusive adversary through a murky, deadly terrain. The film paints a bleak picture. Traversing urban war zone and rural front lines, the story follows Neale's turbulent trek from the asylum to a perilous, war-torn outside world that is an alien web rife with malice and active combat, blackouts, air raids, aerial attacks, explosions, bomb shelters, wreckage and devastation, menacing Nazis, fifth-columnist conspiracies, and betrayal. Paranoid and on the run, he flees cramped train cabins, stark countrysides that have become bomb-ravaged battlegrounds, and a blacked-out London turned to ruins, with chaotic air raids and crowds taking shelter in the subway as bombs explode and sirens wail outside. Neale is lured to a séance by a slinky blonde femme fatale; a gunshot suddenly pierces the silence in a black room, and lights reveal a murder—for which Neale is implicated. A hunted man, wanted by the law and stalked by the enemy, Neale unexpectedly cracks a sabotage plot against the Allies

Gunfire pierces a shrouded séance as Stephen Neale (Ray Milland) is framed in *Ministry of Fear*.
Paramount, 1945.

involving secret military microfilm baked into cakes, sewn into suits, and smuggled by Axis operatives.

Henry Sharp, a veteran pictorialist from the silent era, photographed *Ministry of Fear*. The film was designed by Paramount's art direction team, headed by Hans Dreier and Hal Pereira after designing *This Gun for Hire* and just prior to designing *Double Indemnity*. Lang relies on sound and shadow in its stunning climax. A fair-haired woman, Carla (Marjorie Reynolds), holds a loaded gun pointed at culprit saboteur, Cost/Travers (Dan Duryea), who asks, "You wouldn't shoot your brother, Carla?" He grabs stolen Allied microfilm, punches Neale, flips off the light, and flees. For a moment the audience sees a black screen with no image at all. Then a door swiftly opens, briefly reveals light, and slams shut. A gunshot blasts, and a thump is heard beyond the door in the darkness, as a tiny pinpoint of light pierces the unlit room. Seemingly straight out of Hitchcock's *Scarface*-inspired climax from *The Man Who Knew Too Much* (1934), the finale in *Ministry of Fear* culminates in a masterful Lang-Sharp chiaroscuro tour de force with skewed Dutch-angle shots of cramped stairwells and a rain-drenched shoot-out on a shrouded nocturnal rooftop. This *noir* setting drew on experiences of the front line and tapped into the rough rain-soaked combat circumstances that military troops were forced to endure (often in the dark of night) throughout World War II. Narratively, its pitch-black setting—in interiors and exteriors—directly related to the Nazis, espionage, paranoia, and the war. Its shadowy wartime *noir* streets and claustrophobic confines became a place of anxiety made lethal because of the war—where the military threat is now a civilian crime front.

The patriotic wartime topicality sailed smoothly past Production Code censors. Because the film's civilian setting was located in an overseas city rather than on American soil, *Ministry of Fear* also evaded federal censorship by the Office of War Information. Filmed from July 7 to August 21, 1943, with retakes in November, budgeted at $715,000, its final cost totaled $720,606.[61] Lang's film was completed before *Double Indemnity*, yet it was shelved and stockpiled throughout most of the war. *Ministry of Fear* was not previewed until October 16, 1944, after the studio released *Double Indemnity*, and then not released until February 1945—when Paramount publicized it as "The biggest thriller since 'Double Indemnity.' From the novel by the author of 'This Gun for Hire.'" Ads filled with "demonic" underlighting promised, "Menace Behind Every Shadow . . . Suspense in Every Move!"[62] Paramount touted how *Ministry of Fear* was sent to "Uncle Sam's fighting forces all over the world," highlighting its paranoid psychology and sabotage as a "stark account of a sensitive man seeking the answers to a deep and dark mystery" and appealing to troops in presenting a "study of a lonely Britisher fighting unseen enemies." Taglines read, "His secret meant death to one man if he didn't talk . . . to countless thousands if he did!" Simulating combat, publicity featured a suspicious gun-toting Ray Milland: "Like stealthy steps through a black night . . . They hunt him by day . . . Haunt him by night . . . as he defends the world's most important secret!" The heroine looks over her shoulder, with the caption, "He loved her—but could he trust her?" Questioning the loyalty of women and substituting women with "female" weapons, Paramount's press book sexualized military equipment, giving objects of violence, destruction, and explosive fire power female attributes, giving a "facial" to an army tank explaining that "Fritz Lang is Stickler for Realism in Screen Drama."[63] *Hollywood Reporter* called Lang "brilliant" and the spy ring with enemy agents conveying espionage suspense as "fresh and exciting as tomorrow's newspaper." The *New York World-Telegram* called it a "tense spy story" where the hero, "released from an asylum after the mercy killing of his wife," keeps "far from the police," and the "cryptic heroine" is alternately an "angel" and a "vicious temptress."[64] As its title suggested, *Ministry of Fear* conveyed a dark world where nothing is certain. Its Allied home front is a menacing site of danger, anxiety, and subversive corruption cloaked in the shadow of blackouts and urban violence.

Dark for the Duration

Film noir was imminent as the United States entered World War II. From December 1941 through summer 1943 films such as *This Gun for Hire, Casablanca, Moontide, Street of Chance,* and *Ministry of Fear* illustrated how a complex set of factors in World War II–era Hollywood converged in myriad ways that ultimately influenced and contributed to the development of proto-*noir* style. The PCA's lapses in Code enforcement, the Office of Censorship's banning of "un-American" Hollywood gangsters but condoning of depictions of war-related atrocities, and the Office of War Information's regulation of screen stories depicting the combat front or domestic home front to promote the war effort—all of these developments complicated World War II censorship and encouraged hard-boiled film adaptations that initially reformed gangsters and promoted patriotic crime. However, by 1943—midway into the conflict—Hollywood began to avoid mentioning the war altogether, to evade government regulation during wartime, and also to anticipate the motion picture industry's postwar reconversion, as Allied victory seemed on the horizon. Three films—Paramount's *Ministry of Fear, Double Indemnity,* and Universal's psychological female detective thriller *Phantom Lady*—featured some of the most strikingly dark visual styles and thematics of early films noir and became notable stylistic models for films that followed.[65] Recognized for their definitive *noir* style, these pictures began filming amid tremendous studio rationing of lighting, electricity, film stock, and set materials by late summer–early fall 1943, in an uncharacteristically dark urban Los Angeles basin in response to wartime blackouts—astronomer Walter Baade's optical light measurements from Mount Wilson overlooking the Los Angeles skyline during this period are noted to be the best observations in astronomical history as a result of a blacked-out city cloaked in darkness.[66] These wartime production constraints accentuated the stark style of these films. Thus, it was the *war* that contributed significantly to the deep shadow in such wartime 1940s films noir.

Blackouts were frequent in Los Angeles and across the West Coast after Pearl Harbor, spreading to the Midwest and East Coast by 1942. Realist painter Edward Hopper's *Nighthawks* (1942) is often compared to film noir, and many *noir* filmmakers even cite Hopper's influence on their visual aesthetic style in later *noir* films. In fact, Hopper's *Nighthawks,* like film noir, is a fascinating cultural product that seems to depict the bleak darkness, lonely isolation, claustrophobia, and alienation of a blacked-out urban American setting. Hopper painted the piece in 1942 after a two-month cross-country road trip to California and the West Coast that began in 1941. As the February 28, 1942, *New York Daily Mirror* noted: "It was dark last night in 1,000 square miles of New Jersey and 2,261 square miles of Maryland. Test blackouts, blotting the city of Baltimore off the map—except for defense factories—and erasing 60 miles of Jersey coast including three military posts, were generally termed successful." Even so, "two 15-foot neon signs remained lighted during last night's test."[67] The Second World War had manifested not only a wartime national consciousness but also a variety of war-related conditions and material limitations—rationing lighting and electricity and restricting filming to claustrophobic studio sound stages, tarped or tented back lots, and dark, blacked-out night locations—affecting the Hollywood film industry and its motion picture productions. Compounding wartime filming constraints were weather-related concerns. Coinciding with the emergence of dark, visually confining studio sound stage–bound films in the early 1940s, the *Los Angeles Times* noted rainfall in the basin for the 1940–41 season to be 32.76 inches. (As storms moved east, rainy conditions were a problem on location shooting outside Hollywood: Warners' 1942 production *Air Force* was plagued by Florida downpours.) National Weather Service and City of Pasadena records show that the all-time twenty-four-hour rainfall record for California was 26.12 inches on Mount Wilson in 1943.[68]

As extensive blackouts and war-related production restrictions in Hollywood affected filmmaking conditions during this time, the political climate and harsh realities of the war became darker as war-related crime and brutality grew more apparent. The realities of World War II combat substantiated the heightened depiction of violence, atrocities, and crime indicative of real wartime events. By March 1943 Madison Square Garden's widely publicized rally "We Will Never Die"—in somber memorial to two million Jewish civilians of Europe then known to have perished—illustrated a rising awareness in the United States (particularly by European émigrés) of Nazi atrocities. When Washington's Office of Censorship lifted the ban on showing atrocities onscreen, this precedent not only compromised PCA censorship enforcement; it also contradicted the federal Office of War Information Bureau of Motion Pictures' earlier policy of discouraging unsavory depictions of the United States—from gruesome realistic battle scenes to gangsters and unflattering illegal black-market activities on the American home front—domestically and abroad. This reversal in regulating graphic film content laid the groundwork for a more liberal PCA during (and after) the war.[69]

The wartime production environment would enhance Hollywood's *noir* visuals, but so, too, would the comparatively bleak vision of creative talents such as German émigré writer-director Billy Wilder, who had worked at UFA before fleeing the war in Europe and whose family was killed at Auschwitz. The gravity of escalating wartime conditions no doubt contributed to the increasingly dark German expatriate productions just a few months later. As Lang completed *Ministry of Fear*, former UFA roommates Robert Siodmak and Billy Wilder gained nearly simultaneous PCA approval on separate projects: Siodmak's collaboration with fellow émigré and Hitchcock protégé Joan Harrison on the film noir *Phantom Lady* and Wilder's PCA milestone *Double Indemnity*. Although *Phantom Lady* was released first, in early 1944, it was *Double Indemnity*, a few months later, that would generate a *noir* crime trend in 1944 filmmaking. Wartime conditions and PCA approval culminated in fully articulated film noir, which could finally come into its own. Hollywood's stylized adaptation of James M. Cain's "sordid" novels reveals the complex censorship and production process of *noir* films.

Censorship, Hard-Boiled Fiction, and Hollywood's "Red Meat" Crime Cycle

Hollywood, according to present indications, will depend on so-called "red meat" stories of illicit romance and crime for a major share of its immediate non-war dramatic productions: The apparent trend toward such material, previously shunned for fear of censorship, is traced by observers to Paramount's successful treatment of the James M. Cain novel, "Double Indemnity" which was described by some producers as "an emancipation for Hollywood writing."
—Fred Stanley, *New York Times*, 1944

I think the whole system of Hays censorship, with its effort to establish a list of rules on how to be decent is nonsensical. A studio can obey every one and be salacious—violate them and be decent.
—James M. Cain, *Daily News*, 1944

Documentary technique—what *noir* cinematographers John Seitz and James Wong Howe and director Billy Wilder called "newsreel style" to achieve greater "realism" and production economy during the war—influenced the definitive visual design and stark camerawork of *Double Indemnity*. This dark, newsreel style employed deep shadows to facilitate wartime filming amid urban blackout and dimout regulations in Los Angeles and effectively functioned as a savvy production strategy, creating a sordid milieu while technically complying with the Production Code, thus enabling censorship approval. Banned for a decade, the screen adaptation of James M. Cain's fiction, particularly *Double Indemnity* (followed by *The Postman Always Rings Twice* and *Mildred Pierce*), would be a milestone for censorship endorsement of film noir in this wartime setting and initiate interest in Raymond Chandler's hard-boiled novels *Farewell, My Lovely* and *The Big Sleep*. *Double Indemnity* provided a model for advancing a new "red meat" crime cycle in Hollywood during and after the war, a trend that would later be known as *film noir* in France in 1946.

Censorship and *Double Indemnity*: Adapting James M. Cain during the War

In *Double Indemnity* American audiences finally saw full-blown film noir on Hollywood screens. Industry trade publications and archival records from the 1940s reveal that *Double Indemnity* started a trend of Hollywood crime pictures during the war and indicate that it was a pivotal film in the evolution of Production Code censorship and wartime production restrictions, providing the enabling conditions for the dark style and paranoid thematics of film noir. In 1944 Fred Stanley of the *New York Times* wrote that *Double Indemnity* initiated the dark, "red meat" trend noted for its "renewed interest in certain types of storied sordidness and ultra-sophistication." In accordance with official PCA policy the article assured those concerned with Hollywood's moral decline that the controversial James M. Cain adaptation "has not prompted any easing of Hays office or State censorship regulations. There have been none and none is expected. It is just that Hollywood is learning to use finesse in dealing with a variety of different plot situations which, if treated . . . obviously, would be unsuitable."[1] Such finesse would be a hallmark of wartime films noir.

Contrary to the Hays Office's press spin in 1944, Hollywood's industrial self-censorship by the PCA certainly eased during (and after) World War II, evident in studios producing racy Cain stories. The adaptation of *Double Indemnity* was influenced by the Production Code, but the film itself influenced, in turn, how the Code was (or was not) applied to films that followed. In a sense it opened the floodgates for a darker cinema, accommodating what industry censor Joseph Breen termed "low tone and sordid flavor."[2] *Double Indemnity* enabled a proliferation of Code-approved films noir. In its wake came *Murder, My Sweet* (1944; an adaptation of Raymond Chandler's novel *Farewell, My Lovely*), James M. Cain's *Mildred Pierce* (1945), Chandler's *The Big Sleep*, and Cain's scandalous *The Postman Always Rings Twice* (both produced in 1944–45, released in 1946). The box-office revenue for *Double Indemnity* (some $2.5 million in North American rentals) offered studios tangible incentives for jumping on the *noir* band wagon.[3]

None of the key players had predicted the success of *Double Indemnity*, nor could they have anticipated its influence; at the outset neither studio nor star nor PCA censor Joseph Breen wanted to be involved with it. "I like to set Hollywood back on its heels," director Billy Wilder remarked; "my own studio said I was crazy to attempt it . . . [Even] George Raft turned the role down flat. We knew then that we'd have a good picture."[4] In Wilder's adaptation of Cain's novel married femme fatale Phyllis Dietrichson is out for money and murder in cold blood. Barbara Stanwyck's Phyllis uses her sexuality as bait. Accomplice Walter Neff (Fred MacMurray) is an insurance salesman with a roving eye—for Phyllis and for a little cash. The two have an affair and then plan to murder her husband so they can run off together with the insurance money. (They "get away" with the crime in Cain's book by committing suicide while making a getaway on a boat to Mexico.) Tenacious insurance claims investigator Barton Keyes (Edward G. Robinson) activates a kind of detective framework, solving the case. Cain's sordid story scared off screenwriters; not even Wilder's longtime collaborator Charles Brackett would take on the adaptation, and Cain was unavailable.[5] Wilder turned to a first-time screenwriter and industry outsider, hard-boiled writer Raymond Chandler. But finding a writer was a less daunting problem than overcoming the PCA's opposition.

Double Indemnity pushed the envelope of the Motion Picture Production Code of 1930 to its limit and paved the way for dark, controversial films to be produced in the future; when Joseph Breen approved, and condoned, the film, this initial Cain adaptation set the stage and the tone for how Hollywood film noir could successfully maneuver around the Code. The PCA had been known in the industry as the Hays Office, after Will Hays, president of the Motion Picture Producers and Distributors of America (MPPDA) since 1922. The MPPDA first began to monitor scripts on the West Coast on a regular basis in 1929 and adopted the Production Code, authored by Father Daniel Lord and *Motion Picture Herald* publisher Martin Quigley (with input from Hays, Col. Jason Joy, and industry executives) as its moral blueprint for Hollywood films in 1930. The Motion Picture Production Code of 1930 was loosely enforced until 1934, as can be seen by the content of early 1930s films. But when the National Catholic Legion of Decency threatened to boycott indecent Hollywood films in the spring of 1934, Hays established the Production Code Administration and hired Joseph Breen to begin enforcing industry self-censorship. This system of self-regulation was intended to prevent direct government censorship, as well as to appease the Legion. Threats of Legion boycotts came at a financially crucial time for the industry, during the Great Depression in the spring of 1934. Breen's appointment as head of the PCA was part of an agreement among the "Big Five" vertically integrated major Hollywood studios not to exhibit films without the PCA Seal of approval in their lucrative first-run theaters,[6] which, along with a $25,000 fine imposed on studios that released unapproved films, ensured censorship enforcement by the end of 1934.

At that point in Hollywood history the Production Code (as a result of Breen's vigorous enforcement) wielded considerable power. "The responsible heads of the studios are a cowardly lot," Breen reportedly told Hays. *Film Weekly* called Hays "a mere Hindenberg" and Breen "the Hitler of Hollywood." By 1935 he "cashiered properties, rewrote screenplays, supervised directors, and edited films . . . The Code was the Word, the gospel according to Breen."[7] Breen had his own definitive idea of *Double Indemnity* when MGM originally submitted it for production in 1935. In Cain's words, "The

Hays office knocked it in the head. I didn't see its letter, but was told it was an uncompromising ban of the story in toto, one of those things that begin 'under no circumstances' and wind up 'way, shape or form.'" Cain believed that the PCA's "main objection" was that the story was a " 'blueprint' for murder," showing "wayward persons how to kill for profit."[8] The collision between the censorship restrictions of the Production Code and Cain's crime-and-passion tale almost prevented *Double Indemnity* from being adapted. In a February 1944 interview for the *Daily News* Cain explained how he completed writing *Double Indemnity* in 1935. His unpublished story was based on one of the most sensational American tabloid press incidents of the 1920s: the brutal 1927 New York murder of Albert Snyder by his wife, Ruth, and her lover, Judd Grey, for insurance money.[9] Cain mimeographed his dramatization and sent the first copy to producer Lawrence Weingarten at MGM, who, according to Cain, had expressed interest. Weingarten called Cain the day after he received *Double Indemnity* to inquire about the price. "By now five studios were interested, not independents, but the big ones . . . Warners, Columbia, Paramount and Twentieth Century–Fox" in addition to MGM.[10]

Cain's opportunity to sell *Double Indemnity*—and the studios' interest in producing it—was blocked when Breen read it and launched his unambiguous rejection on October 10, 1935. Breen's response (sent to John Hammell at Paramount, David O. Selznick at MGM, Jack Warner at Warner Bros., Nicholas Schenck at MGM/Loew's Distributing, and Frances Manson at Columbia Reading Department) stated that so many aspects of Cain's story violated the Production Code that he was "compelled to reject" any consideration of it for studio production. He objected to the "details of the vicious cold-blooded murder shown," the "illicit, adult sex relationship" of the lovers that drives the story, its "violent people," and the criminal's "confession to the [insurance] agent who withholds information"—all in all characterizing the story as "a gross miscarriage of justice." Breen took particular issue with the insurance agent's "arranging the escape of the two murderers from the country" and the culmination of "the two committing suicide" in Cain's original story. Overall, Breen concluded, the "low tone and sordid flavor" of Cain's story was "thoroughly unacceptable."[11]

Not surprisingly, Breen's letter threw cold water on the hot project. (Since Paramount was emerging from receivership, Wilder was not yet directing, and Weingarten's *The Bishop Misbehaves* flopped at MGM by the end of 1935; it may, in retrospect, have been just as well that *Double Indemnity* was not produced that year.) Nunnally Johnson, however, a staff writer whom Darryl Zanuck had brought to 20th Century–Fox in 1935, was still interested. According to Cain, after Breen rejected MGM's 1935 submission of *Double Indemnity,* Johnson "tried to devise a method of meeting this objection." Breen actually approved Johnson's version (with an outline treatment by Colonel Joy). As Cain explains, however, 20th Century–Fox's head of production, Darryl Zanuck, preferred the original version and said Johnson's "was not the same story."[12] Zanuck, who had recently left the socially conscious environment of Warner Bros., was interested in the darkness of Cain's story in 1935, but without Breen's endorsement of the original premise, according to PCA records and Cain's 1944 interview, the *Double Indemnity* project sank into limbo for eight years.

In the meantime Cain sold the story in 1936 to *Liberty* magazine as a serial, where it received an enthusiastic reception. Its popularity led to its publication in the collection *Three of a Kind* on April 19, 1943. With the novella about to appear, Cain's agent recirculated advance copies of *Double Indemnity* to the studios. Paramount became interested at the behest of Billy Wilder, who, according to Cain, "had his eye on it for some time."[13] Wilder admitted producer Joseph Sistrom "had read the story and had brought it to the attention of the studio and to *my* attention . . . He *was* the producer, but they only wanted to give him associate producer credit and he refused it; he didn't want to take any credit at all."[14] The *New York Times* noted Sistrom's interest in the project after his secretary disappeared into the ladies' room, reading *Double Indemnity* and then insisting that Cain's "sensational" story was perfect for Billy Wilder.[15] All were keen on taking a crack at Cain's juicy tale.

With interest at Paramount, the story was resubmitted to the Hays Office, whose first response was identical to the 1935 verdict. Indeed, Breen's letter to Luigi Luraschi of Paramount's Censorship Department on March 15, 1943, was a *word-for-word* duplicate of the October 10, 1935, letter he had sent to MGM's Mayer—and other studios—banning Cain's story.[16] (Perhaps Breen thought the studios suffered from memory loss, or possibly he did not think anyone else kept files for eight years.) This time, though, Cain was given a copy of the memo: "It was perhaps as stupid a document as I ever read—for it made not the slightest effort to ascertain whether the picture could be filmed with the changes commonly made in a novel when it is prepared for the screen . . . But Wilder, [Paramount executive William] Dozier and Sistrom are not easily frightened men, and they decided to make a try at it."[17] After a lapse in correspondence Luraschi responded to Breen's letter by submitting a partial story outline for *Double Indemnity* on September 21, 1943.[18]

As Cain described his story, "it is about a married woman who falls in love with another man, kills her husband, fraudulently attempts to collect insurance, attempts to kill her lover and gets killed by him for selfish motives." However, it "presents these people with compassion and understanding."[19] On September 24, 1943, Breen replied to Luraschi's submission: "the basic story seems to meet the requirements of the Production Code." Breen gave very specific restrictions in response to two scenes in the story outline: Phyllis's erotic entrance and the murder of her husband while she is driving him to the train station:

page 6   The towel must properly cover Phyllis . . . below the knees with no unacceptable exposure.

page 8   The flimsy house pajamas must be adequate.

page 43   Omit "And listen don't handle the policy without putting your gloves on."

page 47   Omit "to park *your south end.*"

page 62   Omit details on disposing of the corpse and explicit details of the crime . . . delete the whole scene/sequence . . . therefore, Fade out after they take the body from the car—let the dialogue explain what they did.

page 74   Delete specific poisons in [insurance investigator] Keye's speech sentences.

Breen added that he would be "happy to read your shooting script and report further . . . final judgment is based on the finished picture." Breen and Paramount's Censorship Department would exchange twenty-three letters with revised pages between September 24 and December 1, 1943. Many sequences were written in pieces as production progressed, then submitted for PCA approval, and quickly shot—Wilder made minor changes (pertaining to "displays of the body"), and Breen approved them. Wilder complied with most of Breen's requests—with the exception of Phyllis's towel not being "below the knees."[20]

Not surprisingly, Breen's lifting of the PCA ban did not come soon enough for Cain. David Hanna's February 1944 article, "Hays Censors Rile Jim Cain," noted the hard-boiled author's "high indignation about the manhandling his books received from the Hays guardians of cinematic virtue" and the "tortuous path" *Double Indemnity* traveled in its transition to the screen:

What about the ban on my other stories? For example, *The Postman Always Rings Twice,* still gathering dust at MGM, which could be a fine movie if handled as adroitly as *Double Indemnity.* What about *Mildred*

Pierce which I am told has favorable Hays comment? What about *Serenade* which with obvious changes could become an excellent picture? I'm getting sick of the Hays office and I'm not in the least bit amused at the money it is costing me . . . I am perfectly frank to say . . . It is not only the principle of the thing with me but the money.[21]

The relationship between money and "decency" remained a recurrent Hollywood theme. Paramount production records indicate a May 25, 1943, letter from Jacob H. Karp of the legal department stating that the studio had purchased the story rights for *Double Indemnity* from Cain on May 15, 1943, for $15,000. Interestingly, a March 1943 memo from William Dozier states that Paramount owned the story and assigned a fund to develop the film "produced under the supervision of Mr. Joseph Sistrom." Yet "No writers have been assigned to date."[22]

By 1943 James Cain was considered a leading hard-boiled fiction writer—as was Chandler, who cowrote the screen adaptation. The stature of hard-boiled literature had increased between 1935 and 1944—initially considered seedy during the 1930s but then promoted in the 1940s, growing in popularity over the war years as paperbacks became available after 1939. Although the hard-boiled tradition, in which Cain and Chandler (along with Hammett) were key figures, flourished in American popular fiction during the Great Depression, this trend did not immediately catch on in the film industry. The Code was a major deterrent. In this tradition of Depression-era tales Cain published *The Postman Always Rings Twice* (which MGM bought in 1934, the year of its publication, but could not produce until late 1944–45, following Paramount's *Double Indemnity* precedent). Cain then published *Mildred Pierce* in 1941. One reason for the approval of Cain's story involved the complications of enforcing the Code during World War II; circumstances changed from 1935 to 1943—midway into the war.

Initially, the immoral content in *Double Indemnity,* Cain's reputation as a racy writer, and Cain's timing in attempting to adapt the story (just one year after Breen vigorously began enforcing the PCA Code in 1934) contributed to Breen's hostile response. Eight years later conditions were different. Cain asserted in 1944 that producers "have got hep to the fact that plenty of real crime takes place every day and that it makes a good movie . . . The public is fed up with the old-fashioned melodramatic type of hokum."[23] Certainly, there are significant industrial and cultural considerations for this change in the Code's policy, some of which relate to wartime production circumstances. With the film industry booming during World

War II, profits rose from the early 1940s to peak in 1946, yet producing films during the war required a massive transformation of every sector of the industry, as severe shortages and problems due to wartime restrictions and government (and military) involvement complicated production. Concerns escalated about U.S. and Allied combat overseas by 1942, and Hollywood began to stabilize wartime operations in support of the war effort as American and Allied forces gained control in Europe and the Pacific in 1943.[24]

Double Indemnity, in adeptly beginning its film narrative by stating the prewar date of its story (July 16, 1938), avoided OWI interference because its 1930s setting did not deal with issues immediate to the war or to the home front. Moreover, Paramount was the studio most resistant to federal (wartime propaganda) censorship. In March 1943 the *New York Times* reported that Paramount studio chief and Producers Association president Y. Frank Freeman "was the last holdout against cooperation with the OWI" in agreeing "to submit synopses of proposed pictures to the OWI on request."[25] By early 1943 Hollywood studios—with the exception of Paramount—submitted scripts to OWI on a regular basis. War-related newsreels also became more graphic during this time. A February 6, 1944, *New York Times* article, "Hollywood Turns To 'Hate' Films: Government Lifts Ban on Showing Jap Brutality," cites the depiction of screen violence, previously banned, as condoned by the government's wartime Office of Censorship for propaganda purposes.[26] This policy contradicted the Code and preceded the April 1944 Hollywood preview of *Double Indemnity*. Moreover, Breen's sojourn at RKO—providing a brief lapse in his rigorous administering of the PCA between 1941 and 1942—may well have affected his previous by-the-book approach to Code enforcement and thus benefited the PCA and the industry in producing a more temperate censor in 1943 than in 1935.

Even more significant, however, was the government's investigation into monopolistic practices by the film industry after 1938 and the signing of a consent decree in 1940 prohibiting distributors' booking of films in blocks larger than five. By March 1941 Thomas Brady of the *New York Times* noted, "Hollywood Clears Decks for Consent Decree: Four Studios Revise Production Set-Ups to Meet the New Selling Terms." Exhibition and distribution were the money lifeline of the industry. Four months later Douglas Churchill of the *New York Times* observed, "Hollywood Changes: Quietly the Major Studios Reorganize Executive Staffs to Meet a New Era."[27] These preliminary steps toward antitrust legislation were initially preempted by the urgency of mobilizing Hollywood's propaganda machine with America's entry into World War II. The government, however, reinstituted the Paramount Case in 1944—the year *Double Indemnity* was released. The *New*

York Times heralded "U.S. Renews Battle on Film Monopolies" by August 1944.[28] Since Hollywood's self-regulation was enforced by its vertically integrated oligopoly, these developments must have raised some concerns about how enforceable the Code would be in the absence of cohesive studio system cooperation. (In fact, four years later the landmark 1948 Paramount Decision would effectively dismantle the Hollywood studio system and thereby undermine the industry's mechanism of self-regulation.) It was in this complex wartime context that Paramount was able to produce Cain's fiction after Wilder and Chandler adapted, refined, and presented the hard-boiled material with *noir* nuance and "finesse."

The effort to adapt *Double Indemnity* in 1943 necessitated a savvy production strategy to simultaneously comply with—while maneuvering around—the Code.[29] Wilder and Chandler's primary strategy in collaborating to rework Cain's material was to maximize the use of innuendo and verbal wit. Rarely had so little been directly stated in a film yet so much implied. The following sequence illustrates the suggestive metaphor and cunning repartee in the dialogue of *Double Indemnity*. (The scene was invented for the film and cannot be found in Cain's novel.) The topic of conversation shifts from accident insurance as Walter Neff's eyes drop to Phyllis Dietrichson's anklet. Neff makes a pass at Phyllis. He asks her name, saying he'd have to "drive it around the block a couple of times" and "was sorta getting over the idea" of talking to her husband:

Phyllis: There's a speed limit in this state, Mr. Neff. Forty-five miles an hour.
Neff: How fast was I going officer?
Phyllis: I'd say around ninety.
Neff: Suppose you get down off your motorcycle and give me a ticket.
Phyllis: Suppose I let you off with a warning this time.
Neff: Suppose it doesn't take.
Phyllis: Suppose I have to whack you over the knuckles.
Neff: Suppose I bust out crying and put my head on your shoulder.
Phyllis: Suppose you try putting it on my husband's shoulder.
Neff: That tears it.

The scene concludes with Neff agreeing to return:

Neff: Will you be here . . . same chair, same perfume, same anklet?
Phyllis: I wonder if I know what you mean.
Neff: I wonder if you wonder.

Chandler was instrumental (albeit grossly underpaid and perhaps un-
deracknowledged) for his keen contribution to the moody descriptions and
dialogue of the film.[30] In fact, the opening of the first PCA-approved script
for *Double Indemnity* reads like a good Chandler novel. Chandler had a kind
of "sinuous poetry" in his descriptions of Los Angeles. He wrote "amusingly
vicious dialogue." He had a "gut feeling for the killer instincts of a blonde."[31]
(Wilder and Chandler wanted Phyllis to appear tawdry—she was after all a
gold-digger. Stanwyck's donning a brassy platinum-blonde wig and anklet
added not only hard-boiled sexuality under a misleading angelic guise but
also, like other *noir* femme fatales Lana Turner, Marjorie Reynolds, and
Claire Trevor, made Phyllis a more Aryan-looking villain.) A Chandleresque
voice-over is laid over Neff's drive home: "It was a hot afternoon, and I can
still remember the smell of honeysuckle all along that street. How could I
have known that murder can sometimes smell like honeysuckle?"[32] Chandler was also noted for his signature voice-over narration writing style and
infamous for his late-night dictation into his machine. Significantly, it was
the very restrictions of the Code that made necessary this devious transformation of Cain's gruff material. Wilder and Chandler's innuendo was designed to conform with the brittle semantics of the aged Code (in theory),
while defying it through dark metaphor (in practice). In fact, the film version successfully capitalized on the fact that the Code was rather ill
equipped to handle nuance. The rigid framework of specific taboos about
individual words and actions enabled a writer (and director) to paint a portrait of criminality without using prohibited words and without showing
censorable deeds. As Wilder and Chandler ingeniously discovered, the Code
could be manipulated.

To oblige the Code, the "morally correct" position is foregrounded in
the story's cinematic adaptation. The film specifically utilizes a flashback
structure with voice-over narration to simulate a voice of morality, reinforced by the tenacity of claims examiner Keyes, in an obvious attempt to
pay obeisance to Breen's compensating moral-values clause requiring criminals to get their just and fatal due by the film's conclusion. The PCA's compensating moral-values regulation reinforced the happy ending in many
Hollywood genres. Yet in film noir it adds to the fatalism of an oppressive
environment and the doom of a flawed, conflicted protagonist. *Noir*'s central voice-over narration frames and structures the action with a guilt-ridden male point of view, tapping into a destabilized wartime psyche. While
this narrative device evokes the hard-boiled detective story, it reveals the
criminal up front—as self-destructive antihero—to emphasize the futility
of the perpetrator's immoral deeds. For example, the script specifies a "dark

street near Neff's apt. house," where the story's protagonist takes a walk following the murder. Embedded in Neff's voice-over is the film's inevitably fatal moral retribution: "That was all there was to it. Nothing had slipped, nothing had been overlooked, there was nothing to give us away." But there is growing paranoia: "And yet, Keyes, as I was walking down the street to the drug store, suddenly it came over me that everything would go wrong. It sounds crazy, Keyes, but it's true, so help me: I couldn't hear my own footsteps. It was the walk of a dead man."[33] Neff's personal confession to Keyes by dictating the story's narration also adds an intimate male-bonding camaraderie that would have appealed to men in military units. Cain praised the film's narration and flashback structure. "It's the only picture made from my books that had things in it I wish I had thought of." The "device of letting the guy tell the story by taking out the office dictating machine" was "much better than my ending . . . I would have done it if I had thought of it."[34]

Because censors "exercised more power while films were in the planning stages than in the review of completed features,"[35] once Chandler and Wilder's script was approved by Breen and the footage already shot, *Double Indemnity* was basically finished. Wilder could film the images any way he wanted to, keeping within the approved dialogue and action of the script; he was thus free to be creative with lighting, photography, and sound to evoke a dark, seedy milieu rife with dark themes and malicious deeds—with the exception of one particularly infamous sequence. According to Paramount production files Wilder devised the film's ending after the PCA objected to the narrative payoff in Cain's original story. Breen was scandalized that the novel allowed the criminals to flee the country with no retribution for their crime—with the aid of the insurance agent—then ended in the couple's suicide instead of their apprehension by the authorities. In an effort to comply with these Code objections Wilder shot a sequence detailing the criminal's execution in a gas chamber (for which he spent $4,695 on the set alone);[36] that ending was shelved after the film's preview—and after the PCA determined the "whole sequence in the death chamber to be very questionable in its present form . . . specifically the details of the execution . . . are unduly gruesome to the Code."[37] In the final ending, like a war film, Neff lies dying as Keyes lights his cigarette, waiting for the police to arrive.

The Code restricted specific references to sex and violence—these were to be implied rather than shown. Omitting direct references to sex and violence capitalized on innuendo in dialogue (a clever fusion of hard-boiled Chandleresque style with Wilder's black comedic wit) and the dark, seductive visual design. Sordidly suggestive and definitively *noir,* the "black" film showcased the splintering venetian blinds, pronounced shadow, and chiaroscuro low-key mise-en-scène of Billy Wilder's direction, Hans Dreier and Hal Pereira's art direction, and cinematographer John Seitz's stark newsreel-style camerawork. The dark photography created a corrupt, mysterious setting that undermined those censorship restrictions that were followed. Wilder used many striking images, such as the pitch-black night-for-night exterior shots of the railroad tracks where Neff and Phyllis drop her husband's body after they murder him in the car. The deep blackness surrounding the sedan (with headlights off) suggested a murderous milieu as the engine fails in the dark. The completely black exterior of the neighborhood street seemed to visually swallow Neff as he walks home (unable to hear his own footsteps) after the murder. In fact, Wilder's film was suspenseful and unsettling from the moment it opened as Neff, shot (by Phyllis just prior to murdering her) and bleeding, swerves his car, screeching through dark, wet city streets in this black urban environment. To avoid showing censored violence and sex, the film suggested action offscreen, using sound and visuals to convey taboo material in an unseen space. For example, Wilder framed a tight close-up of Phyllis's reaction to her husband's murder (as the horn blows and Neff strangles him offscreen) to imply violence rather than show any details of the crime. Viewers could use their imagination to fill in the void. Wilder's clever devices included seating the couple at opposite ends of a couch in Neff's apartment, fully dressed and smoking cigarettes, after fading from a passionate embrace to imply sex, splintered by venetian blind shadows to forebode their fatally doomed affair. These cinematic elements added sultry eroticism and a dark, ominous setting.

The chiaroscuro lighting and shadowy visual design that today is considered so characteristic of film noir style was in large measure a savvy aesthetic response to the Code and the war. The quintessential *noir* images in *Double Indemnity* effectively utilized its mise-en-scène to reveal the corrupt American city; its sordidness is suggested by scenes shrouded in shadow, fog, and smoke and by light splintered into oblique patterns or glistening reflections on rain-slicked streets, pools of water, shattered windows, and mirrored surfaces. Cinematographer John Seitz acknowledges the influence of the war on the visual technique of *Double Indemnity:* "The film was shot in 'newsreel style.' We attempted to keep it extremely realistic . . . The effect of waning sunlight" was created by using "some silver dust mixed with smoke" to accentuate the shimmering contrast of low-key lighting.[38] Hollywood's new trend toward realism as an outgrowth of the war influenced both fictional and documentary films during 1943 to 1945. Wilder noted that in filming *Double Indemnity* with director of photography Seitz, "We had to be very realistic. You had to believe the situation and the characters, or all was lost ... *Double Indemnity* was based on the principal of *M* ... I tried for a very realistic picture—a few little tricks, but not very tricky. *M* was the look ... It was a picture that looked like a newsreel. You never realized it was staged. But like a newsreel, you look to grab the moment of truth, and exploit it." Room interiors were shot in art director Hans Dreier's house, and Wilder described the image he wanted to achieve: "whenever I opened the door and the sun was coming in, there was always dust in the air. Because they [femme fatale Phyllis and her husband] never dusted it." Wilder insisted realism influenced the visual style of *Double Indemnity* even more than earlier German expressionist films. "There was *some* dramatic lighting, yes, but it was newsreel lighting. That was ideal. I'm not saying that every shot was a masterpiece, but sometimes even in a newsreel you get a masterpiece shot. That was the approach. No phoney setups ... Everything was meant to support the realism of the story."[39]

The war played a key role in Wilder's bleak vision of authenticity. Shortly before directing and coscripting *Double Indemnity*, Wilder directed the World War II desert combat drama *Five Graves to Cairo* (1943) while actual fighting was still going on in Africa. Wilder noted, "In serious films like *Five Graves, Double Indemnity*, and *The Lost Weekend* I strove for a stronger sense of realism in the settings in order to match the kind of story we were telling. I wanted to get away from what we described in those days as the white satin decor associated with MGM's chief set designer, Cedric Gibbons." Wilder recalled, "Once the set was ready for shooting on *Double Indemnity* ... I would go around and overturn a few ashtrays in order to give the house in which Phyllis lived an appropriately grubby look because she was not much of a housekeeper. I worked with the cameraman to get dust into the air to give the house a sort of musty look. We blew illuminant particles into the air and when they floated down into a shaft of light it looked just like dust." He added, "Shortly afterwards MGM made another James M. Cain novel into a picture, *The Postman Always Rings Twice*, with Lana Turner as the wife of a proprietor of a hot dog stand. She was made up to look glamorous instead of slightly tarnished the way we made up Barbara Stanwyck for *Double Indemnity* and I think *Postman* was less authentic as a result."[40] Cain's journalistic background informed his style; the gritty nonfiction source of his story was derived from newspaper headlines—not unlike the realistic newsreel style of documentary films being produced during the war. Hard-hitting material began changing the cultural and production climate during the 1940s to accommodate serious topics that posed challenges to the Code. A July 30, 1944, *New York Times* article, written just prior to the release of *Double Indemnity*, projects greater popularity of documentary subjects related to the war and "increasing use of documentary methods in the telling of screen fictional dramas."[41] The wartime trend toward newsreel style inflected a visually and thematically dark film in *Double Indemnity*.

Double Indemnity was truly a breakthrough film in definitively inaugurating this sophisticated wartime *noir* strategy as a means of cloaking illicit material while it disguised cheap or recycled sets to accommodate the wartime restrictions on production. On October 6, 1943—ten days into shooting—a Paramount memo from Norman Lacey to Frank Caffey noted that "existing dimout regulations will not permit such use of light" during three night-location shoots scheduled at the Union Pacific East Los Angeles and Glendale train stations.[42] Several memos referred to these dimout restrictions—in fact, the crew actually considered renting Santa Fe railcars and filming the train sequence in Las Vegas. (They finally were allowed to film in Los Angeles and Glendale at night using very little light.) Such restrictions contributed to the film's definitive *noir* style. For example, Cain's story reads: "There's nothing so dark as a railroad track in the middle of the night."[43] The lighting restrictions actually aided in creating such an ambience. The car's headlights are turned off in this scene—the script notes a "dark landscape" at the railroad tracks where the lights of the sedan's "dark bulk . . . blink twice and go out."[44] The film's visual rendering of Cain's material not only establishes a model for the dark, cynical thematics and style of film noir but also achieves this amid—and because of—industrial wartime production restrictions.

The wartime environment and its production constraints directly contributed to the psychological paranoia and claustrophobia of Wilder's film noir. As wartime dimout restrictions enhanced the film's dark style and judicious use of lighting, a Paramount production memo for *Double Indemnity* shows that the studio hired "plainclothes detectives and OPA [Office of Price Administration] officials" to patrol the shoot at the market. The studio wanted to prevent theft of grocery items by the cast and crew during filming, a likely possibility due to wartime rationing. Thus Paramount provided a material base of embedded paranoia into the actual production of the film. Ironically these production circumstances inform the scene's clandestine rendezvous at this seemingly mundane site following the murder. Moreover, these rationed grocery items were used to accentuate the cluttered claustrophobia of the market's interior mise-en-scène, suggesting the paranoid criminal couple's physical and moral entrapment; they'll not evade the law.[45]

Wilder had tremendous influence as a writer-director, with increased creative control and power in getting controversial material produced.

Wilder referred to *Double Indemnity* as having "the fewest mistakes" of his films "because it was taut and moved in the staccato manner of Cain's style."[46] The tight pace of the film was effectively enhanced by the strict rationing of film stock, tighter budgets, and scarcity of set materials (and even talent), all of which accelerated shooting schedules. Wilder and Sistrom ran a tight ship. The total production cost for *Double Indemnity* was $927,262.86 —well under their $980,000 budget, even though they exceeded their forty-two-day shooting schedule by nine days.[47] James Cain called Wilder's adaptation of his novel "one of the finest pictures ever made . . . There are situations in that movie that can make your hands wet, you get so nervous . . . I tell you, it is just beautiful." Yet the author noted that the film "violates practically all the rules imposed by the Hays office."[48] Wilder's *noir* stylistics certainly provided a dark, efficient, imaginative way to subvert the strictures of the Production Code. Casting even created ingenious ambiguity by casting all three prominent stars—comedic Fred MacMurray as Neff, Barbara Stanwyck as Phyllis, even former gangster Edward G. Robinson as the insurance claims examiner Keyes—against type. A third of the film's overall production budget, roughly $300,000, was allocated to star salaries (at $100,000 apiece), securing these players—almost half the film's $725,000 direct cost.[49] The screen couple's deadly illicit affair was promoted, and compensating moral values were embedded in the film's advertising as the studio's publicity slogans clamored: "You can't kiss away a Murder!" and "From the Moment they met it was Murder!" *Double Indemnity* was "Paramount's terrific drama of an unholy love and an almost perfect crime."[50]

After previewing in April, *Double Indemnity* was released in Los Angeles in August 1944 (opening in New York in September 1944) to nearly unanimous critical accolades and box-office revenues. Reviewers agreed—it was a sordid smash. As Philip Scheuer stated in August 1944, "Wilder deliberately set out to 'out-Hitch Hitch,'" citing Alfred Hitchcock's wire to Wilder: "Since 'Double Indemnity,' the two most important words in motion pictures are Billy Wilder." In an August 6, 1944, *Los Angeles Times* article, "Film History Made by 'Double Indemnity,'" Scheuer noted the Code taboos that *Double Indemnity* overrides: "It details the actual commission of a crime . . . of passion . . . But it never tries to whitewash the criminals." He adds, "Like the great French cinemas, it is adult," evocative of film noir.[51] Wilder and Chandler's "sordid" adaptation garnered popularity and seven Academy Award nominations. Barbara Stanwyck's deadly cool performance as cold-blooded femme fatale Phyllis Dietrichson won her an Oscar nomination for Best Actress.[52] Soon a prominent wartime red-meat trend spread through Hollywood like wildfire, capitalizing on Paramount's feat in ob-

"From the Moment they met it was Murder!" Barbara Stanwyck and Fred MacMurray in *Double Indemnity.*
Paramount, 1944.

taining a seal of approval despite the "low tone and sordid flavor" of *Double Indemnity.*[53] Successfully maneuvering around the Production Code to produce a visually and thematically bleaker wartime-postwar American cinema, filmmakers launched a series of film noir productions intended to simulate the unique style of *Double Indemnity* and replicate its box-office returns.[54] Hollywood crime and romance proliferated. The critical and financial success of *Double Indemnity* encouraged other stylistically "black" 1940s films, raising expectations for hard-boiled adaptations.[55] Wilder's film certainly invigorated RKO's interest in one of its shelved properties, Chandler's *Farewell, My Lovely.*

Adapting Chandler: RKO's *Murder, My Sweet*

On June 3, 1941, as Orson Welles produced *Citizen Kane* and Alfred Hitchcock completed *Suspicion,* and after Joseph Breen had left the PCA to head production at RKO, the studio purchased the screen rights to Raymond Chandler's hard-boiled novel *Farewell, My Lovely* for a mere $2,000. Following Boris Ingster's impressive *noir* debut *Stranger on the Third Floor* the year before, RKO could have produced a fabulous film noir of Chandler's book. But Chandler was an unknown in Hollywood, and Ingster's film was far from financially successful. Instead, RKO threw out much of Chandler's fascinating tale and ambience in *Farewell, My Lovely*, reformulating it into a cheap, second-bill B movie titled *The Falcon Takes Over* (part of its low budget *Falcon* series) starring George Sanders and Ward Bond. Although it was the best of the *Falcon* series, RKO (and ill-suited production chief Breen) had no idea how to maximize and profit from Chandler's moody atmospheric story about shady urban detective Philip Marlowe in seedy 1940s Los Angeles. In retrospect, it was a missed opportunity. Chandler's property collected dust for another three years at the studio. Yet tough crime novels, like those of Cain and Chandler, became coveted screen material by spring 1944, when Paramount unveiled *Double Indemnity*. As Chandler gained Hollywood recognition for collaborating on the soon-to-be-Oscar-nominated screenplay, RKO producer Adrian Scott wisely surmised that *Farewell, My Lovely* could be remade and upgraded into a better film that more fully realized Chandler's milieu.

In adapting Chandler's fiction, screenwriter John Paxton remained faithful to the hard-boiled novel's mood and witty, sardonic dialogue. The film opens as Marlowe (Dick Powell), brutally beaten, nearly blind, and interrogated by police, launches into a flashback in which the cynical detective navigates a series of mysterious traps. In Chandler's elaborate story—a nocturnal web of lies, deceit, blackmail, bribery, adultery, drug-induced hallucination, and murder in the seedy underbelly of the "City of Angels"—a motley array of characters from the streets and corrupt affluent society appear suddenly and then disappear. A hulking, psychologically volatile ex-con, Moose Malloy (Mike Mazurki), lures the private eye into a wild labyrinth to find his former girl, a dancer named Velma, who turns out to be a deadly married femme fatale, Mrs. Grayle (Claire Trevor). Marlowe pursues the elusive femme who leaves a trail of multiple identities and dangerous dead ends. He is watched, betrayed, clobbered on a deserted roadside, and framed for murder at every turn but finally manages to find her. Grayle seduces him, and they have a brief affair; but she is mixed up with the mob and leaves him hanging. Gangsters abduct, beat, and drug the private eye, a scientist wants to use him as a guinea pig for experiments, and he lapses into a head trip, a nightmare shown in a series of montages. Marlowe tries to break free of his altered state and escapes; the cops question him, and his alluring knockout sets him up. Grayle emerges with a gun in a blacked-out beach house and tries to kill Marlowe, her elderly wealthy husband appears and kills her, and Moose breaks in to shoot her husband

Police interrogate Philip Marlowe (Dick Powell), wounded in action and nearly blinded by gunfire in *Murder, My Sweet*.
RKO, 1944.

for murdering his girl. In the end the hard-boiled dick is cleared and falls for Grayle's redeeming stepdaughter, Ann (Anne Shirley, who originally wanted the duplicitous evil temptress role).

In April 1944 RKO submitted *Farewell, My Lovely* for PCA consideration—a project that Breen, now back at the PCA, had already endorsed as RKO production head three years earlier. On April 13 Breen replied to RKO's William Gordon that the preliminary estimating script and basic story for the proposed picture "seems to meet the requirements of the Production Code." However, Breen requested specific corrections to eliminate sexual innuendo: "Cute as lace pants," "He could use *that* too," and "I hope *they give him* enough cheap blondes where he is now" would all have to go. He purged references to homosexuality, omitting what he called "pansy" characterizations, and toned down the narrative adultery: Since the femme fatale is a married woman, "the physical contact between her and Marlowe should be kept to a minimum . . . We request that you cut down the embracing and kissing between Marlowe and Mrs. Grayle. We recommend that they only kiss once in this sequence." Breen advised minimizing erotic displays of the female body ("Care will be needed with costuming and movements of the dancer"), loose women ("The expression 'broad' is on the Association's list of forbidden words, and must be changed"), and illicit sex ("Please rewrite the line, 'Maybe you were just *making love* to me' . . . This scene with the man's clothes in with Mrs. Grayle's, is unacceptable and should be omitted entirely from the finished picture"). He specified not showing violence—inflicted on or by Marlowe—onscreen:

page 80   We suggest you mask this action of Amthor hitting Marlowe on the face with his gun butt. Otherwise, the scene will probably be deleted by several censor boards.

page 86   Again, we suggest masking this action of Marlowe hitting the man behind the ear.

For safety the censor denied free speech to avoid panic in crowded theaters:

page 83–6 In line with standard industry procedure, there must be no cries of "Fire." Some other word must be substituted.

And he banned onscreen suicide:

page 154   It will not be permissible to suggest that Mr. Grayle escapes punishment by committing suicide. Please, therefore, change the line, "Yeah, he did it himself?"—possibly indicating that Moose killed the old man before he died himself.

Breen concluded with his customary disclaimer, "You understand, of course, that our final judgement will be based upon the finished picture."[56] The endorsement of *Farewell, My Lovely* in the wake of Hollywood insiders viewing *Double Indemnity* for the first time showed that Breen expediently approved Chandler's hard-boiled material. The crime-and-passion bandwagon had begun.

In late spring–early summer 1944 Adrian Scott produced *Farewell, My Lovely* and assigned Edward Dmytryk to direct. Dmytryk was a young RKO director with a well-deserved reputation for delivering tightly paced, modestly budgeted, and highly profitable pictures such as the proto-*noir* anti-Nazi *Hitler's Children* (1943) and racist anti-Japanese political potboiler *Behind the Rising Sun* (1943). *Farewell, My Lovely* was Dmytryk's first A-class picture. Scott and Dmytryk cast former Warner Bros. musical star Dick Powell against type as hard-boiled detective Philip Marlowe. After years of typecasting, Powell was ready to try something new. He had actually auditioned for the lead in *Double Indemnity*, Walter Neff, but lost the role because Wilder felt the public would never accept the 1930s Busby Berkeley song-and-dance man as a tough crime character capable of murder. After Powell had been freelancing, RKO president Charles Koerner, keen on producing musicals in the future, made a deal, signing the actor up for two RKO pictures a year and promising Powell a shot at Philip Marlowe in *Farewell, My Lovely,* then suggesting him for the role. In person Dmytryk found the actor to be taller and tougher than he had anticipated (absent the heavy stage makeup used in Powell's customary musical films). It turned out to be excellent casting. In fact, Chandler regarded Powell's performance as the truest detective Marlowe onscreen and RKO's adaptation as the best film of his hard-boiled novels.

As in *Double Indemnity,* low-budget financial limitations and wartime material constraints enhanced the vivid film noir style in *Murder, My Sweet.* Because RKO viewed the film as a risky project, and did not have large sums of money for sets and production, Dmytryk's project was budgeted under $500,000 with a short shooting schedule. The film, completed July 1, 1944, cost a modest $479,000—nearly half as much as *Double Indemnity* or *Citizen Kane.*[57] In visualizing Marlowe's confusion and paranoia, images accentuated the dark mood of Chandler's story with brilliantly stylized drug-induced dream sequences. *Stranger on the Third Floor* special-effects veteran Vernon L. Walker collaborated with Douglas Travers on the film's psychological montages, art director Albert S. D'Agostino collaborated with Carroll Clark, and Dmytryk gave cinematographer Harry Wild a chiaroscuro painting to illustrate the tone and style that he wanted to capture onscreen. Like *Stranger on the Third Floor, Citizen Kane,* and earlier horror films, Dmytryk shot far below normal camera angles to distort the perspective and view of people in the frame. Dmytryk described the film as "utter realism, but it wasn't shot realistically at all." Originally released as *Farewell, My Lovely* in late 1944, the film was retitled *Murder, My Sweet* to capitalize on its crime and romance component (and to avoid any possibility that audiences would think it was a Powell musical) and then released in early 1945.[58]

RKO blitzed racy publicity for *Murder, My Sweet.* Since the Advertising Code for publicity was more lenient than Production Code censorship, ads (featuring Claire Trevor's unbelievably ample display of legs spilling out of a split skirt) ran in *Life* magazine on February 18, 1945, with the salacious tagline: "Careful Dick . . . She's as Cute as Lace Pants . . . But you can't stop a Murderess . . . if you stop a Bullet First!" (The banned line was even used twice in the film.) Exploiting the femme fatale for a returning GI audience in 1945, ads capitalized on infidelity and gender distress: "DON'T FALL FOR THAT FEELING . . . SHE KILLS LIKE SHE KISSES!" Below, a gritty image of Pow-

ell with an open shirt, holding a cigarette, looms next to the caption: "Dick
Powell . . . Different, Greater than Ever . . . in a NEW Characterization!"
RKO's press book publicity headline screamed: "Dick Powell Wins Red-
Blooded Role." Yet unlike earlier detectives such as Sam Spade, RKO's new
private detective was publicized as "more often wrong than right and does-
n't get on the real track until near the end. Furthermore, when it comes to
actual physical contact with his enemies, he gets badly beaten up" (much
like troops on the front line). However, ads did not mention Chandler, his
Farewell, My Lovely book, or the detective Philip Marlowe character. Instead,
RKO's focus was weapons and women, not necessarily in that order. On
February 17 *Liberty* magazine featured the tagline, "Forget that look in her
eyes . . . SHE'S GOT *MURDER* IN HER HEART," describing the film as a shady
"murder-mystery." By March 3, suggesting Hollywood's growing propensity for crime, *Collier's* ran a similar ad: "ROUGH! TOUGH! TERRIFIC! Sensational is the word for the NEW Dick Powell! Hardboiled, Two-Fisted, he Follows a Trail of Violence, Blackmail and Murder . . . in this new kind of
Red-Blooded Mystery!" Beside the blaring headline, a rugged unkempt
Powell wears a fedora and holds a gun, targeting the detective market while
simulating combat. Trevor leans twisting on a sofa with an open (un)dress-
ing robe exposing abundant legs and her erotic bikini brassiere. By April a
plethora of detective and screen magazines ran ads with the tagline "Trouble ahead, Mister! That Fellow who Hired You to Find His Woman Won't
Stop at Murder . . . if you Don't Deliver! Neither will She . . . if you Do!"
(Ads suggested the film's adulterous love triangle with Shirley's smaller
headshot, in the lower corner, looking up at Powell's dominating virile image.)[59] *Murder, My Sweet* was a sensation. The modestly budgeted film
earned $1,150,000 domestically and $565,000 overseas, totaling $1,715,000—
and a sweet $597,000 profit for RKO.[60] On the heels of *Double Indemnity,
Murder, My Sweet* reinforced the red-meat crime trend, as Cain and Chandler's fiction became lucrative and popular in wartime 1940s Hollywood.
As the success of these films became known in the industry, another studio
reassessed its hard-boiled holdings with interest: MGM owned Cain's most
scandalous story, *The Postman Always Rings Twice.*

Censorship, Red Meat, and *The Postman Always Rings Twice*

James M. Cain's *The Postman Always Rings Twice,* like *Double Indemnity,*
was another example of a 1930s novel that the Production Code censors
would not touch but later endorsed during World War II, when conditions
were more appropriate. These potentially scandalous stories were reacti-
vated as a cycle of dark film adaptations when it was institutionally viable

and profitable. But even if censors' resistance subsided, the film cycle itself caused controversy. *The Postman Always Rings Twice* (produced in 1944–45 but not released until 1946) could not be produced in the same way that *Double Indemnity* had been—MGM had to visually lighten it up, whitewash it, and sanitize it. These wartime crime films were indicative of Hollywood's new tendency toward film noir, which developed in relation to industry censorship during the 1940s. Paradoxically, film noir both complied with, yet undermined, PCA censorship. While a darker wartime economic and cultural environment informed the production context of this influential film noir, Cain's provocative crime-and-passion tale, banned by censors since its sale to MGM in 1934, would not have been deemed appropriate by this grand and conservative studio had *Double Indemnity* not set an industry precedent in navigating around the PCA, overturning Breen's ban, and becoming a profitable sensation.[61] In a sense MGM's project was a sequel effort responding to the success of Cain's initial screen adaptation. Following the August-September 1944 release of *Double Indemnity,* by November 19, 1944, the *New York Times* reported, "Last week's high mark in the 'red meat' trend was the disclosure that Metro-Goldwyn-Mayer intends to co-star John Garfield and Lana Turner in Mr. Cain's 'The Postman Always Rings Twice.' The property, bought several years ago, was kept in the studio's archives until now because (to use a favored Hollywood expression) of Metro's 'inability to clean it up.'" Industry analysts observed: "Closer to the cameras is another of Mr. Cain's novels, 'Mildred Pierce' . . . scheduled to go into production this week at Warner Brothers . . . reported to be negotiating for the author's 'Serenade.' The screen version of Raymond Chandler's 'The Big Sleep,' in production at Warners, is said to be another example of ingenuity in treating of psychopathic and physiological matters."[62] The PCA's endorsement of Cain's *Double Indemnity,* and the film's commercial success, actually motivated a proper representational context for *The Postman Always Rings Twice* and other hard-boiled adaptations.

Cain had written *Bar-B-Q* at the peak of the Depression, during the Bank Holiday in March 1933, after losing his screenwriting job at Columbia Studio. He finished the story in September.[63] By January 1934 advance galleys of the book were sent to the studios, who were *very* interested. Alfred Knopf published the book as *The Postman Always Rings Twice* in February. This hard-boiled novel, Cain's first, established his trademark terse, first-person narration and tight plot, entangling sex, money, and violence. It was a story of a young drifter who has an affair with an unhappily married woman and then conspires with her to murder her husband so the two can run off together. This narrative formula was more than a bit scandalous when the book was published, the same year the MPPDA established the PCA and Joseph Breen began enforcing industry self-regulated censorship. In fact, *The Postman Always Rings Twice* was alarming censors even *before* the PCA was officially established in July 1934. The PCA would be formed (and the National Catholic Legion of Decency threatened box-office boycotts) in response to violent screen crime, gangster films, and sexually explicit material. Already, by February 1934, however, the *New York Times Book Review* called Cain's novel "strong men's meat and not for those who mind blood and raw lust. It has vigor and economy of method . . . but its artistic merit won't keep it from giving the sensitive nightmares."[64] Cain's story was hot. Although MPPDA president Will Hays and Breen immediately discouraged RKO, Warner Bros., and Columbia from adapting it, MGM purchased the screen rights for $25,000 in March—without consulting Hays or Breen. In a March 9, 1934, MPPDA Production Code memo Breen noted his "shock" on learning about the purchase and stated he was not responsible.[65]

The story was banned.[66] March 22, 1934, correspondence between Hays and counsel Gabriel Hess reveals an *eight-page* indictment, "Exhibit A," to support the rejection, listing restrictions and "objectionable features," calling Cain's story "salacious in essence" and a "deception to the public," and concluding it would be "IMPOSSIBLE TO MAKE A PICTURE OF THE BOOK AT ALL."[67] Apparently, *The Postman Always Rings Twice* would pose a big problem vis-à-vis Production Code enforcement. By March 30, 1934, P. S. Harrison (publisher of the industry trade *Harrison's Reports*) wrote to Louis B. Mayer on behalf of independent theater owners to "protest" MGM's "decision to produce" Cain's novel.[68] By April 2 the Hays Office referred to *The Postman Always Rings Twice* as a "particularly dangerous story." Hays questioned whether it could be made at all on April 4. On April 21, 1934, Breen spoke to Hays at length regarding MGM's script property—and Metro decided to abandon the project. *The Postman Always Rings Twice* was dropped.

Within a few months, by summer 1934, Breen and the newly formed PCA would consistently enforce the Production Code. Cain's hard-boiled novel was such a scandalous sensation that after drawing controversy prior to the PCA's inception, it faced scrutiny after Hays censored—and MGM canceled—its production. For good measure, on September 4, 1934, Hays sent a letter to Breen initiating the PCA policy of forwarding Code rejection of *The Postman Always Rings Twice* to other studios. Banning the property industry-wide, it outlined how the industry MPPDA board of directors went through the formal process of officially rejecting a story when "one member company" of its studio organization attempted to produce questionable material. In this case the industry board firmly enforced the Production Code.[69]

Ten years later Paramount released *Double Indemnity.*

Hollywood was not the only party interested in James M. Cain. Others adapted Cain overseas during wartime. In what would become a seminal adaptation for Italian neorealism, French director Jean Renoir gave Italian director Luchino Visconte a copy of Cain's *The Postman Always Rings Twice.* Visconte filmed *Ossessione* in 1942—another controversial and banned Cain adaptation not seen for many years after it was pulled from release. In Hollywood the next year, as a preemptive strike, Breen reiterated in March the ban on Cain's *The Postman Always Rings Twice* and warned Paramount's censorship department against purchasing it. However, PCA records suggest that Paramount was considering the property. On March 15, 1943, Breen sent two letters to Paramount: (1) an exact copy of an October 10, 1935, letter to MGM (and other studios) banning *Double Indemnity* and (2) a letter restating the rejection of *The Postman Always Rings Twice* by quoting passages from a March 1934 letter banning MGM's purchase of the story.[70] (Breen later approved Paramount's production of *Double Indemnity* on September 24, 1943.)[71] By April 1944 (as *Double Indemnity* was being previewed) Paramount's censorship department denied any interest in Cain's *The Postman Always Rings Twice.*[72] Nonetheless, whether industry fact or rumor, in August 1944 (as *Double Indemnity* was being released in Los Angeles) Hedda Hopper of the *Los Angeles Times* reported Paramount and director Billy Wilder were negotiating for the rights to *The Postman Always Rings Twice:* "Billy Wilder who ain't afraid of nothin' is deep in the throes of trying to buy James Cain's *Postman* from Metro. If he gets it—and he will—Barbara Stanwyck says she'll make it with him. You can look for lots of Wilder-Stanwyck pictures since *Double Indemnity.* They rang the bell and I don't mean the postman's."[73] By October 1944, however, it was MGM producer Carey Wilson (better known for his Andy Hardy movies) who submitted a treatment to the PCA and negotiated a deal with Breen to produce Cain's story—the success of *Double Indemnity* was indeed a Code precedent. Interest in Cain's meaty properties had ignited. Wilson worked with writers Harry Ruskin and Niven Busch to adapt the screenplay. MGM and the PCA exchanged numerous letters and script revisions through May 1945, when Breen finally approved changes and production began.[74] PCA endorsement of *The Postman Always Rings Twice* was a milestone. The film's scorching beach scenes, previewed in *Life,* had "driven director Tay Garnett to drink" and caused Breen to issue a warning to Wilson regarding the studio's racy publicity.[75]

An August 20, 1945, *Life* magazine article, "Love at Laguna Beach," stated that MGM bought Cain's "tough novel of adultery and murder" in 1934 but thought it was "too hot to handle" and "did not dare make it into a movie. Times changed, however, and so did MGM's mind." Citing MGM's decision to "go ahead" with production of Cain's "hot story," *Life* announced that the studio was "giving it everything, including a sizzling beach scene" where Turner, "wearing a white bathing suit which may become historic, tests the true love" of Garfield, who "helped murder her husband."[76] Several steamy, suggestive beach photos of the couple accompanied the piece. The *Life* item mortified Reverend H. Parr Armstrong of the Oklahoma City Council of Churches.[77] Surprisingly, though, Breen defended MGM's production of Cain's story—and its potentially scandalous publicity—to national religious organizations. In fact, on September 19, 1945, Breen wrote to Dr. Samuel McCrea Cavert of the Federal Council of Churches of Christ in America: "We believe the finished picture will not be offensive to anyone. It is a psychological study of two murderers who seek to cheat justice, but who fail in the attempt. I need not tell you that Metro, in its screen production, has made many drastic changes in the story as told in the novel. I am certain that, while the film story is 'strong meat,' it will be an acceptable picture for adults."[78]

Several savvy production and marketing strategies account for Breen's about-face in support of the MGM project. After all, *Double Indemnity* had been nominated for several Academy Awards, including Best Picture, and Stanwyck's performance was winning accolades. Rather than the Chandleresque repartee of *Double Indemnity*, *The Postman Always Rings Twice* evaded censors by suggesting innuendo in scenes without the use of dialogue. Carey Wilson called *Postman* a "Study in White."[79] In a 1946 publicity interview, "'The Postman' Emerges as Torrid Movie," Wilson highlights "Miss Turner's charms," explaining, "Except for one costume, everything she wears is white . . . In one scene she wears a bra and shorts. And I'm afraid Miss Turner's legs are very, very nice."[80] (Actually, there are several black costumes—such as a black robe and dress—strategically positioned at the murderous end of the film for dramatic femme fatale effect.) Cain noted that MGM writer Harry Ruskin diffused the erotic steam of his story by clothing Lana Turner in scores of white costumes to suggest purity (and obviously appease the PCA).[81] Still, there was theory, and there was practice. As evident in the lurid beach promotion for *The Postman Always Rings*

Twice, white could still blaze by way of Turner's two-piece bathing suit and did not necessarily imply demureness. The MGM production used high-key lighting and a bright set, which countered the shadowy *noir* visual design of *Double Indemnity.* Unlike the stark newsreel style Seitz employed in *Double Indemnity, The Postman Always Rings Twice* is shot in MGM's slick, flat, big-budget, polished style. Consequently, Metro's film is not very dark photographically—certainly not at all as visually black and hard-hitting in cinematography as the earlier Paramount film. An exception is the ominous climax, where Garfield returns to a black-robed Turner, as the classic femme holds a gleaming butcher knife, in a shadowy kitchen just prior to plotting the murder of her husband.

Overall, however, the film was decidedly sanitized. To appease Breen, many of the graphic references to sex and violence in Cain's novel were eliminated. Particularly suggestive passages of carnal lust and savagery were supplanted with metaphor and innuendo. Perhaps the best example illustrating metaphor in Cain's "red-meat" story is Garnett's actual cut to hamburgers sizzling and burning on the grill following Garfield's introduction to Turner early in the film. The way the sequence is shot is highly suggestive, relative to the PCA-approved screenplay. Garnett's shooting script references Frank (Garfield) looking over at Cora (Turner) near the kitchen door. Cora's entrance is precipitated by an "opened lipstick" rolling in from the adjacent room, which Garnett adroitly circled, adding a fairly innocuous transition: "Insert lipstick—*Pan* slowly from lipstick to Cora." The script then reads: "Standing in the kitchen doorway, almost imperiously . . . is Cora . . . wearing a white playsuit, shorts and a halter, plain white high-heeled pumps . . . looking at Frank impassively."[82] What is less obvious from this description—and Garnett's handwritten directions—is how the scene is actually executed onscreen. Turner's neckline, bare midriff, and tight, white shorts contradict her mild demeanor. Furthermore, the point of view of Garnett's (low-angle) pan from the opened lipstick on the floor, up Turner's legs, added a sexually charged means of introducing the star—while technically complying with the Code. To this strategy MGM added punitive retribution and compensating moral values—the bad guys get it in the end. Like Cain's story, although illicit lovers Frank and Cora get away with killing her husband and attempt to flee, rather than the murderous couple going off (or even going down) together, they are fatally separated, Cora being killed in a car accident and Frank arrested for her murder. As the film ends, he awaits the electric chair. As Breen required, if characters commit adultery or crime, they will die or do time. A flashback narration

"Their Love was a Flame that Destroyed!" John Garfield and Lana Turner in *The Postman Always Rings Twice*.
MGM, 1946.

foregrounded the *noir* antihero's psychology, guilt, and impending doom as a consequence of his crimes and uncontrollable obsessions—thus reinforcing a voice of morality throughout the film.

Publicity for *The Postman Always Rings Twice* featured Cain's novel prominently as "The Book that Blazed to Best-Seller Fame!" and described the film as "More Sensational than 'Double Indemnity!' And by the same Best-Seller author!" MGM was indeed capitalizing on Cain's growing reputation—and exploiting it. Advertising for the MGM film made its Paramount predecessor look tame by comparison. MGM paid no homage to Breen's ethical proscription for *The Postman Always Rings Twice*. Instead, Metro's publicity featured Lana undressing to reveal a risqué two-piece white bathing suit (resembling a bra and underwear) with the caption, "You must be a she-devil . . . You couldn't make me feel like this if you weren't . . . ," along with "Their Love was a Flame that Destroyed!" And finally, "I had to have her love even if I hung for it!" Images included Garfield about to strangle (or caress) Turner. The press book's salacious ad featured blonde, bare-shouldered Lana with a cigarette in her mouth as Garfield fires up his lighter, next to an insert where the black-garbed, gun-toting femme sticks up another man. It clamored: "The Story of A Babe Who Married the Wrong Guy!" A caricature of a huge hand cleaves a butcher knife above the tagline: "Her name is CORA . . . *She Gets Into Men's Blood . . . And Stays There!* His name is FRANK . . . *His Savage Boldness Will Thrill the Women!*"[83]

Rarely had so many raw, libidinous, and murderous screen narratives involving flesh—in both graphic brutality and illicit sex—been condoned by industry PCA censors. The stories showcased violence, bold women, and twisted love triangles with sensational publicity. MGM spared no expense in its comparatively brighter $1,683,000 *noir* film. *The Postman Always Rings Twice* rollicked to the box office, reinforcing Hollywood's wartime *noir* cycle, earning $3,741,000 in North American rentals, even more than *Double Indemnity*, and outpacing its predecessor abroad as well, where it earned another $1,345,000, totaling $5,086,000 and a handsome $1,626,000 profit for MGM.[84] Like MGM with *The Postman Always Rings Twice*, Warner Bros. was jumping on the *noir* bandwagon. Producer Jerry Wald secured the purchase of *Mildred Pierce* on the tails of Breen's *Double Indemnity* approval. Wald used a similar narrative strategy to maneuver PCA restrictions and Warners' studio brass pushed to heighten scandalous topics yet still gain Code approval. Studios lost no time in producing crime-and-passion adaptations. RKO filmed Chandler's *Farewell, My Lovely* shortly after *Double Indemnity* premiered, and Warner Bros. rushed to produce Chandler's *The Big Sleep*. Cain's stories were hot properties: *Mildred Pierce* was already in production, and *Serenade* had been purchased by Warner Bros. as MGM was making *The Postman Always Rings Twice*.[85] Cain's tough fiction encouraged an abundance of Code-approved hard-boiled film noir by the end of the war. Because studios had stockpiled roughly 200 films, completed but not released, throughout the duration, these wartime production trends also resulted in a proliferation of crime pictures in 1946, a delayed reaction to Hollywood's booming war industry.[86] As women entered creative positions in Hollywood over the course of the war, the face of *noir* would also change, offering more nuanced and multifaceted images of femme heroines.

Rosie the Riveter Goes to Hollywood

mages of the hard-boiled femme fatale crystallized in such classic *noir* films as Billy Wilder's *Double Indemnity,* Tay Garnett's *The Postman Always Rings Twice,* Edgar Ulmer's *Detour,* Fritz Lang's *Scarlet Street,* and Howard Hawks's *The Big Sleep.* Embodying the evil, alluring "spider woman," Barbara Stanwyck's deadly cool Phyllis Dietrichson calls the shots, disposes of her husband and his first wife, manipulates and shoots her lover, and generally raises the bar on female badness in *Double Indemnity.* Stanwyck's Phyllis, as well as Lana Turner's lethal Cora in James M. Cain's other "sordid" and censorable novel, *The Postman Always Rings Twice,* was based on a real-life femme fatale, Ruth Snyder, who conspired with her lover to brutally murder her husband for cold, hard cash—tabloids had a field day as her unforgettable image in the electric chair splashed across the front page of the *New York Daily News.* Joan Bennett's unabashedly irreverent, double-crossing Kitty in *Scarlet Street* is the ultimate duplicitous temptress. These images of women were often created and developed by men in a historically male-dominated industry. But women, both as characters and as a force behind the camera, grew increasingly influential during the war years. The World War II labor shortage created a need in Hollywood that women (and men who were unable to serve in the military) filled. As the war progressed, female screen images eventually coincided with women's acquisition of greater power in creative and executive positions in Hollywood—and in many classic film noir productions.

Defense assembly-line worker "Rosie the Riveter" was an empowering icon transcending gender stereotypes throughout World War II for the purpose of promoting a much-needed female workforce to aid in military production.[1] As millions of men departed for military duty overseas, millions of women held down the home front—taking traditionally male jobs, working in factories and elsewhere to support the war effort. Women and minorities became essential to American military production as employment-aged white males left the domestic labor force. (Taking the hint from Washington, Hollywood even promoted a multiethnic national workforce in wartime industries—federal incentive for studios to mobilize African Americans for the war effort led to the production of all-black musicals *Stormy Weather* and *Cabin in the Sky,* which were encouraged by the government and specifically aimed at targeting more active, less peripheral depictions of ethnicity for propaganda purposes.)[2] Hollywood relied on keen efforts by men unable to serve, like European émigrés, and women contributing vital roles in the film industry throughout the conflict. It is not that studios and male production executives necessarily wanted greater numbers of women for creative positions; rather, they needed them to fill the talent void resulting from the large numbers of men who were away. By July 1944 the *New York Times* noted the film industry's "shortage of male acting talent"—Clark Gable had been gone, Mickey Rooney and Red Skelton left to enlist, and no male stars or creative talent at 20th Century–Fox had returned from the war.[3] As women played important roles behind the scenes and onscreen, many wartime *noir* motion pictures featured stronger, active female characters. The representation of independent, transgressive femme fatales and complex career women coincided with a wartime female labor force, nationally and inside the film industry. *Phantom Lady, Mildred Pierce,* and *Gilda* offer notable examples of women becoming more creatively involved in the studio production process, often gaining executive authority, in wartime Hollywood films noir.

These films targeted motion picture audiences stratified by gender (female home front / male combat front) during wartime, a demographic that changed as the war ended. America's mobilization for the war involved a tremendous cultural and industrial transformation. At home and abroad World War II labor needs redistributed the U.S. population, geographically and demographically. The absence of millions of men serving in the armed forces shifted demographics as women dominated the domestic market. In the patriotic effort to bolster military morale abroad, a massive wartime distribution network facilitated an industry-wide operation to internationally screen films to troops overseas. By February 1942 the government's War Activities Committee (WAC) worked with the army, the War Department, and Hollywood studios to send 16-mm film prints free of charge to soldiers at the front.[4] This worldwide distribution and exhibition became a vast supplemental parallel industry aimed at Allied forces and coinciding with the domestic release and exhibition of Hollywood films at home. Dual homefront versus military-front distribution operations coincided with an effort by the studios to initiate narrative strategies that targeted a World War II audience segregated by gender. Hollywood made wartime films with female home-front and male military-front viewers in mind.

Film genres, studio production, and promotion strategies responded to changes in gender demographics brought about by the conflict. War films, for instance, were directed toward male combat troops overseas while enjoying enormous popularity at home; female-oriented genres like domestic melodramas were aimed at women in the home front. *Noir* crime films targeted a masculine audience yet included strong femme fatales, redefining *femininity* and "love-interest" characters and capitalizing on wartime easing of PCA censorship. Films noir featured the savvy strategy to target, market, and appeal to an audience stratified by gender with audacious romantic female lead characters aimed at a 1940s home-front audience and brazen sex appeal with heightened violence for combat troops abroad. The growing number of femme fatale screen divas during World War II recognized the increasing female autonomy and independence of women working in factories to support the military. The depiction of strong, bold women in wartime films noir represented this cultural shift in traditional gender roles over the course of the war.

Wartime promotion, advertising, and media narratives reinforced these images. The *Magazine War Guide* recommended media plots to facilitate male workers accepting women in the workplace: "The men in these fields must be prepared to receive women as coworkers. This can be done through stories showing the advent of women logging camps, on the railroads, riding the ranges, and showing them NOT as weak sisters but as coming through in manly style." Even advertising directed at women took a significantly different approach during World War II. With war-related rationing, Fleischmann's Yeast featured a military uniformed woman on a motorcycle with the bold caption: "This is no time to be FRAIL!" and "The dainty days are done for the duration." Philco showed an aproned housewife pummeling a Nazi and a Japanese soldier with a kitchen sink (alongside a rifle-wielding U.S. serviceman and mallet-wielding male factory worker): "With Everything—Including the Kitchen Sink!" DuBarry cosmetics showed a woman boarding a military plane: "Wartime living has taught many women to simplify their beauty care."[5] The pragmatic and necessary austerity of wartime affected women's fashions and grooming aesthetics—or lack thereof. Veronica Lake's popular peek-a-boo, over-the-eye hairdo (spoofed in Billy Wilder's comedy *The Major and the Minor* just after the successful release of *This Gun for Hire*) became a serious hazard to enormous numbers of women copying the glamorous style yet working in factories where machinery made dangling locks a dangerous liability. In the interest of safety and the war effort the star was instructed to adopt a hairstyle with stray locks pulled back and away from her face for working women to emulate. This stylistic shift unfortunately proved a devastating move for Lake's screen image. Such utilitarian functionality undermined the star's glamour mystique and eventually her career. Not surprisingly, many wartime 1940s female stars and models, particularly during the 1942–43 period, sported hairstyles pulled up and back off the face in promoting a fashionable, functional aesthetic.

Given the male talent shortage and lucrative female home-front demographic, female stars and women in production roles enjoyed opportunity during the war years. A number of screen actresses gained prominence, ideally coming into their prime in the 1940s—including Katharine Hepburn, Bette Davis, Ingrid Bergman, Rosalind Russell, Betty Grable, Rita Hayworth, Barbara Stanwyck, Lana Turner, Olivia de Havilland, Joan Fontaine, Greer Garson, Joan Bennett, and Joan Crawford. Women stars like Bennett, Grable, Hayworth, and Hepburn acquired more power during this period than other women before or after the conflict. World War II also provided an arena for talented women to make significant strides in the film industry behind the scenes and often "above the line," moving into writing, editing, producing, and even production executive ranks. In "Hollywood Bows to the Ladies" the *New York Times* noted growing involvement of women in the studio filmmaking process by January 1945. "Picture-making, like everything else, is coming more and more under feminine influence. The ladies, no longer content with being just glamorous, are invading in increasing numbers the production field, a sphere hitherto almost entirely masculine."[6] Studios certainly capitalized on the ability of female talent to tap into the lucrative home-front audience—particularly with the predominance of working women earning substantial disposable income and having little to spend it on with the wartime rationing of consumer goods. After losing many international markets in wartime, Hollywood relied on targeting this domestic female audience. Women worked on several *noir* crime films and influenced the assertive, often working, heroines in films such as *Phantom Lady, Mildred Pierce, Gilda,* and *The Big Sleep,* where images of *noir* women evolved beyond the typical femme fatale. *Mildred Pierce* and *The Big Sleep,* coscripted by female screenwriters like Catherine Turney and Leigh Brackett, showcased a variety of working girls—from self-employed entrepreneurs to taxi drivers and rare-book clerks. Writers like Joan Harrison and Virginia Van Upp actually became producers and creative production executives—a remarkable feat during the studio system era. Hitchcock's former associate Joan Harrison moved into producer ranks to acquire greater creative and executive control. As a female writer-producer, Harrison en-joyed authority and autonomy few women writers attained.[7] Harrison's *Phantom Lady* is a fine example of women working in Hollywood, produc-ing strong images of working women in film noir, during the war years.

Joan Harrison, Robert Siodmak, and *Phantom Lady*

In *Phantom Lady* Ella Raines's working *noir* heroine, Kansas, takes time off her job to moonlight for the police and track down criminals. Tapping into a home-front audience of working wartime women, Raines's active female character was the product of working woman Hitchcock protégé, writer-producer Joan Harrison, who coscripted Hitchcock's *roman noir* gothic films *Rebecca* and *Suspicion*. Based on a hard-boiled novel by William Irish, a pseudonym for writer Cornell Woolrich, whose early writing had con-tributed to *Dime Detective* and *Detective Fiction Weekly*, Universal's *Phan-tom Lady* was adapted by Bernard Schoenfeld, and Harrison was involved in story and script development for the screenplay. *Phantom Lady* is notable as a *female* hard-boiled detective *noir* crime film, where the protagonist is neither a male nor a female victim (as in gothic Hitchcock thrillers *Rebecca* and *Suspicion*) nor a lethal femme fatale. Instead, the film centers on a strong, independent career-woman-turned-professional-female-detective who reluctantly poses as a loose, erotic femme to solve a case clearing her male employer of a crime he did not commit. Visually deceptive and nar-ratively unpredictable, *Phantom Lady* opens with what appears to be the main character of the story: a man picks a woman up at a bar, takes the ex-otic stranger to a show, and then returns home to find menacing gangster-like police who interrogate him about his beautiful murdered wife in the bedroom. His alibi date vanishes—a phantom lady whose absence struc-tures the film—while the presumed guilty hero is hauled off to jail and out of most of the picture. Enter his female office assistant, Kansas. Convinced of his innocence, she decides to solve the crime and save her boss from the chair. Donning a sexy femme alter ego, she picks up lascivious drummer Elisha Cook Jr. (one of his best roles) in a now famous orgiastic jazz sequence (unbelievably approved by the PCA), entering a corrupt urban underworld of lies, payoffs, betrayal, and murder—where her boss's best friend and professional colleague turns out to be the psychopathic killer (who had an affair with his wife before strangling her and framing him for the crime). In the classic "wrong-man" scenario Harrison cast both hero and villain against type—reversing customary roles to create ambiguity in the male characters. Universal publicized framed good guy Alan Curtis as a "once villain" who "makes [a] romantic bid." Harrison's casting provided a "good looking" and "romantic" antagonist with masculine sex appeal to target women, referring to "the fair sex" to describe the female home-front audience. An anti-intellectual bent infused the film's "mysterious killer," played by Franchot Tone, described as a "psychopathic intellectual." Emphasizing the film's realism, promotional material describes how Tone "consulted a noted Beverly Hills psychiatrist to obtain authentic information on the physical and nervous reactions of a psychopathic depressive." Initially, even the police seem to more closely resemble thugs than law-enforcement officials.[8]

Produced in late 1943, Universal's *Phantom Lady* combined male and female European émigrés—newly autonomous British producer Harrison and director Robert Siodmak. Harrison had just negotiated a producing project for herself at Universal when she happened to meet Siodmak in a restaurant frequented by émigrés near the studio in 1943. The two hit it off, initiating discussions that resulted in their collaborating on *Phantom Lady*. Harrison had graduated from Oxford, where she wrote film reviews for the student newspaper. In Britain Harrison worked as a copy editor before responding to Hitchcock's ad for a "producer's assistant." She received cowriting credit on the script for Hitchcock's 1939 British film, *Jamaica Inn*. Harrison rose from secretary to script reader / story analyst to screenwriter, moved with the prominent British producer-director to America, and collaborated on Hitchcock's Hollywood gothic mystery films with female protagonists and wartime espionage thrillers *Foreign Correspondent* (1940) and *Saboteur* (1942). Considerable media and press attention was given to Joan Harrison as Universal's *Phantom Lady* project commenced in fall 1943 through its January 1944 release. Not only did Harrison's innovative role as female studio producer grant her rare, heightened creative control as a woman, but the former writer was also prominently regarded as Alfred Hitchcock's protégé. Such sought-after achievement and recognition for a female producer in the Hollywood studio system still held several challenges, however. In a February 1944 interview with the *Los Angeles Times* Harrison described herself as a "thwarted writer." She explained that her scripts had been so butchered that she had requested to have her name removed from the credits and became a producer to gain greater creative authority. When she was given the opportunity to produce, Harrison asserted, "the front office attitude resents a woman in authority and it probably always will—they recognize women writers but prefer to keep us in prescribed groves [*sic*]. Some day they will have to admit that a woman can function successfully as an executive, too."[9] Harrison was known for keenly infusing the "women's angle" into films, a particularly marketable skill during the war. Yet rather than standard female melodrama, Harrison's interest was in crime, notably crime a bit darker than the conventional weepie.

Universal publicized *Phantom Lady* as an innovative mystery drama from a woman's point of view, "based on feminine psychology for its essential appeal," describing this "formula" for the film as "never before . . . translated for the screen." Its narrative is "in no sense a 'horror' film, nor is it just another 'whodunit' of the cops-and-criminals pattern," but rather a "highly ingenious tale dealing with the obstacles to justice often presented by chance, circumstance and human psychology." Studio press books promoted the female protagonist's independence and determination. Publicity heralded the film's "spirited" and "level-headed" heroine as "wholly unstereotyped" in an "adventure into the mystic realm of psychological conflict, rather than the ordinary crime detective thriller."[10] Louis Black observes that *Phantom Lady* "differs dramatically" from other *noir* films because it refrains from "portraying women as the bitch goddesses of the hard-boiled tradition" to, instead, depict independent women "rather benevolently."[11] Tapping wartime working-women audiences, publicity noted a female player's former wartime occupation in "Girl Quits Truck for Film Career." The film's promotion recognizes Harrison as a forerunner in female studio producers and describes her casting an actress who could dress plainly without being "glamorous" in the role. Consistent with an effort to target an employed female audience "getting their hands dirty" during wartime military production, it quotes Harrison explaining the part to Raines: "I told Ella the girl in 'Phantom Lady' would have to be made quite plain, that the nature of the character wouldn't permit her to be beautiful. That her clothes would be ordinary, some of them downright shabby." A March 29, 1944, *Los Angeles Times* review of *Phantom Lady* even describes the film as "the story of a girl who goes to the defense of her employer when he is accused of murder and helps discover a maniacal killer."[12]

Phantom Lady was progressive for its innovative creative authority granted a woman, its stark *noir* style, and its central, active female protagonist. In fact, a February 28, 1944, *Life* magazine article, "Ella Raines: The Pretty Young Star of 'Phantom Lady' Began Her Career by Being Incorporated for $1,000,000 by a Production Firm," said it all. The piece highlighted a photo-feature of *Phantom Lady* star Ella Raines. It described how the twenty-two-year-old former University of Washington drama coed was initially signed and "incorporated" by Howard Hawks and Charles Boyer as the "sole asset" of their independent producing company, B-H Productions, Inc. Hawks and Boyer then "passed her [Raines] on" to Universal for the role of the assertive, resourceful independent female protagonist in Harrison and Siodmak's film. (The feature also made sure to mention Raines's military husband, "bemedaled captain in the Army Air Forces," being ordered back to duty during their wartime honeymoon—an obvious human-interest item to the prominently female domestic audience.)[13] The business strategy of "woman as independent production commodity" highlighted in the article is certainly noteworthy. Like Selznick, Hawks purchased, "owned," developed, and refined new feminine star talent, grooming actresses and "manufacturing" female screen images—as Selznick "made" starlets and loaned them to other studios, Hawks sold his actresses' contracts to various Hollywood studios and made a profit.

Despite Harrison's position of production authority, Universal capitalized on her femininity and attractive physicality in studio publicity designed to mold, promote, and "package" the female producer and to provide a novel industry production image for the studio. Much like Columbia glamorized production executive Virginia Van Upp, Universal marketed Harrison's gender as a desirable young female producer. Studio publicity noted: "A girl with wavy blonde hair, dimples and a 24-inch waistline could entertain people with something besides crime stories. But not Joan Harrison. She lives and breathes crime—in her imagination, of course—and then tells it to others via the motion picture screen. Miss Harrison is a woman movie producer, one of the few in Hollywood. Her feminine slant has added freshness to 'cops and robbers' plots."[14]

Publications often capitalized on emphasizing the producer's feminine "allure." One piece even made a point of publicizing Harrison's "ah-inspiring legs." Harrison, however, referred to herself as a "specialist" in psychological crime narratives, explaining, "I don't want to make pictures with the Andrews sisters."[15] In an October 23, 1944, article for the *Hollywood Reporter* entitled "Why I Envy Men Producers," Harrison facetiously commented on the wartime challenges facing a woman producing in the Hollywood studio system in the 1940s. She complained that men producers "don't care if nylons ever come back"; furthermore, the "shortage of girdles doesn't even attract their attention in the newspapers." She adds that her wartime male counterparts are not even "disturbed" if the "laundry's making confetti of the linen sheets, which can't be replaced in these times," nor do they "worry about menus or stretch ration points."[16] The war-related scarcity of rationed materials influenced 1940s fashions and simplified Hollywood costume designs, paring down wardrobes and eliminating an array of garment items—unexpectedly aiding the intended heightening of eroticism in wartime films. Lana Turner's bare legs (which were safely covered in coarse rayon hose for a close-up) and midriff in *The Postman Always Rings Twice* were both spicy *and* economical. Rita Hayworth's seductive attire in *Gilda,* shot during the nylon and girdle shortage, liberated women's bodies from constrictive intimate apparel, cleverly draping the torso of gowns to conceal the fact that the star had recently had a baby.

Because Harrison's mentor, Hitchcock, had worked at Germany's UFA studio early in his British career, bringing a somber vision to his films, Harrison was credited with Hitchcock's bleak stylistic predilection by association, especially since *Phantom Lady* had such a beautifully black visual style. As creative Hollywood studio executive, Harrison's remarkable female production coup and her Hitchcock lineage were so heralded in the film's publicity and critical reception that its director, UFA alumnus Robert Siodmak, was barely mentioned. Siodmak's first film had been a realistic German documentary, *Menschen am Sonntag* (People on Sunday, 1928), a collaboration with brother Curt, roommate Billy Wilder, Edgar Ulmer, Fred Zinnemann, and Eugen Schufftan. While in Germany, Siodmak even worked for famed UFA producer Erich Pommer (who produced *The Cabinet of Dr. Caligari*) and "discovered" Emeric Pressburger while working as a writing talent scout. Siodmak left Germany specifically because of Nazi objections to his racy films. Goebbels condemned Siodmak's last UFA film for its illicit sex affair, which the propaganda minister perceived as corrupting German families. Like other émigré filmmakers, Siodmak found work in France. Joining a prominent German-exile community in Paris, that included Fritz Lang and Billy Wilder, Siodmak directed many of the era's major French film stars, such as Danielle Darrieux, Maurice Chevalier, and Charles Boyer. Several of Siodmak's French films have been cited as precursors to his American films noir, especially *Cargaison Blanche* (French White Cargo / Traffic in Souls, 1937) and *Pièges* (Snares, 1939), a crime film starring Pierre Renoir, Eric von Stroheim, and Maurice Chevalier. Fleeing the war and wartime occupation, Siodmak departed for the United States the day before Hitler and the Nazis marched into Paris in 1940. In Hollywood Siodmak directed *Son of Dracula* in 1943, and Universal signed him to a seven-year contract before he collaborated with fellow émigré writer-producer Harrison on *Phantom Lady.* A veteran craftsman, Siodmak's rich expressionist style no doubt aided Harrison's film. In fact, when auteur critic Andrew Sarris reconsidered Siodmak's contribution in exporting his UFA stylistic background to the United States, Sarris actually argued that Siodmak's 1940s American films, with shadowy interiors and dark night settings, were more "Germanic" and expressionistic than his earlier European films.[17]

Completed just prior to *Double Indemnity, Phantom Lady* is a unique wartime effort by these European expatriates and influential as a prototype for film noir. Full of thematic duplicity and dark visual stylization, the unusual crime film ends with the female protagonist communicating via the office Dictaphone with her boss (used as a murder confessional device in *Double Indemnity*). Both films were submitted to the PCA on the same day, and the salacious and censorable content of *Phantom Lady* was approved two days before *Double Indemnity*. *Phantom Lady*, like *Double Indemnity*, started filming in September 1943, with tight wartime production constraints, electricity rationing, and a blacked-out skyline during the darkest period in the history of the Los Angeles basin. It is no wonder both films were so recognized for their definitive *noir* style. *Phantom Lady* was considered the "last great burst of expressionism in Hollywood" by Raymond Durgnat and Andrew Sarris.[18] Consistent with wartime bans on daytime location filming, most of the film is shot at night on a dark studio sound stage or tarped back lot. Studio publicity cites the film's unique cinematography, attributing its "unusual 'minor key' photography" to the "artistry" of famous *noir* cameraman Elwood "Woody" Bredell, who, according to Warner Bros. editor George Amy (*Air Force, Objective Burma*), could allegedly "light an entire football stadium with a single match."[19] Just months after Fritz Lang's chiaroscuro in *Ministry of Fear*, Siodmak and Bredell captured and epitomized film noir style in *Phantom Lady*, using extreme low-key (nearly pitch-black) lighting of a silhouetted couple meeting in jail, rear-lit via a single barred window—a stark image that became iconic of the dark 1940s trend. Siodmak achieved mood in the film by using silence on the sound track and filming almost all the action at night—certainly consistent with and facilitated by wartime daylight shooting limitations. Studio publicity noted that a "pre-war canvas shades 'Phantom'" in constructing and utilizing the "biggest" 810-foot black tarpaulin set at Universal "in years" (with a forty-two-foot ceiling) for night exterior shots on the back lot—alluding to the well-known production shortages and recycling of sets over the course of World War II, heightened by actual external location limitations by day and blackout/dimout regulations by night. Filming almost entirely on a sound stage, emulating exteriors rather than navigating the production "mine-fields" of wartime location restrictions, complications and disruptions certainly justified this canopying over "two intersecting 'brownstone streets'" on the "tented" studio back lot to facilitate greater control over shooting during the war.[20]

As the *Phantom Lady* project commenced, Universal's Maurice Pivar initially submitted a script to Joseph Breen on September 1, 1943. Two days later Breen declined Production Code approval. He cited "excessive drinking" and banned references to sex, suggestive dancing, any condoning of di-

vorce, and the terms *lousy, lousing,* and *brassiere.* Songs and costumes would
require PCA approval, and he added that the "jive sequence" should be
"handled with the greatest care to avoid any possible suggestion that Cliff
[Elisha Cook Jr.] and the rest of the musicians are dope addicts." (This
rather short-sighted comment makes no reference to sexual innuendo in
the jazz sequence.) As a final note indicating multiple wartime censorship
considerations, Breen sent the script to Addison Durland, "our Latin American advisor," regarding "Latin American angles of the story." With a much-
restricted wartime international market, Latin American and domestic audiences were crucial for Hollywood.[21] Universal resubmitted a script for
Phantom Lady on September 14. On September 16 Breen stated that changes
had not been made. The censor reiterated his ban on drinking and suggestive dialogue.[22] As it happened, *Phantom Lady* and *Double Indemnity* were
then resubmitted to the Hays Office for PCA approval on September 21,
1943—Universal sent the script for Harrison/Siodmak's project for consideration as Paramount (after a pronounced lapse in correspondence) sent
Wilder/Chandler's script to Breen.[23] One wonders whether former roommates Siodmak and Wilder were in cahoots. *Phantom Lady* was approved
by the PCA the next day—followed by the milestone endorsement of *Double Indemnity* two days later. Whatever transpired proved a strategy for success. Wilder and Chandler had certainly been working through the summer
to gain PCA approval on *Double Indemnity,* yet it is remarkable that these
potentially scandalous projects gained such swift, sudden, and comparatively easy PCA endorsement by the fall of 1943 and that Harrison and Siodmak's less-than-subtle orgiastic jazz jam session sailed so painlessly by the
censors. Perhaps the strategy of "bombard them and keep them busy" resulted in divided (and diluted) efforts by the guardians of cinematic virtue
to strictly enforce censorship based on a 1930 moral blueprint that was increasingly contradicted by violence and political propaganda during the war.

   Phantom Lady was filmed from the end of September through late October, and postproduction continued into November. Breen was busy approving changes through October, while he was approving Wilder's *Double
Indemnity* revisions from September 24 to December 1. By December 7,
1943, *Phantom Lady* was reviewed by PCA members Pettijohn, Zehmer, and
Durland—with Breen noticeably absent—in a report by L. Greenhouse that
classified the film as a melodrama-murder mystery, citing "murder" and
"some social drinking," no "adultery or illicit sex," an "unsympathetic drunk
character," and a "Latin American singer" (portrayed by Brazilian star Au-
rora, Carmen Miranda's sister).[24] A PCA seal was granted the next day, on
December 8, yet Universal publicity for *Phantom Lady,* like many of these

films noir described as "red meat," heralded and eroticized how the female heroine is "roughed up" by male costars during production; in this case the brutal encounter ensues after jazz drummer Elisha Cook Jr. leads our undercover detective heroine up to his shady bachelor pad just after the jam session and learns that Raines is on the job rather than on the make. Publicity often conflated sex and violence to titillate. Studio promotion narratives capitalized on suggesting more than censors would visually allow onscreen. In "Star's Portion Not All Roses" Universal's studio press book for *Phantom Lady* describes female star Raines as having "paid off three-to-one for her acting ability on the set one day. Teamed with Elisha Cook, Jr., in the 'jive' sequence," she did "seven 'takes' of one of the wildest scenes recently put on the screen." Surprisingly reminiscent of wartime espionage thrillers (like *This Gun for Hire*), publicity explains how Raines "drops her purse while searching for a cigarette" for the male character, who "discovers her 'secret orders' to apprehend him. He has been making love to her, but his emotion changes to hate and fear." As the film capitalizes on bona fide violence, the press piece details how "Cook grabs her, tries to get the truth from her. In the struggle, a lamp is overturned and a divan gets kicked around. Director Robert Siodmak, wanting to put a punch into the sequence, had the pair run through it seven times. Next day Miss Raines appeared on the set with 21 bruises. The make-up man was summoned to 'cover up.'"[25] Universal's efforts to accommodate the PCA continued through January 6, 1944, when Pivar submitted a revised ending for *Phantom Lady* to Breen, but according to MPAA/PCA files the censor sent no reply.[26] With both *Phantom* and *Indemnity* completing production and nearing release Breen may have resigned himself to a losing battle with both films.

Wartime industry, critics, and the public struggled with how to classify and conceive of the film. A January 21, 1944, *Motion Picture Daily* review noted Universal's deviation from its earlier horror tradition, describing *Phantom Lady* as "not just another horror film. On the contrary, as produced by Joan Harrison and directed by Robert Siodmak, is top-notch psychological murder mystery melodrama packed with 87 minutes of suspense and action in the best Alfred Hitchcock manner." Drawing on Hitchcock's female gothic thrillers *Rebecca, Suspicion, Shadow of a Doubt,* and espionage thrillers *Foreign Correspondent* and *Saboteur*, it praised *Phantom Lady* as "guaranteed to leave limp hearty devotees of this type of film." Trades called Raines "romantic," the "surreptitious" jive session "unique," and the jazz music "part of the action." Evoking a wartime male psyche, Tone's "personable sculptor" is "afflicted with paranoia" that "leads him" to commit a "series of vicious murders" in a "grand performance."[27] Yet *New York Times* critic Bosley Crowther noted the film's pronounced style rather than narrative in a lukewarm February 18, 1944, review:

> We wish we could recommend [*Phantom Lady*] as a perfect combination of the styles of the eminent Mr. Hitchcock and the old German psychological films, for that is plainly and precisely what it tries very hard to be. It is full of the play of light and shadow, of macabre atmosphere, of sharply realistic faces and dramatic injections of sound. People sit around in gloomy places looking blankly and silently into space, music blares forth from empty darkness, and odd characters turn up and disappear. It is all very studiously constructed for weird and disturbing effects. But, unfortunately, Miss Harrison and Mr. Siodmak forgot one basic thing—they forgot to provide their picture with a plausible, reasonable plot.[28]

Phantom Lady was a sleeper, and although it was released in January-February 1944, a few months before *Double Indemnity,* it was the Paramount A film, rather than the more modest Universal production, that received all the critical and industry attention and initiated Hollywood's crime cycle. Such reception may also have been aided by the fact that *Phantom Lady* was disqualified from Academy Award consideration because of its January-February 1944 release date. (*Double Indemnity* received numerous Oscar nominations later in 1944 for the following year's Academy Awards.)[29] While Harrison was promoted as Hitchcock's protégé in producing *Phantom Lady* in wartime, not long after her celebrated status as the female "master of suspense," men were increasingly emphasized after the war. By February 1946 the *New York Times* noted that Siodmak—who went on to direct *noir* films *Christmas Holiday* (1944), *The Suspect* (1945), *The Spiral Staircase* (1946), *The Killers* (1946), *The Dark Mirror* (1946), *Cry of the City* (1948), and *Criss Cross* (1949)—"rebelled" against directorial typecasting in making exclusively psychological mystery and suspense films. Soon it was male director Siodmak, not female producer Harrison, who was "disturbed" to be repeatedly called "a second Alfred Hitchcock."[30] As a hyphenate producer, Joan Harrison had the power to realize her vision in *Phantom Lady* as a dark, psychological female detective film. Harrison would go on to write the gothic *Dark Waters* (1944) and then produced the films noir *Uncle Harry* (1945, directed by Siodmak), *Nocturne* (1946), *They Won't Believe Me* (1947), and *Ride the Pink Horse* (1947). Not all women writers were as fortunate as Harrison, however. Without hyphenate producer status, writer Catherine

Turney's role in scripting *Mildred Pierce* shows how the Hollywood film-making process was more typically dominated by men.

Catherine Turney, Jerry Wald, and *Mildred Pierce*

Mildred Pierce—like *Laura* and *Gilda*—revolves around a female protagonist whose presence is so intrinsic to the film that she not only structures the story but also becomes the namesake of the entire picture. The classic *noir* picture employs gothic *roman noir* conventions in its central working-redeemer character. *Mildred Pierce* combines female melodrama with a hard-boiled detective narrative to create a heroine that, like Kansas, Laura, and Gilda, defies conventional notions of a gothic ingenue or femme fatale. Mildred is presented as an amalgam of *noir* redeemer, working woman, and mysterious, possibly guilty, femme fatale who is a humane, compassionate character. Warner Bros. adapted James M. Cain's *Mildred Pierce* in 1944–45, shifting a women's sex melodrama novel to a crime film using a flashback to frame the story, not unlike *Double Indemnity*. Warners' version begins with a murder and a police interrogation, changing the weepie to a murder mystery—where the darkest points in the crime investigation set up the framing narrative.[31] The film opens with gunfire. The camera, skewed in an extremely low Dutch angle, shows a man, shot several times, in a dark beach house. He calls out, "Mildred," before he crumbles and dies. Like *Laura*, the picture becomes a whodunit, implicating the heroine. Seemingly admitting her guilt, Mildred (Joan Crawford) contemplates suicide shortly after the murder. Police detectives suspect she committed the crime and interrogate her to discover her story and reveal her past. The film flashes back to her life as an unhappy housewife and mother of two daughters who becomes a Rosie the Riveter–style career woman after her husband, Bert (Bruce Bennett), leaves. Mildred builds her own business as a restaurant entrepreneur to support her family. She spoils her irresponsible eldest daughter, Veda (Ann Blyth), who becomes a monster, and neglects the other, who dies. Mildred carries on with other (shady) men and has affairs. Although her opportunistic suitors (Jack Carson, Zachary Scott) are the sexual aggressors, she is reluctant and far more interested in material status to impress and indulge Veda. Mildred marries a broke con artist with a wealthy name, Monte (Scott), rises in her career, then loses almost everything. She is ultimately victimized not only by the dubious men who betray her for money and destroy her business once she achieves success but also by ruthless, greedy Veda. After she and Monte leach all Mildred's cash, Veda runs off to pursue a cabaret career, steals her mother's disreputable husband, and turns out to be a lethal femme murderess who kills him (when he calls her a tramp and refuses to dump Mildred and marry her). Mildred tries to take the blame for Veda, but in the end she reunites with Bert, who validates her innocence as police haul irredeemable Veda off to jail.

Mildred Pierce reflects Hollywood's effort to modify Cain's story for a male, as well as female, audience. Screenwriter Catherine Turney, who collaborated on the script, had started at MGM and was one of the first women writers to work at Warner Bros. in the 1940s. Turney was known as a "woman's writer," and her first assignment at the studio was *Mildred Pierce*. According to Turney, "Jack Warner didn't really like women writers," but he realized they could make money for the studio. (Turney also notes that female salaries were only a fraction of male salaries.) Turney explains, "One of the reasons they hired me is that the men were off at the war, and they had all these big female stars" wanting "roles that served them well"—not passively "sitting around being a simpering nobody" but rather taking action and often "battling against the odds."[32] Producer Jerry Wald cast Joan Crawford as Mildred, an ideal comeback for the former MGM diva who had refused mediocre scripts and middle-aged, past-her-prime roles during a two-year hiatus from the screen prior to signing with Warner Bros. in 1944. Crawford demonstrated that she could battle the odds and beat out the competition in fighting for the role—impressing Wald and Curtiz after *Double Indemnity* spider woman Barbara Stanwyck and Warner femme Bette Davis turned it down. The Warner Bros. project featured a woman's story, a major female star, and a woman writer to appeal to a female audience.

Men, however, still dominated many aspects of the production for *Mildred Pierce*. Jerry Wald had just finished a series of action-oriented war films, or "men's pictures," such as *Objective Burma, Destination Tokyo,* and *Pride of the Marines.* Michael Curtiz had recently directed *Casablanca, Dodge City, Yankee Doodle Dandy,* and *Passage to Marseille.* Male executive Jack Warner ran the Warner Bros. Hollywood studio. Other male screenwriters on the project included male-action specialist Albert Maltz (who adapted *This Gun for Hire* and scripted *Destination Tokyo*), Ranald MacDougall (the only writer to receive screen credit for *Mildred Pierce,* a favorite writer of Wald's who scripted *Objective Burma*), and William Faulkner (who worked with Howard Hawks on *Air Force, To Have and Have Not,* and *The Big Sleep,* opting not to receive screen credit on *Mildred Pierce*). The male author collective of producer Wald, director Curtiz, executive Warner, and writers such as Maltz, Faulkner, and MacDougall presided. Turney was initially used for the "female angle," but her input on *Mildred Pierce* was rewritten, produced, and directed by males to reinforce a macho crime ethos in order to capitalize on the framework and success of *Double Indemnity.*

Wald initially sought not a woman but Cain himself for the project; however, Cain was under contract to MGM at the time. In the box-office glow of *Double Indemnity* Cain wrote to Wald "stressing that *Mildred Pierce* was an attempt to develop a serious theme" and "objecting to Warner's attempt to exploit his literary and cinematic reputation—based, as it was, on *Postman* and *Double Indemnity*—by turning *Mildred* into that kind of Cain thriller." Cain told Wald the opening of Warners' screen adaptation has "tingle, the promise of great photographic effectiveness, and that curious quality describable only as style, which I imagine Curtiz had a great deal to do with." Cain, however, asserted that the "only point developed in this footage is: Who done it? This, it seems to me, is a very thin springboard for a story." He argued, "*Mildred Pierce* is one woman's struggle against a great social injustice—which is the mother's necessity to support her children even though husband and community give her not the slightest assistance." It was a great wartime theme for the home front. Both Cain and Turney opposed "superimposing the murder on the story" of *Mildred Pierce* in an effort to turn it into what Cain described as "another *Double Indemnity.*"[33] Yet Cain and Turney were unsuccessful in discouraging a male-oriented suspense flashback framework. Though Turney worked on the screenplay, Wald added a *Double Indemnity*-like flashback structure with voice-over narration to the story in spite of her objection. Turney described Wald's "introduction of the flashback idea" into Warners' adaptation of Cain's novel as "pure gimmick," along with using a murder to open the film—devices that turned a straight female melodrama into a crime thriller.[34] Wald again sought Cain, who suggested female writer Margaret Gruen for the project; Wald hired her and then put male action specialist Maltz on the script to revise Gruen's work. Wald later brought Turney back onto the project yet instructed her to follow Maltz's outline and narrative framework—which included a more masculine murder/flashback narration structuring the story.

In a 1944 Paramount press release Cain noted the impact of the adaptation of *Double Indemnity* on Hollywood film trends, referring to it as his most censorable story: "It may be, since the word 'adult' is the one reviewers use most frequently in connection with it, that a new field for moving pictures has been opened up."[35] Cain acknowledged the significance of the sordid, formerly banned film adaptation being approved as a censorship precedent in Hollywood during the war. "If Breen would approve a script of *Double Indemnity* that adhered so closely to the original story, he would approve anything. Warner Brothers, having bought *Mildred Pierce,* even began negotiating to buy *Serenade.* And about the same time, MGM dusted off *Postman* and writer-producer Carey Wilson quietly went to work on a script that would satisfy the new, more liberal Hays Office."[36] Given the momentum of this red-meat crime trend, its industry context and bandwagon production climate noted in the *New York Times* from November 1944 to August 1945 (two and a half months prior to the October 1945 release of *Mildred Pierce*), Wald and Warner no doubt saw the good fortune of adapting another "sordid" Cain novel at such an opportune time.[37] Cain biographer Roy Hoopes calls Wald an opportunistic "live-wire hustler" known for male-oriented productions, particularly war productions, yet "aware that the war would not last forever and that postwar America would probably go back to its old ways, with theater audiences dominated by women. So he wanted a 'women's picture.' When Jack Warner, caught up in the *Double Indemnity* excitement, gave him *Mildred Pierce* to read, he thought, this was it."[38] Gender demographics were actually reversed, or at least more complicated. Domestic wartime audiences were predominantly female, with a parallel combat male audience overseas—thus the market stratification. In anticipating postwar demographics, with men returning from military duty and reintegrating a masculine market into the domestic home-front audience, it made sense for studios to target both male and female sexes simultaneously, as in *noir* crime films with strong independent glamorous women and masculine crime, violence, and erotic appeal. Like other *noir* films, *Mildred Pierce* capitalized on drawing both men and women into theaters.

Although Wald may have been interested in the *Mildred Pierce* project since the book's 1941 publication, Warner Bros. production records indicate that Wald's initial treatment by Thames Williamson was sent to Joseph Breen for PCA consideration in January 1944, the month after *Double Indemnity* completed shooting at Paramount. Although *Mildred Pierce* was published during the war, Cain's story was set in 1931 during the Depression years. Williamson's January 12, 1944, treatment for Warners' film changed the book's setting to wartime Los Angeles. On January 14, 1944, Williamson sent Wald a memo: "In contrast with some of Cain's other novels, the elimination of sexual rough stuff from *Mildred Pierce* does not materially affect the rich meaty story . . . Mildred is naturally and normally inclined toward sexual satisfaction with both Wally and Monty, but *she never steps over the line.*"[39] Williamson made an effort to sanitize the raw sex from Cain's story to gain PCA approval in January and February 1944. Breen nixed Warners' *Mildred Pierce* project on February 2, 1944, as containing "so many sordid and repellent elements" that he suggested the studio "dismiss this story from any further consideration." Breen, however, had already given the go-ahead to the equally "sordid" *Double Indemnity*, signing off on the Paramount project that had already completed production and was nearing release. Studios were well aware of this after ten years of PCA bans on Cain's novels across the industry. In this production context, although Breen was adamant against adapting *Mildred Pierce* in early February, he capitulated by the end of the month. After a lapse in correspondence Breen suddenly wrote to Jack Warner of the "pleasure" he had discussing the project with Jerry Geller and Wald on February 22. In a more obliging tone Breen was ready to accommodate "some of the details" that "may creep in" that "would not be acceptable in the finished picture. We feel, however, that these can be handled as, and when, the screen play comes along."[40] Giving approval to Warners' project before a screenplay was written, Breen had no consistent way to enforce the Code with the precedent of Cain's *Double Indemnity* at Paramount.

It was not until mid-March and into April 1944, as *Double Indemnity* proceeded into previews, that Wald assigned Catherine Turney to script a straight adaptation of *Mildred Pierce*, true to Cain's novel (there was no flashback at this point) to see how much racy content could be submitted to the PCA. Following Turney's work on the script in aiming female melodrama past the censors, and after the *Double Indemnity* preview, Jack Warner sent a wire from Warners' New York office to the Hollywood studio on May 15, 1944. Warner informed Wald and executive assistant Steve Trilling that Shumlin thought "too much of [the] sex angle" was "removed" from *Mildred Pierce* to appease the Hays Office. (If Paramount could get away with it in *Double Indemnity*, he reasoned, Warner Bros. should be able to exploit the same meaty potential.) Warner instructed Wald and Trilling to put more sex into the story and beef up its raw appeal. "Maybe some of this could be put back and still not have Breen on our necks. Told Shumlin sex angle would be put in, in playing."[41] As in Wilder's adaptation of Cain, Warner favored metaphor and suggestion to get around the Code. As in *Double Indemnity*, the model of applying a flashback framework to Cain's novel (with proper narrative retribution for committed crimes) would facilitate PCA approval.

As Lizzie Francke has noted, Wald keenly considered commercial aims in producing *Mildred Pierce*:

> *Double Indemnity*'s dark story of homicide and adultery marked not only a stylistic breakthrough for film-makers but also signaled some relaxation in the Hays Office's moral patrol of the screens. It was en-

couraging news to Wald and other producers who wanted to take more risks. Murder could make money, murder spiked with love and lust could make twice as much. With such ingredients added to *Mildred Pierce,* Wald deduced that he would have a hot property on his hands since the film would appeal to more than just the women's audience.[42]

Rewriting *Mildred Pierce* continued through the release of *Double Indemnity* (from April to October 1944). By late October–early November 1944, after the successful *Double Indemnity* Cain adaptation framework on which to model *Mildred Pierce* and gain PCA approval, Wald began screening other influential dark films like Alfred Hitchcock's *Rebecca* and Fritz Lang's *Woman in the Window* to study flashback technique. By November 1944, just before filming began on December 7, Wald called *Mildred Pierce* "basically a murder mystery" (having altered the original female melodrama focus à la Turney). On February 6, 1945, Wald even specified shooting inserts of Crawford using "low-key lighting."[43]

The war certainly affected the project's production. Filming was subject to location shooting restrictions, which still persisted by late 1944 and early 1945. As in so many of *Mildred Pierce*'s *noir* and proto-*noir* predecessors, wartime limitations on studio lighting, electricity, set and costume materials, and filming locations facilitated the dark visual design. Warner Bros. repeatedly had to obtain permission from the U.S. Navy to film coastal beach locations near Santa Monica, Malibu, Redondo, and Laguna beaches—and the military even required viewing all shot footage.[44] The navy allowed nighttime shooting for *Mildred Pierce* but banned daytime filming of coastal regions for national security reasons. The use of blacked-out evening shots enabled military approval—and created a definitive style from the very opening of the story. The film was shot chronologically (highly unorthodox, starting without a finished screenplay), and the opening murder scene was filmed at director Michael Curtiz's beach house at night—for which military permission was still required. Warner Bros. delayed the 1945 release of this wartime production until after the war. As studios shifted to non-war-related story material to capitalize on a female and returning veteran audience while seeking long-term postwar marketability, *Mildred Pierce* avoids mentioning the war in its home-front story. In fact, a 1945 viewer wrote to Warner asking whether the film is set during wartime, a question based on inconsistent references to nylon rationing.

Like Lake's androgynous male-garbed publicity in *This Gun for Hire,* Crawford's independent female entrepreneurial protagonist in *Mildred*

Pierce taps into blurring gender roles, with working women ably filling traditionally male jobs. The picture's hard-hitting crime ethos, homicide, and investigative framework undermined the sentimentality of conventional weepies, broadening the appeal of *Mildred Pierce* by targeting Warners' male-oriented crime (previously gangster) film audience with suspense. Wald's mystery saga included a cultural moral. Mildred is depicted as grossly negligent in her motherly duties. Her self-reliant career ambitions not only destroy her family, home, and love life but also encourage her spoiled, neglected, and undisciplined daughter, Veda—another transgressively independent woman turned domestic threat—to ruin Mildred's chances at success in business, wealth, marriage, or a happy life until Mildred returns to her first husband. Ideologically, *Mildred Pierce* demonstrates Hollywood's effort late in World War II to representationally rechannel working women back into the home to resume maternal duties and anticipate returning veterans. As demographics shifted from a wartime market to an increasing postwar focus in 1945, the film industry foresaw and began preparing for the end of war.

Warners' effort to masculinize the female melodrama along the lines of the *noir* crime trend seemed to have paid off by September 29, 1945, as Alton Cook of the *New York World Telegram* praised the film: "Warners Banish Three-Year Jinx: 'Mildred Pierce' Rings Bell in Non-War Category." Cook cited the film as a distinguished non-war-related complement to Warner Bros.' war films, and a "worthy companion piece" to that "other remarkable picture from a James M. Cain novel, 'Double Indemnity.'"[45] Budgeted at $1,342,000 *Mildred Pierce* cost $1,453,000 and earned $3,470,000 domestically and another $2,141,000 once international markets opened after the war.[46] Nominated for Academy Awards, including Best Screenplay, *Mildred Pierce* was hailed by critics, who called it "smashing" and a "triumph." Crawford won a Best Actress Oscar for her role as Pierce. Warners' 1945 publicity featured a woman with a gun alongside the tagline: "The kind of Woman most men want—BUT SHOULDN'T HAVE!" Ads read, "A mother's love leads to murder," and "She knew there was trouble coming—trouble she made for herself—a love affair—and a loaded gun . . . she had no right to play around with either!" The marketing strategy fueled the film's popularity, luring first-time viewers with a gimmick: "What Did Mildred Pierce Do?" and "Please don't tell anyone what Mildred Pierce did." A year later the *Detroit News* reported, "More than a million customers stormed box offices to find out."[47]

Mildred Pierce shows Wald's creative influence and authority as studio system producer, capitalizing on a shifting commercial market and super-

"The kind of Woman most men want—BUT SHOULDN'T HAVE!" Joan Crawford as the eponymous Mildred Pierce. Warner Bros., 1945.

seding Turney's creative concerns as a female writer. But at Columbia another woman reversed this power dynamic. By 1945 Virginia Van Upp achieved tremendous creative power—perhaps more than any other female contemporary—in actually rising from writer to studio executive. Along the way she also produced the film noir *Gilda*.

Virginia Van Upp and *Gilda*

Gilda is another classic *noir* film that combines female gothic melodrama with a hard-boiled, gangster-detective crime narrative. Set in Buenos Aires, *Gilda* features a South American locale as the war began to wind down and combat-hardened veterans began to return home. Like wartime London in *Ministry of Fear* and French Martinique in *To Have and Have Not,* Hollywood sound stages doubled for exotic locations abroad. Actor Glenn Ford, recently home after four years of wartime duty, plays a scrappy, war-scarred antihero, Johnny, renegade American exile-turned-bum-turned-gangster, who mixes with the underworld, working for a Nazi-turned-international-espionage-cartel-boss Ballin Mundson (George Macready) after gambling (and presumably living) on the street. He finds his former lover, Gilda (tantalizingly portrayed by Rita Hayworth), married to his Aryan employer. Mysterious and disreputable, Mundson hires Johnny to run his gambling casino and keep an eye on his beautiful, defiant, sexually independent wife. Argentinean police detective, Obregon (Joseph Calliea), seeking to break the illegal Axis cartel, pursues Johnny and Mundson, who conveniently fakes his death in the middle of the movie. Fiercely loyal to Mundson, yet jealously conflicted over his relationship with Gilda, Johnny marries her to possess, control, punish, and seek vengeance via psychological abuse and by confining her in an effort to tame her strong persona and transgressive sexuality. Cold-blooded Mundson menacingly reappears from the "dead" to complicate matters and threaten the dysfunctional couple. In the end Mundson is killed, the police detective arrests his German underworld co-conspirators for breaking antitrust laws, the casino is taken over by the government, and Johnny and Gilda can finally fly off to America together.

Rita Hayworth's bold performance as sex siren translates into one of the all-time great femme fatales. Gilda, a woman with much bravado accentuating her smoldering sensuality, was also terribly vulnerable and had been treated sadistically. Hayworth's charismatic heroine was an alluring role "manufactured" and emphasized by a powerful creative executive woman involved in the production of the film, producer (and former writer) Virginia Van Upp, who was also head of production at Columbia studio beginning in early 1945. As Hayworth's real-life marriage to Orson Welles unraveled during the making of the film, Van Upp had a close relationship with the actress, provided her a safe haven, mentored the star, and supervised the writing of the project (by screenwriter Marion Parsonnet) while producing the picture. When compared to earlier gothic heroines (manufactured and refined by male filmmaking personnel such as Selznick and Hitchcock), women more actively involved in such creative or executive positions as writing or producing *noir* films—whether Turney coscripting *Mildred Pierce,* Brackett coscripting *The Big Sleep,* Harrison producing *Phantom Lady,* or Van Upp producing *Gilda*—contributed to more fully developed and unpredictable *noir* heroines who were more complex and assertive (often nontraditional or career women) variations on the conventional femme fatale.

Gilda, Mildred Pierce, and *Laura* are female-centered *noir* stories that become sex melodramas within a male crime milieu, where the central heroine is surrounded by men who find her sexually attractive and consorts with many of them. Gilda is brazen, openly defiant, and cognizant of her own sexuality. She is irreverent in her active pursuit of her independence. As a dangerous femme, Gilda is deviant in using the power of her erotic female image to arouse and manipulate men for her own pleasure. She strives to be a "working girl," pursuing a career singing, dancing, and performing striptease in a cabaret of wildly ecstatic male patrons. Hayworth's beautiful, strong-willed temptress in *Gilda* is daringly aware of her female allure and boldly uses her sexuality to titillate and elicit applause. Hayworth's performance—like her dangerous spider woman in *Lady from Shanghai* or Turner's role in *The Postman Always Rings Twice*—is a fine example of how classical Hollywood cinema sells fascinating gender roles codified as "male threat" by the end of the war.

Despite her transgressive behavior, however, like the female gothic ingenue, Gilda is not evil or malicious but, instead, a victim of the abusive, violent men around her, entangled in a series of bizarre relationships that accentuate her gender distress. Openly rebellious rather than demure, Gilda does not behave like a typical bride or widow. Although she is married to Mundson, she taunts and tantalizes Johnny as he manages her husband's illegal business affairs and then agrees to wed her ex-flame when the kingpin is believed dead. Marital bliss is rather a wedded nightmare for Gilda as twisted intimate relations imprison her in these domestic unions. Like Mildred and Laura, Gilda transcends her diva sexuality and image as a femme who men desire, evolving into a sympathetic, multidimensional *noir* heroine. She is human, has flaws, and even exhibits self-destructive behavior. In *Gilda* Van Upp and Hayworth create a complex protagonist who simultaneously embodies an independent woman, a victim, a redeemer, an active working girl pursuing a career of sorts (albeit interrupted by a violent slap from her tormented tough-guy husband), and a sexual femme fatale wreaking havoc in men's lives (as they battle their own demons). Ultimately defying lethal femme stereotypes, however, this dangerous classic *noir* woman has a heart. Gilda's provocative and alluring image as quintessential 1940s femme fatale—like Hayworth's famous wartime pinup poster—is ultimately all for show, an act, a masquerade to save her pride (and no doubt appease censors). Her sexual exploits are allegedly not for real, just meant to emotionally hurt her tormented beau, with whom she has a history. In the end Gilda actually turns out to be a "good girl" (despite her bad-girl image) who is less naive than other gothic redeemers (such as Fontaine in *Suspicion*), and more comfortable with her own sexuality, but who ultimately tames her unruly independence, makes amends, and gets together with her man—in a *noir* finale where the Hollywood couple disappears into the dark.

Virginia Van Upp was a production executive at Columbia Pictures from 1945 to 1947. She began as a writer, scripting the 1938 Paramount gangster film *You and Me*, directed by Fritz Lang (with songs by Kurt Weill), and later the wartime Columbia musical *Cover Girl* (1944), starring Rita Hayworth and Gene Kelly. Van Upp "tailored" the female role in *Cover Girl* for Columbia's star Hayworth, groomed the actress, and even organized her costumes.[48] Moving on to producer ranks, she became a powerful female writer-producer, working with Hayworth at the studio. Van Upp eventually rose as an executive to Columbia's head of production for two years during, and after, the war. On January 7, 1945, the *New York Times* noted: "This week Virginia Van Upp, the scenarist, will step into the position of executive producer at Columbia . . . Miss Van Upp's new berth is considered to be the most important executive position yet for a woman at a major studio. She will have the over-all supervision of the preparation and actual filming of twelve to fourteen top-budget pictures to be made by Columbia during the year. Working under her will be several associate producers—all men."[49] The *Hollywood Reporter* elaborated on Van Upp's executive promotion at Columbia, stating that the producer "will select stories, okay casting, and generally keep an eye on the biggest attractions the company will make. Needless to say the 'woman's angle' will be kept in mind," and this would "undoubtedly please exhibitors everywhere when they start counting the take. Women have long edited some of the nation's most popular magazines, and their policy, in most instances, has upped circulation and profits."[50]

Van Upp personally produced *Gilda* from 1944 to 1946, supervising Hungarian expatriate director Charles Vidor (who had worked at UFA and had directed *Blind Alley* and *Cover Girl*), cinematographer Rudolph Maté, and art directors Stephen Goosson and Van Nest Polglase. In fact, powerful female star Hayworth insisted Van Upp produce the project. *Gilda* affirms Columbia studio chief Harry Cohn's confidence in Van Upp as an influential female executive producer overseeing other female, as well as male, creative talent. Women penned the screenplay and produced the project, and the crime film was clearly female-centered. Columbia Pictures publicity called it a "tense and realistic" screenplay based on Jo Eisinger's adaptation of E. A. Ellington's original story. When Van Upp sent a first draft of the script to Humphrey Bogart, he rejected the role of Johnny Farrell, considering it a minor male costar for Columbia's headliner Hayworth in a woman's picture. Ironically, a September 16, 1945, *New York Times* article stated that the project was initially intended as a gangster film set in the United States. Columbia and Van Upp no doubt entertained high hopes of once again getting gangsters by the Code as the war neared its end. The unpatriotic taint of gangster pictures, however, fueled enough censorship resistance that the film's setting was moved to Buenos Aires. The role of Gilda solidified Rita Hayworth as a 1940s sex goddess. Although the film was initially banned in 1944 as a gangster picture during wartime, like *Mildred Pierce* the female melodrama was masculinized as a *noir* crime narrative. Showcasing Hayworth with wild provocative musical song-and-dance sequences, it also included male camaraderie, homoerotic underpinnings, and an underworld milieu.[51]

On November 16, 1944, following the momentum of the release of *Double Indemnity* (and just three days before the *New York Times* cited the industry's red-meat trend), Columbia's Silvia Stein submitted the proposed story to the "Gentlemen" of the "Association of Motion Picture Producers" for PCA consideration. By November 20 Breen had rejected the story on the basis of its illicit sex and adultery without compensating moral values.[52] Work on the project eventually resumed, however, particularly after Van Upp took over the production reins at Columbia. Revisions of the story and lyrics for *Gilda* were resubmitted to the PCA on August 4, 1945. Two days later Breen rejected lyrics for the song "Amado Mio" because of its "sex suggestiveness." (The song remained in the film anyway.) Stein resubmitted the script on August 24; Breen rejected it on September 4 as shooting began. Revisions were resubmitted on September 8, and Breen finally granted PCA approval on September 11. A few weeks later, however, he objected to Hayworth's line "If I were a ranch, they'd call me the Bar Nothing"; and by late

October he wanted Van Upp's assurance that a suggestive "first class rib" involving stockings would defuse sexual innuendo. The censor continued to haggle over sex and violence in the story through December, when filming concluded. By early December Breen banned suicide and noted Van Upp's revision, "Didn't you ever hear of a thing called justifiable homicide?" On February 1, 1946, *Gilda* was reviewed by the PCA—in the absence of Breen—and granted a seal of approval on February 25.[53] Sexually charged *noir* innuendo—as in Hayworth's hair tossing and Gilda's transgressive independence and coded striptease of the glove-peeling "Put the Blame on Mame" song-and-dance number—at once responded to and played havoc with PCA censorship. In the association between pleasure and violence *Gilda* wonderfully illustrates a recurring female dilemma and conflict in film noir—the clash between classical motifs of personal romance, love, and private life versus career / public life. This narrative tension related to gender in the ambivalent role of American women by the end of World War II, coinciding with their desire to retain careers they had begun during the war.

Gilda premiered in March 1946. *Variety* called Hayworth "ravishing," noting the film's "melodramatic" war-related espionage narrative involving "German agents demanding" her sadistic husband "return certain patents and tungsten mines." The review also mentioned Van Upp's prominent production role and "step upward" as female producer of the "drama."[54] *Gilda* reformulated Nazis into underworld Aryan gangsters, yet its espionage slant had a unique spin as a female star vehicle Van Upp developed for Hayworth in her first dramatic role. The film established Hayworth as a femme fatale. Her unmistakably erotic and independent feminine character transcends "fallen women" or passive victims and becomes a "misunderstood" woman who is "wronged" but refuses to wallow in self-pity.[55] Impudent, strong, and liberated (in every sense of the word) despite a sadistic masculine power structure, Rita's femme flies in the face of the men around her. She embodies a sexual threat that males in the narrative seek to contain. Not surprisingly, Van Upp's involvement and authority as a female studio executive contributed to Hayworth's strong, independent, transgressive screen diva. Columbia's film and its sensational publicity for *Gilda* capitalized on the film's audacious femme fatale.

In appealing to men overseas and a returning combat audience, studio press books also described Ford's Johnny as a disheveled transient—a "hard-bitten young American" on a "South American waterfront" who is "making his own luck with a pair of loaded dice. Attacked, he is saved by a sinister stranger" in a "gambling casino." Promoting military male camaraderie, Johnny then becomes the stranger's "trusted lieutenant." Publicity

clamored that his "past is a secret" and that "a woman is the cause of his bit-
terness." In tapping into the social terrain of returnees from military duty
abroad (many of them absentee husbands in hasty marriages immediately
prior to or during the war), Ford's character meets his employer's bride:
"Tension electrifies the air" as Johnny "faces the woman in his life! But their
love has turned to hate as they pretend not to know each other." Reflecting
the paranoia and suspected infidelity of a masculine wartime psyche, "Gilda
appears to carry on sordidly with other men, while Johnny, jealous in his
own right and deeply aware of his allegiance to his boss," a surrogate for
Uncle Sam, "grimly forges her alibis." He thinks "Gilda's infidelity is the
cause" for his friend's death. Johnny marries her but "makes her a virtual
prisoner" to "avenge" him. But she "escapes" and "becomes a cafe singer."[56]

Rarely had Hollywood narrative been so steeped in the fantasy and
nightmare of a war-related psyche and cultural mythology. The film and
publicity targeted an audience divided by gender at the end of the war, in
both American home-front society and Allied combat fronts overseas (and
even after the war with ongoing American occupation abroad, in Europe
and Japan). In shifting from wartime espionage to cold war paranoia, 1946
publicity added: "Although the war is over, Johnny learns that the casino is
a front for German business interests. A German suspicious of Mundson is
murdered," but a "government agent" later "smashes the cartel." The war influenced Columbia's advertising campaign. The studio press book promoted Ford's recent return from military service and explained that "production of 'Gilda' took place during the nylon shortage. As a result, Miss
Hayworth's ultra-lavish wardrobe . . . included a pair of rayon—not nylon!—stockings." It publicized Hayworth's wartime popularity overseas after troops voted her number-one pinup girl in 1945. "GI's began writing,
telephoning and wiring the studio, saying they wanted their favorite pinup gal to sing and dance and show her legs." A press book feature, "Glamour Gals vs. Tanks," even promoted *Gilda* cinematographer Rudolph Maté's
filming of the combat movie *Sahara*. In "Hollywood Photographer Dis-
cusses His Subjects: Rudy Mate Finds Lensing Hayworth Easy but Tank in
'Sahara' Worried Him for Weeks," the famous émigré cameraman explained,
"It's easier to photograph a glamour girl than it is an army tank." Maté compared shooting the tank *Lulubelle* in the masculine, hard-hitting realism of
Sahara to photographing Hayworth in *Gilda*—in an odd transference from
weapons to women.[57] The comparatively rugged *Lulubelle* was the sole
"woman" in the earlier Columbia war film, costarring opposite Bogart and
the boys at the front. The ultimate publicity for Hayworth and *Gilda* was
another linking of weaponry and women, with a "smart plug"—this time

on the atomic bomb. By July 3, 1946, Hollywood Bureau correspondent Harold Heffernan of the *Detroit News* commended the film's explosive "A-Bomb Tieup":

> Occasionally the slogan boys have their chores done for them and wholly unsolicited. This happened many times during the war when GI's branded stars with their own designations, which stuck and received wide exploitation. Probably the greatest piece of unplanned publicity ever applied to a picture and a star was the A-bomb blast for "Gilda" and Rita Hayworth, which came up from Bikini to hit every newspaper story and every radio broadcast of the proceedings last Sunday. Columbia estimates the plug will add close to a million dollars to the gross of "Gilda" and boost Miss Hayworth's standing immeasurably.[58]

Violence became sexy. The independent *noir* female screen images seen late in the war were not without hard knocks. Sensational publicity showcased violence for sex symbol Rita Hayworth in Columbia's *Gilda*—interestingly combined with cross-promotion for Fritz Lang's *Scarlet Street* at Universal, starring femme fatale Joan Bennett. Film noir promotion strategies for *Gilda* capitalized on ads featuring the female star being "roughed up" by Ford's Johnny. Studio press book publicity observes, "Rita Takes Punishment," and compares the two films and female stars. The studio's feature taps into increasing gender distress, even growing labor dissension throughout the industry:

> Two of Hollywood's most popular glamour girls, Rita Hayworth and Joan Bennett, are undoubtedly toying with the ideas of either donning boxing gloves and learning the art of fisticuffs, or picketing their studios with placards proclaiming their leading men to be unfair to organized feminine pulchritude. All because of the indignities these two ladies suffered in their latest pictures. To put it bluntly, Rita and Joan get slapped around. They both are recipients of stinging blows to the face lustily administered by their respective leading men, Glenn Ford and Dan Duryea, and there's little they can do about it at the time.[59]

Ads featured seductive images of Hayworth in her strapless black gown with taglines like: "There NEVER was a woman like Gilda"; "Now they all know what I am . . . "; and "'Bewitchy' is the word for *Gilda!*" Several offered an alternative photo of Ford slapping Hayworth that read, "I was true to one man once . . . and look what happened!" Another showed a smug, satisfied Rita leaning back with a cigarette under the line " . . . now I do what I please, when I please!" A few included Ford towering over Hayworth as she clung to him from the floor below: "Johnny, let me go. Please let me go. I can't stand it any more . . . " Others revealed a laughing siren in a white beaded two-piece with a slit-skirt flashing a bare leg and open waist: "Gilda used men the way other women use makeup!" Columbia's press book splashed images of its star: "*Rita Hayworth* A SUCCESS STORY . . . who made something of an atomic impression on all the GI's." It announced, "Hollywood Actors Return from Wars to Renew Careers. The movie Johnnies are back home from the war, and the actors who have replaced them in Hollywood films will have to fight hard to retain their new positions." Promotions included a "gallery of Hayworth art" and clamored: "Editors Today Want 'Cheesecake' to Offset Serious News—These 'Gilda' Photos Will Sell Tickets and Newspapers!" It described Rita as "'Luscious,' 'seductive,' 'glamorous,' 'alluring'—and an extra 'hubba hubba' for good measure." Drawing on Hayworth's *Cover Girl* and wartime pinup appeal, "From Dancing Glamour to Success in Drama!" compared Rita to Ginger Rogers and Joan Crawford in *Mildred Pierce* as joining "Ranks of Former Dancers Who Won Fame In Straight Roles." The piece "They Made Good by Playing Screen 'Meanies'!" called Hayworth "bewitchiest," "glamorous," and "tantalizing" and also mentioned Barbara Stanwyck in *Double Indemnity,* as well as Bette Davis, Vivian Leigh, and Joan Bennett making a "startling impression . . . switched to being a minx" in *Woman in the Window.*

Publicity for *Gilda* reproaches strong, independent women as responsible for violent male behavior. Columbia's press book indicts Hayworth: "After leading Glenn Ford a torrid chase through most of the picture, she finally enrages him to the point where he hauls off and lets her have it."[60] It blames women and autonomous, unrestrained female sexuality—shown in Rita's wild abandon in Gilda's famed "Put the Blame on Mame" number— as the cause for male anger and then justifies it as a "natural" claim, describing women as the "previously" so-called "fairer sex." In such films, drawing on sex and violence, the *noir* crime trend became a highly successful and profitable narrative cycle in the transition and reconversion from wartime to postwar culture, economy, and industry in the United States and evolved into distinctive cinematic style even before French critical recognition in 1946. This sexy, crime-oriented marketing strategy related to an initial move by Hollywood studios to target returning male veterans exposed to inordinate amounts of violence in wartime combat. The trauma of several years

Rita Hayworth as quintessential *noir* femme Gilda.
Columbia, 1946.

of bloodshed, death, and devastation had left pronounced battle scars—
psychically, as well as physically.

Following *Gilda*, Hayworth began work on the *noir* film *The Lady from
Shanghai* (1947), written, costarring, and directed by the star's ex-husband
Orson Welles, in the midst of futile reconciliation efforts at marriage between star and director. To appease Columbia studio boss Harry Cohn's objections to Welles, Van Upp contributed uncredited writing. The close rapport between Hayworth and Van Upp, coupled with distress at home,

contributed to the *noir* film's ambivalent sexual tension. Van Upp also flew to Acapulco to provide Hayworth with emotional support and counsel when the relationship with Welles collapsed a second time during filming. Van Upp left her powerful female executive position at Columbia in 1947. Many commended Van Upp's "ability to survive in a man's world without losing her femininity," describing the woman producer-executive as "the perfect Hayworth scenarist" because she was "very tough, very funny and very feminine."[61] Yet some attributed Van Upp's Columbia departure to her no longer being able to "take the pressures of production."[62] Ironically, Van Upp had been reluctant to accept the Columbia executive appointment and increased studio authority during the war because it alienated the female producer from her male peers and added personal strain on her family. In fact, the female executive had to be "pushed into accepting" the post because she was so concerned about how the "new work pressures might infringe" on her domestic life.[63] Her husband, radio producer Ralph Nelson, was away on military duty, and Van Upp was supporting a young daughter from a previous marriage. Ultimately, Van Upp's relationship suffered because of her career. The executive producer resigned from her duties to "resume her marriage" as her husband pursued a producing career. The couple divorced two years later. A reporter asked if professional jealousy was the cause of the breakup. Van Upp responded, "I suppose so. How can you ever explain these things?" Van Upp later asserted: "I am going to marry my work—I think that's safer."[64] Van Upp was never again able to reach the creative and executive pinnacle she attained as Columbia's head of production.

As the male labor shortage evaporated, with men returning from military service, women—including Harrison and Van Upp—found less opportunity in Hollywood. (Other talent—even émigrés like Fritz Lang—were also caught in a bind: "Jobs were drying up as Hollywood personnel flooded back from wartime service, and the nervous Lang saw no immediate prospects on the horizon." Lang assistant and confidant Andries Dienum explained that after *Scarlet Street* and the war, "Fritz took *Cloak and Dagger* because nothing else was available." By April 1946 the *Hollywood Reporter* observed that *Gilda* director Charles Vidor sued Columbia for terminating his contract after completing the film.)[65] The need for creative talent during World War II, with large numbers of men leaving for military duty, had benefited new talent such as European émigrés and particularly women. As the Hollywood film industry transitioned from wartime production toward economic reconversion in a postwar economy, things changed. Studios now had an ample, ready supply of talent. As in other domestic industries, women had filled a temporary talent void. The film industry's reconversion coincided with provocative film narratives, promotional strategies, and gender implications coinciding with the employment and executive authority given to women. Even in the personal lives of female star Hayworth and producer Van Upp, the distress at home ironically paralleled the doomed sexual relations in the films with which they were creatively involved, *Gilda* and *The Lady from Shanghai*. As growing numbers of men resumed civilian life, reentered Hollywood's production workforce, and transformed gender demographics of audiences, macho narratives increased. Images of women in films noir began to change by the late 1940s and 1950s as home-front working women were channeled back into the home with more domestic roles after the war. Given these leaner employment prospects, Van Upp left at an inopportune time and eventually lost her powerful professional status like so many women redirected from the workplace in a tight immediate postwar environment. Despite these challenges, however, Harrison persevered, segueing from features into independent telefilm production in the 1950s and later gained notable recognition producing Hitchcock's television series *Alfred Hitchcock Presents*.

6 Hyphenates and Hard-Boiled Crime

World War II had left an indelible mark on Hollywood—changing the industry and its players, complicating censorship, modifying films the studio system produced and how they were publicized, and ushering in a bold new film cycle. Even overseas a few began to take notice. On February 4, 1945, screen critic Joan Lester of London's *Reynold's News* penned "Professor in Love with Picture." She recognized a number of new films coming out of Hollywood. "It is not only the quality of films which varies," Lester explains, "but the tastes of film-goers. Now and then comes a well-directed, well-acted thriller which has universal appeal. 'Double Indemnity' and 'Laura' were outstanding examples. 'The Woman in the Window,' though lacking the macabre brutality of the former and the smooth subtlety of the latter, is still rattling good entertainment, and pretty well everybody's cup of tea, choc-a-block with suspense and brilliantly photographed."[1]

Late in the war Hollywood crime films became more masculine. Simulating combat and targeting a growing audience of veterans returning home from the war abroad, tough wartime *noir* crime films exploited violence. Already by 1943 Hollywood studios anticipated the end of the war and produced screen narratives depicting a seedier American home front involving crime, corrupt detectives, and former GIs, tapping into the psychic identity of tough "destabilized" males exposed to inordinate violence in combat. Screen violence was heightened as federal regulation changed and screen gender roles shifted—from weapons to women. Encouraging male camaraderie (though homosexuality was censored) and reformulating "un-American" gangsters, red-meat crime men roughed up tough, sexually transgressive, dangerous women in late wartime and early postwar narratives. Publicity promoted violence and male stars beating up female costars as hard-hitting realism.

The war had affected audiences, the film industry, and American culture. By the mid-1940s, publications such as the *New York Times* noted the graphic death and violence of the conflict itself, as well as its newsreel and photojournalism coverage, which had corresponded with a wartime psyche.[2] World War II profoundly influenced filmmakers who enlisted—evident in the stark images filmed on their return. It heightened wartime documentary newsreel production and accentuated the dramatic trend toward realism during (and after) this period. In targeting a growing male audience, studios tapped into popular conventions during the war (combat, action films with graphic, real-life naturalism) to reformulate for a postwar market. The impact of the war and war-related newsreels refined depictions of onscreen crime, violence, and increasing realism. In turn, the growing trend toward realism influenced the emerging *noir* crime cycle. Such realism contributed to stark cinematic style and hard-hitting topics—not only topical socially conscious concerns but also narrative violence (evocative of combat), often rechanneled into sexual violence. Crimes of violence and passion were key to Hollywood's red-meat trend, soon to be coined film noir, which flourished with a more lenient PCA.

The rise of the "hyphenate" writer-director, producer-director, and writer-producer coincided with unique conditions in 1940s Hollywood and the initial move toward independent production that accelerated during the war. Filmmakers like producer-directors Howard Hawks and Fritz Lang negotiated more autonomous production deals during this time. Hyphenate and independent production allowed creative writer-directors, producer-directors, and writer-producers notable artistic freedom over the filmmaking process and provided substantial wartime tax advantages for highly paid "above-the-line" (creative and executive) talent. These hyphenate filmmaking arrangements not only gave filmmakers greater creative control to experiment in their films but also evaded a steep 90 percent wartime income tax on their large salaries because these quasi-independent production deals allowed hyphenate filmmakers to be paid in capital gains (at a mere 25 percent) rather than taxable salary—so the incentive was certainly lucrative. Because filmmakers sometimes earned a percentage of the film's gross box-office receipts in lieu of a huge salary, in many cases these hyphenate production deals also encouraged higher quality, first-run A-film product—in an effort to maximize financial returns.

Often working in-house at various Hollywood studios, hyphenates gained coveted independence. By the early 1940s *Variety* observed that studio-based independent filmmaking was growing, and the *New York Times* noted, "Unit production—that system by which independent producers operating under protective wings of major lots are encouraged to use initiative and imagination while obtaining the benefits of factory costs and methods—has become an accepted practice at four studios: Warners, RKO, Universal, and Columbia." As the war wound down and in the postwar era, independent production proliferated. By the end of World War II, in "New Hollywood Units," *New York Times* industry analyst Fred Stanley wrote:

> The recent increase in the number of active independent companies and the current popularity for the profit-participation field on the part of acting talent are indicative, to Hollywood observers, of the rapidly changing over-all complexion of motion-picture production. Some industry leaders predict that in the not-too-distant future the larger percentage by far of top pictures going to the theatres will be contributed by independent and semi-autonomous companies.
>
> Several factors enter into the changing production vista. Not the least is an attitude of independence on the part of name actors, directors, and writers, who since returning from war service, now desire to be their own bosses and accomplish cinematically things which perhaps they were restricted from doing when previously under contract to major companies . . .
>
> Finance for independent productions has never been more free, thanks to a three-year bonanza box office. Moreover, in the eyes of the larger bracket stars there are income tax attractions in an occasional film "on their own." Also fitting into, and prompting to a great degree, the decentralization move is the desire on the part of most major companies to veer from mass production methods of the past and depend more on the individuality—and gambles—of self-financed independence . . .
>
> "Scarlet Street," the initial film of Diana Productions, the Walter Wanger–Joan Bennett–Dudley Nichols–Fritz Lang unit, only could have been made, according to Mr. Lang, as an independent venture in which those involved were willing to gamble their money and services.[3]

As hyphenates and independents gained more creative control, power shifted away from the old guard in Hollywood. The era of executive studio bosses making all the filmmaking decisions was over. Increasingly, power moved into the hands of talented creative individuals. As the industry made fewer films during the war, and more of these releases were A pictures with higher budgets, comparatively autonomous creative personnel enjoyed unprecedented "authorship," becoming involved in all aspects of filmmaking and making crucial production decisions. This shift in Hollywood's power dynamic encouraged innovation and led to more sophisticated handling of screen material, style (visual nuance), writing, dialogue, and characterizations ("off-type," with more realistic combinations of good and bad qualities) that moved beyond superficial genre formulas. Rather than blandly churning out studio product, these creative hyphenate filmmakers strived to transcend mediocrity and raise the overall quality of Hollywood's product to achieve an aesthetic. And, remarkably, they accomplished this by also making films efficiently, capitalizing on wartime constraints.

As these filmmakers were given greater freedom to experiment, manipulate, and subvert cinematic conventions, the result was more original work. In this way creative hyphenates and independents refined the American film product, enabled the development of a distinctive wartime trend, and contributed to film noir style. By 1944 to 1945 pictures like *Laura, Detour, The Woman in the Window, Scarlet Street, To Have and Have Not,* and *The Big Sleep* showcased an emerging *noir* visual aesthetic and a growing effort to capitalize on sensational narrative and promotion strategies. Wartime Hollywood industry trends featured red-meat publicity strategies exploiting sex and violence as realism and, along with the move toward hyphenate and independent production, the retargeting of star talent to anticipate a postwar market.

From Madison Avenue to Poverty Row: Preminger's *Laura* and Ulmer's *Detour*

Like men overseas longing for photographs of sweethearts and pinups of desirable all-American girls, several *noir* films like *Laura, The Woman in the Window,* and *Scarlet Street* revolve around male protagonists enthralled with the image of a woman. Gene Tierney's good-girl-turned-advertising-executive in producer-director Otto Preminger's classic *Laura* (1944), like Kansas and Mildred Pierce, is another example of a working *noir* heroine. As a successful career woman Laura is an intriguing character—complex, elusive, yet almost ethereal, like a ghost or supernatural spirit that haunts the narrative and whom no one in the film really understands. The film begins after Laura has apparently been brutally murdered in her own apartment, and Detective Mark McPherson (Dana Andrews) proceeds to piece together various stories to solve the crime. Laura, however, turns out to be alive but remains mysterious and absent from the first half of the film, despite the fact that she appears in her painted portrait, in flashback memories, and in fantasies of the male characters. Ultimately, we are introduced to Laura through her image as it is constructed in the minds of the men around her. She becomes an object that many different male characters (from a wide variety of social backgrounds and classes) aspire to, seek to attain, and even kill for.

There are many appealing facets to Laura's *noir* heroine. Tierney captures the everywoman quality of Laura's character, tapping into issues important to home-front working women, while simultaneously appearing otherworldly. In many ways, however, she is not fully formed. As the story unfolds this absentee career girl becomes an ambiguous figure whose very nature is suspect. While Laura is characterized by those around her as a sweet, warm, and earnest all-American girl-next-door, she demonstrates that she is secretive and capable of duplicity. It is not exactly clear as the film progresses whether she is a femme fatale who commits murder and lies to detectives (and whose motives are called into question) or whether she is an innocent victim with good intentions who serves as a redeemer for the crooked men in her life. In fact, as the film fuses a gothic thriller narrative with a hard-boiled detective story, Tierney's *noir* heroine becomes all these things: bad girl, good girl, working woman, and male fantasy.

Laura's reappearance "from the dead" in the doorway of her dark apartment transpires like a dream. Detective Mark McPherson is lost in the fragile beauty of her portrait and has drifted into unconsciousness to ponder her deceased visage. At that point it is not even clear to Mark (or viewers) whether he is awake or in a trance or whether the female figure before him is real or just a figment of his imagination. When it becomes clear that she is very much alive and not a masculine fantasy, we realize there may be a disparity between her image, in mind and on canvas, and the real woman. Laura becomes a kind of mythic *noir* heroine who contradicts her mystique (while ironically adding to it) with her sudden mysterious appearance. We don't really know who she is, and neither does Mark. Her entry calls every crime-solving fact (and our understanding of her character and the film's story) into question as she uproots the detective's methodical piecing together of the case. Moreover, in creating a new dilemma of mistaken identity, Laura's belated arrival implicates her for the murder of another woman (with her fiancé) in her own apartment.

Ultimately, Preminger's film is as much about deciphering who Laura is as it is about solving a homicide case. The myth and mystery of Laura, and of her ever-present image in the painting, reinforce the disparity between a projected female persona and the unraveling layers of who she is. Laura's character is, in fact, manufactured not only by the men in the narrative but also by the male production executives involved in making the film. Otto Preminger, who had initiated the project, had a great deal of creative control as the film's producer-director. Darryl Zanuck, 20th Century–Fox studio chief, also had very different ideas about the nature of her female gothic crime heroine than did Preminger. Zanuck was influential in developing Laura more fully and in removing Tierney's voice-over narration by her character, which was originally in Vera Caspary's 1943 novel and in early versions of the studio's film adaptation. Zanuck urged Preminger to expand Laura's *noir* heroine beyond a naive gothic ingenue victim yet to maintain enough fresh innocence to indicate that she does not realize how much trouble she is in and to avoid making her a cheap tramp or loose femme fatale.[4] Preminger considered Laura a more sexual woman of the night. The creative tension between Zanuck and Preminger added more depth and intrigue to Tierney's screen character. Laura's evolution from career woman to dream-girl fantasy to deceitful femme and finally a more multifaceted variation of the gothic victim by the end of the film—almost killed but ultimately redeemed by her cynical newspaper columnist mentor, Waldo's (Clifton Webb) murderous attempt on her life (proving her innocence)—is fascinating. Laura emerges as a contradictory *noir* heroine with flaws, virtues, and dimensions that do not fit the classical mold of hard-boiled femme fatale and whose feminine presence permeates the film. Based on a story penned by a female author, *Laura* was scripted by Jay Dratler, Samuel Hoffenstein, and Betty Reinhardt, with uncredited writing by Ring Lardner Jr., Jerome Cady, George Bricker, Robert Spencer Carr, and Philip Lewis—like *Mildred Pierce*, men rewriting female contributions.

Originally considered for low-budget production in Fox's B unit under the supervision of Bryan Foy, *Laura* was elevated to a more lavish A-picture status under Zanuck's supervision after he became interested in the project. Submitted to Breen in late October 1943 on the heels of the PCA's *Double Indemnity* endorsement, and produced from late April to late June 1944, the film elicited concern at the Hays Office over a suggested sexual relationship between Laura and Waldo, as well as Waldo's potentially questionable sexual orientation and any hanky-panky going on in Laura's apartment during her absence. *Laura* was filmed after *Double Indemnity* had already previewed, and Preminger complied with only a few of Breen's suggestions. A scene where Waldo describes how he grooms Laura and chooses her clothes and hairstyles was removed because 20th Century–Fox "was worried that declaration would offend World War II soldiers overseas with its depiction of decadent luxury and non-military obsessions happening on the home front." Ads for *Laura* featured luscious images of Tierney with the tagline "Laura was all woman ... Loved by all Men ... Loving None! Then in a moment of terror she found the one man she was ready to live for ...

or die with!" Critics raved about the film. The *Hollywood Reporter* called it a "masterpiece . . . terrific . . . flawless." *Variety* considered it "smart . . . fresh . . . honest, real and adult." And *Daily Variety* gave high praise, calling it "a crime story connoisseur's dish. Rarely does a serious crime drama get such sound and brilliant professional treatment . . . Otto Preminger scores an extraordinary success both as director and producer."[5] Nominated for several Academy Awards, *Laura* beat out *Double Indemnity* by winning Best Cinematography (Black and White, for director of photography Joseph La Shelle) in 1944. *Laura* presents a classy, refined, "Cafe Society" variation on film noir, very much a polished prestige production. A story beginning with and revolving around such a grisly murder would no doubt be handled differently in a James M. Cain novel or any other *noir* picture. The case that Mark is investigating involves a vicious murder in which a young woman has been shot in the face at close range with a shotgun so that she is rendered unrecognizable. Neither the murder nor its gruesome aftermath are shown or even sensationalized, as one might expect. Rather, the story unfolds with savvy nuance, subtlety, and restraint—as does Laura's character.

Quite a different approach is taken by another director on a production far more rough around the edges. Gritty, raw, and frugal, Edgar Ulmer's low-budget cult classic *Detour* (1945) made no bones about cutting to the chase. Expatriate designer Ulmer had worked uncredited on *The Cabinet of Dr. Caligari, Metropolis,* and *M* and collaborated with Wilder and Siodmak in prewar Germany on *Menschen am Sonntag.* He apprenticed with F. W. Murnau on *Sunrise* and *The Last Laugh,* emigrating as the Nazis gained power. A master at shadow, Ulmer directed *The Black Cat* (1934), *Bluebeard* (1944), and *Strange Illusion / Out of the Dark* (1945) in Hollywood and achieved remarkably stylish, powerful, innovative *noir* images on a shoestring budget. Ulmer shot his tight, super-lean B picture *Detour,* packed into sixty-seven minutes, in six days with rear-projected locations and only four (and a half) modest sets at notoriously cheap Producers Releasing Corporation (PRC), a Poverty Row studio. President and executive in charge of production at PRC Leon Fromkess was the picture's credited producer and Martin Mooney its assistant producer. Working at a frenetic pace, without big stars, top salary, or any official hyphenate title, Ulmer enjoyed substantial creative freedom in making his economical films. In effect he acted as an uncredited producer-director—briefly rehearsing, then often shooting sixty to eighty camera setups a day. In the 1940s and 1950s Ulmer "did not make these films as a hack director on salary, on commissioned assignments. Ulmer *chose* to make these films, frequently serving as his own producer when the ubiquitous Leon Fromkess of PRC was elsewhere . . . Once

Laura publicity sexualized Gene Tierney in a love triangle with Dana Andrews and shotgun-toting Vincent Price.
20th Century–Fox, 1944.

Ulmer was typed as a cheapie director, it became nearly impossible for him to command any budget whatever, but it was more important to Ulmer to do his work as he wanted it done than to compromise in the attempt to mount more expensive productions."[6]

Based on Martin Goldsmith's 1939 novel *Detour: An Extraordinary Tale* and scripted by Goldsmith (and an uncredited Mooney), the film is a model of concentrated *noir*. Its aimless, antisocial drifter and toxic romance entangling shady crime, murder, cash, and an agonizing existential journey down a highway to nowhere was the stuff of James M. Cain fiction. In fact *Detour* in many ways becomes a *noir* road movie that seems to pick up where Cain's *The Postman Always Rings Twice* leaves off—that is, if Cain's disreputable couple had continued rather than aborted their hitchhiking odyssey in an effort to extricate themselves from their undesirable love triangle. Unlike the polish in MGM's extravagant A production of *The Post-*

man Always Rings Twice or Fox's prestige Oscar contender *Laura,* Ulmer boils things down to their very essence in his almost minimalist Poverty Row picture. *Detour* still manages, however, to boast convoluted *noir* plot twists. Tom Neal's frustrated, self-pitying hothead Greenwich Village–piano-player-turned-hitchhiker Al Roberts—in pursuit of his starstruck ex-girlfriend, Sue Harvey (Claudia Drake), who moves to Los Angeles—is the ultimate fall guy, self-destructive to the core. Ann Savage's Vera is the film's unforgettable femme fatale, a no-frills, low-down venomous shrew and downright unruly woman. No subtlety about it—this tough, mean, conniving antagonizer goes straight for the jugular. And she looks it. Al's voice-over narration describes Vera: "She looked like she'd just been thrown off the crummiest freight train in the world," and she had "a beauty that's almost homely it's so real." The film's brutally acerbic, caustic, and bitter dialogue pulls no punches as his doomed adventure escalates. When a pill-popping convertible driver, Charlie Haskell (Edmund MacDonald)—going "all the way" with a clawed hand from "tussling with the most dangerous animal in the world—a woman!"—picks Al up and gives him a ride out west and then suddenly drops dead, things get very interesting. Al's awkward predicament becomes more dubious, intriguing, and complicated when he assumes Haskell's identity and makes off with his clothes, car, and money—then, like a shamefully unlucky fool, manages to give a lift to Vera, who personifies bad news for him. Having recently ridden with and clawed dead Charlie, she is immediately on to Al's sham and ready to spell big trouble, blackmailing him and threatening to call the cops. "If you act wise, well, mister, you'll pop into jail so fast it'll give you the bends! I'd hate to see a fellow as young as you wind up sniffin' that perfume Arizona hands out free to murderers!" Like a twisted low-budget Bonnie and Clyde, the couple ride to Los Angeles together and miserably share an apartment, where Al accidentally murders a drunken Vera with the telephone cord before she can do him in. As Al tries to hit the road and flee his rotten surroundings, a patrol car pulls up and hauls him away in a plume of desert dust.

As Hollywood's red-meat cycle and Cain adaptations proliferated by late October 1944, PRC's Martin Mooney submitted the story in a sixteen-page treatment of the novel to the PCA. Breen replied on November 1, agreeing that the studio "could produce *Detour if* its criminal antihero is absolutely in the hands of police with a guilty regretful narration" by the end of the film. It nixed sexual relations between Sue and other men, as well as Al and Vera's having any "suggestion of a sex affair," and took issue with the couple registering as man and wife (Breen insisted they needed separate apartments). The Hays Office had no problem with Vera's being a crook, but she could not be portrayed as a prostitute. If the story was set in Hollywood, the film should not "reflect discredit on the motion picture industry." PRC submitted C. R. Metzger's synopsis of the crime story and a first draft of the script on December 29. After a January conference haggling and negotiating, Breen responded to the final shooting script on February 13, 1945, reporting that the basic story met the Production Code and thanking Fromkess for the excellent manner in which PRC corrected details. He called attention to sexual dialogue, suggestions of homosexuality, nudity above the shoulders, a "flash" of gruesomeness in the murders, and offensive drunkenness, although in this case he encouraged smoking: "Omit Vera's drinking at this point and possibly have her getting a cigarette."[7] (This was, of course, an iconic *noir* motif.) While Breen reiterated his directive on Vera's drinking by May 29, despite the couple's constant bickering, they certainly cohabited. Al tells Vera, "My favorite sport is being kept prisoner," not unlike a dysfunctional marriage as absentee husbands returned to their independent wives. The film's culmination no doubt satisfied the PCA, bringing narrative justice and compensating moral values as its futile antihero mutters, "Fate, or some mysterious force, can put the finger on you or me, for no good reason at all."

Filmed as the war was approaching its end, in June 1945, *Detour* capitalized on extreme production constraints and gender distress in its *noir* style. With abundant artificial fog and a street sign Ulmer cleverly did away with an entire costly urban exterior set of New York City. The fog was so excessive even the actors disappear in it. In another scene, using deep shadow, precise lighting, and a tight zoom in on Al's eyes as he sits wallowing at a counter, Ulmer not only avoids the expense of a more lavish interior set but memorably exploits his antihero's voice-over narration to launch into a flashback of his past without any other special effects. Like an efficient B western, Ulmer's filming on location with outdoor daytime shots was less artificial and far less expensive than constructing an elaborate set. Scenes filmed on a set or on location often relied even more expediently on a mere two-shot of actors sitting in a car and shown from the chest up with rear projection of the desert beyond. This technique also complied with wartime limits on location shooting and revealed only barren open desert and sagebrush rather than vital coastline for security reasons.

Publicity for *Detour* featured Neal, looking like a hobo, leaning against a lamppost and holding a cigarette while he eyes Savage, who wears a clingy dress and ankle straps and resembles a prostitute taking a drag on a cigarette of her own. Next to a clutter of characters and a disheveled Neal holding dead bodies, a tagline read, "He went searching for love . . . but Fate

Ann Savage as hooker, Tom Neal as hobo. "He went searching for love . . . but Fate forced a *DETOUR* to . . . violence."
PRC, 1945.

forced a DETOUR to Revelry . . . Violence . . . Mystery!" Posters showed images racier than the film with an "Adults Only" warning and a wanton Savage with a feline look and a cigarette dangling from her mouth alongside
three taglines: "I Used My Body for BLACKMAIL!" "Men like me too much
. . . and the police too little," and "I could be a one-man woman . . . if I could
find the right man." Despite Al's masculine "woe-is-me" narration in the
film, Vera is publicized as a siren to attract male viewers returning to the
domestic home front. After the war, by October 29, 1945, Jim Henaghan of
the *Hollywood Reporter* called *Detour* "excellent . . . unquestionably the best
film PRC has ever produced," and "an artistic success." He praised the
"mood created," which is "a difficult accomplishment in any budget film.
The achievement is most unmistakably attributable to Ulmer." Commending its "gripping realism" Henaghan called Benjamin Kline's photography
"superb, fluid and exciting in its departure from the usual."[8]

Fritz Lang's *Woman in the Window* and *Scarlet Street*

The Woman in the Window and *Scarlet Street* are two of Lang's best 1940s
films noir. In *The Woman in the Window* Richard Wanley (Edward G.

Robinson), a mild-mannered, married psychology professor, fascinated with a portrait of a woman, meets the alluring femme (Joan Bennett) and murders her lover with a pair of scissors in self-defense. Rather than call the police, he drives to the woods in pouring rain on a stormy night and dumps the body. Former-crooked-cop-turned-blackmailing-bodyguard Heidt (Dan Duryea)—having tailed her lover–dead guy and the professor—threatens Bennett, blackmails her for $5,000, slaps her around, and demands more. She fails to poison the blackmailer, but police track him down and shoot him, thinking he committed the murder. When the professor attempts suicide with a drug overdose, he wakes up and realizes it was all just a dream. *The Woman in the Window,* like *Double Indemnity,* shows the process of crime, the cracking of a case, a couple trying to get away with murder and evade fate, and blackmailers and authorities to accommodate Breen's "compensating moral values." This formula of crime and illicit sex posed problems for the Production Code, but a "crime does not pay" framework enabled approval. *The Woman in the Window* is much lighter than *Double Indemnity*—narratively, thematically, and visually. The brutality and stark, uncompromising ending of *Double Indemnity* was much bleaker, yet *The Woman in the Window* owes something to the eight-year preproduction effort to get Cain's provocative story by the censors.

Nunnally Johnson, a writer-producer on *The Woman in the Window,* had been a writer at 20th Century-Fox in the mid 1930s and early 1940s, where he wrote a preliminary treatment script for *Double Indemnity.* Although Breen had approved Johnson's sanitized outline of *Double Indemnity,* Fox's head of production, Darryl Zanuck, had felt Johnson's version compromised Cain's novel. When *Double Indemnity* finally did get past the censors, in 1943, Johnson was certainly aware of its censorship precedent in deviously complying with, while circumventing, the Code and the marketability for this kind of salacious, Cain-like red-meat material. Johnson was offered a lucrative, creative opportunity to leave Zanuck and his 20th Century–Fox position to become a writer-producer at the newly formed independent production company, International Pictures, initiated by former 20th Century–Fox production executive William Goetz and former RKO corporate president Leo Spitz. International began releasing through RKO in 1944 and would later merge with Universal. Johnson was savvy in eyeing the 1942 J. H. Wallis novel *Once Off Guard* in 1943—as was Zanuck, having returned from active military duty in mid-1943, in developing *Laura* by the end of the year, as *Double Indemnity* was completing production. Johnson also had the presence of mind to cast *Double Indemnity* star Edward G. Robinson as the middle-aged male lead in adapting *Once Off Guard,* retitled *The Woman in the Window*, Robinson's next project following *Double Indemnity*. Robinson, a freelance star by 1943 and trying to get away from typecast gangster roles, had almost rejected the *Double Indemnity* part because it was the third lead.[9] Johnson provided him the title role in International's picture. Johnson scripted, produced, cast costars Joan Bennett and Dan Duryea, and secured director Fritz Lang. Except for bad guy Duryea, the film's gender ratio very much reflects the absence of young men of fighting age, although it is not explicitly set during wartime. Shot by cinematographer Milton Krasner, who filmed Lang's *Scarlet Street*, with process photography by Vernon Walker, who shot special effects for *Stranger on the Third Floor*, *The Woman in the Window* included women behind the scenes, censorable sex and violence, and an effort to design the film in documentary realism style. Editor Gene Fowler Jr. had to resign early in production to join the army. Lang lobbied for rookie assistant editor Marjorie Fowler, Johnson's daughter, to take over and edit the project—enabling a greater role by a woman in the process. Lang's effort also afforded the director more creative license during the editing process in assisting the novice editor. Johnson opposed Lang's dream finale.

International Pictures general manager John Beck Jr. submitted *Once Off Guard* to Breen for PCA consideration in November 1943. Background footage of New York City was filmed on location in December. Art director Duncan Cramer's design illustrations for *The Woman in the Window* relied on a series of stark realistic photos of urban streets, subways, Grand Central Station, and strikingly dark exteriors, with images of a deserted toll booth in a blacked-out night. The streets are wet; only one or two toll lights punctuate the darkness. On March 21, 1944, the Hays Office approved the project but advised avoiding "illicit sex," no opium, no suggested "streetwalker," no disrobing, and requested cleaning up the "blood." By April sets budgeted at $57,500 did not include tarping over back-lot streets for urban exteriors, and the PCA complained changes had not been made.[10] The film was shot from April 11 to June 9 at Goldwyn, RKO, Paramount, and PRC studios on dark, tented, enclosed sound stages for claustrophobic "night" sequences (outside the apartment and men's club buildings), which enabled wartime filming and allowed greater control over lighting.[11] Members of the PCA reviewed the film on September 15—in the absence of Breen—and granted a seal of approval on September 21, 1944.[12]

An International Pictures press book for *The Woman in the Window* noted the Fritz Lang–Nunnally Johnson collaboration was stripped of patriotic flag-waving propaganda. The film's war-related realism, violence, and crime remained, however, and *The Woman in the Window* was plugged as "real," with everyday situations of what could happen to "everyman."[13] Released in October of 1944, on the tails of *Double Indemnity* and repeatedly compared to it, *The Woman in the Window* was heralded by Philip Scheuer of the *Los Angeles Times* as an "adroit exercise in crime": "Like 'Double Indemnity,' it is written and directed without such outmoded devices as creeping hands, screams and dumb flatfeet for 'comedy relief.' Compared to obvious melodramas, its story is almost an intellectual exercise in crime" that "projects a double moral."[14]

Ads for *The Woman in the Window* plugged the film as "an evening of flirtation that ended in a nightmare of MURDER!" International Pictures press book publicity refers to the film as "psychological." Bennett is described as a "volatile, love-hungry, desperate woman" whose "anxiety to escape a despair [with which] she cannot cope draws an innocent man into an abyss." Despite her rather sympathetic screen heroine's being manipulated by blackmailer Duryea, publicity promotes Bennett's femme as bringing about the hero's demise in the story. It notes the "web of circumstances closes tighter and tighter" around Robinson. Suggesting the male bonding of wartime combat, it highlights the male camaraderie of his friendship with the district attorney: "Conflict between lifelong friends, who try to hide their feelings for each other, is an anguish of emotional restraint."[15] An October 10, 1944, *Variety* review called the film the "femme star's best," involving a man "innocently mixed up in murder" who then "dumps the body of the murdered man."[16] RKO premiered *The Woman in the Window* in Los Angeles in October 1944 and released the film in New York on January 25, 1945. The film earned $2,010,000 domestically and $1,315,000 in foreign release as postwar markets began to reopen during 1945—totaling $3,325,000. (After accounting for production costs and RKO's distribution arrangement, though, RKO's profit was a mere $26,000.)[17] While Bert McCord of the *New York Herald-Tribune* thought the film's ending keeps *The Woman in the Window* from "easily" taking its "place beside *Double Indemnity*" as a superior "murder mystery packed with suspense," by January 26, 1945, the *New York Times* called it a "humdinger" of a "mystery melodrama," sporting "sophistication" and "penetrating satiric thrusts at radio advertising and newsreel coverage of crime stories" with a "police homicide bureau chief" and praised Robinson's performance, calling it as high caliber as his performance in *Double Indemnity*.[18]

As *The Woman in the Window* was in production, Lang moved into a hyphenate arrangement—from independent International Pictures at RKO to independent Diana Productions at Universal. Universal "sponsored" Diana Productions as an in-house independent production unit, and it was there that Lang assumed a producer-director role, teaming up with Joan Bennett and her executive producer husband, Walter Wanger. *Scarlet Street* was their first project. On November 18, 1945, the *New York Times* noted that the Diana Productions deal was initiated by Bennett during filming of *The Woman in the Window* at RKO. Trade papers in 1945 described it as an independent company comprising partners Lang, Wanger, Bennett, writer Dudley Nichols, and twelve others. The *Times* explained that "the unit . . . was organized to make 'Scarlet Street,' then considered highly censorable."[19] Although actress Joan Bennett was not officially involved in writing, producing, or directing these hyphenate film collaborations, the prominent glamorous female star of *The Woman in the Window* had considerable behind-the-scenes power on *Scarlet Street*.[20]

Despite the seminal status of *The Woman in the Window* in French *noir* criticism, many consider *Scarlet Street*, with its pessimistic themes and black visual style, to be Lang's *noir* masterwork. "Victory over Germany had come on May 8, 1945, as *Scarlet Street* was in preparation, and V-J day arrived during its filming on August 14. The Axis was defeated. World War II was over, but the director was one of millions who harbored no forgiveness for the Nazis."[21] *Scarlet Street* was produced as grim newsreel footage of the horrors of the European war—Nazi atrocities and genocide in concentration camps—hit American screens.[22] Corresponding with Bennett's business interest as an independent partner in the Diana production, *Scarlet Street* also depicted her alarmingly bold, sexually transgressive femme fatale—like opportunistic Vera and duplicitous Phyllis, a woman whose independence encourages illicit crime and brings about the *noir* antihero's demise. Just as *The Woman in the Window* capitalized on common narrative and star elements of *Double Indemnity, Scarlet Street* drew on many key narrative and star elements of *The Woman in the Window* and then added a darker edge and look, creating a brooding tone and deep shadowy design much sought after in the industry after Wilder's success with similarly stark imagery in *Double Indemnity*. In a wartime filmmaking environment transitioning to a postwar economy, Lang was especially able to achieve bleak aesthetic style as a producer-director in *Scarlet Street* and as a financial partner in the independent production company. With Bennett and Wanger handling financial matters, Lang had greater overall control over production with more creative power.

Director Jean Renoir first adapted Georges de la Fouchardiere's novel *La Chienne* (The Bitch [published in the United States as *Poor Sap* by Alfred Knopf in 1930]) as a social realist film in France in 1931. Director Ernst Lubitsch and Paramount purchased the screen rights in the 1930s but, unable to produce a screenplay satisfactory to the PCA, abandoned it. Lang wanted to take on the controversial project and "make a new film and not just a copy of the Renoir film which we had seen in the Thirties. We wanted to use the idea in a new way with reference to the Greenwich Village atmosphere and the American characters—'Lazy Legs' and Chris Cross."[23] Rough, raw, and sexual, the story involves a truly lethal, duplicitous femme fatale, Kitty "Lazy Legs" March (Joan Bennett), a thinly disguised prostitute who uses, seduces, and betrays a mild-mannered, unhappily married bank clerk and amateur painter, Chris Cross (Edward G. Robinson). Kitty takes all Cross's money and even usurps his artistic identity while sexually and financially double-crossing him to provide favors for her sadistic criminal boyfriend, Johnny Prince (Dan Duryea), who slaps her around. "You wouldn't know love if it hit you in the face," Kitty complains to her working girlfriend, Millie (Margaret Lindsay), who replies: "If that's where it hits you—you ought to know." In the end Cross murders his beloved, deceitful Kitty by stabbing her repeatedly with an ice pick, and Johnny ends up the fall guy sent to the chair.

Like *La Chienne*, *Scarlet Street* featured abundant crime, shady characters, and an antihero that gets away with murdering his two-timing female companion. In *La Chienne* the passive antihero is clearly sleeping with the streetwalker. In *Scarlet Street* this illicit affair is handled with greater ambiguity and nuance to indirectly imply a sexual relationship but gain PCA approval by claiming it is merely platonic and one-sided, the product of a passionate dreamer without the will to take action—until the final blow. Bennett's bold "Kitty" seems more deplorable than her female predecessor in *La Chienne* even though Renoir's heroine (Janie Mareze), openly a prostitute in the seedy alleys of Montmartre, tells the painfully shy protagonist (Michel Simon) that she cohabits with her pimp. The blood-streaked stare of the murdered prostitute in *La Chienne* is a grisly image. The killer's kissing her lifeless body following his crime of passion would certainly alarm Joseph Breen. Simon gets off scot-free without guilt in *La Chienne*. Having lost his job and given up his bourgeois career, he proceeds with everyday life, happier as a bum. Lang showcases Robinson's self-destructive descent in *Scarlet Street*. After his company honors him with an award, he plunges into the depths of despair and humiliation. Cross's fatal attraction to Kitty, combined with the loss of his job and his artistic passion, utterly ruins him. Jail and the chair would be a kinder fate for Robinson's antihero. Completely devastated by guilt and remorse—to the point that they drive him mad—his very existence is ultimately worse.

Lang cultivates a blacker, tragic, heavily chiaroscuro variation on

Renoir's realism. One of the bleakest films in the *noir* canon, *Scarlet Street* culminates in an existential tour de force: Robinson's botched suicide in the final reel. In an oppressive black room lit only by a harsh streak from beyond a crisscrossing window, Cross, depressed and tormented by voices of Kitty and Johnny haunting his conscience, miserably chooses to end his life. He almost succeeds. Lang shows the shadow of his lifeless body hanging from the ceiling in the dark. Two men hear the chair topple to the floor and bust open the door. But once they remove the noose from Cross's neck, he hears voices again. He becomes a delirious bum, bereft of his identity, wandering the streets. He sleeps on park benches, watches his painting of Kitty being sold for a hefty sum, and tries to confess to police, but they don't believe him. The film's conclusion is all the more remarkable given the Code and shows the extent that the war and independent production permitted lapses. The PCA not only allowed a killer a shot at suicide, but the guilty man went free—while an innocent one was electrocuted. Although the Hays Office "bought" Chris's self-inflicted narrative punishment, Lang insisted Robinson's polite, considerate protagonist remained unrepentant about those criminal injustices. Like the gender distress of returning absentee husbands and unfaithful wives at the end of the war, Cross "suffers only from a jealousy which cannot be assuaged even by the death of the two people involved. He still hears their love talk, is tortured by it, and this is what turns him into a bum."[24]

A provocative independent film, and certainly no B movie, *Scarlet Street* was a top-tiered A picture for Universal, budgeted at $1,149,600. Production ran for sixty-two shooting days, from July 23 to October 8, 1945.[25] The Universal Collection cites its final cost at either $1,202,007 or $1,232,179 (the film's financial budgets vary). Budget overages may have motivated Wanger and Universal to recut the film in Lang's absence.[26] Wanger was potentially upset that Lang began another Warner Bros. project before *Scarlet Street* was completed—and thus may have re-edited the film with this in mind.[27] Comparatively, the increasing female star role of Bennett as independent business partner and corresponding defiant femme fatale representation was magnified in her portrayal of "the bitch" in *Scarlet Street*. Her role was also mediated by male authorship concerns—yet within a complex rubric of implicit power in both her marriage to producer Wanger and her relationship with Lang, who allegedly was in love with the star and excessively doted on her during the production of both films. It is possible that an affair was going on between star and director right under Wanger's nose. (Any or all of such intrigue would potentially contribute to significantly enhanced power on the part of the female star, although not in the most out-

Joan Bennett's spider woman, Kitty March, is Robinson's fatal attraction in *Scarlet Street*.
Universal, 1945.

right or conventional terms, via adept political maneuvering behind the scenes to achieve feminine power.) Despite Robinson's major star stature in the film's casting, publicity positioned Bennett at center stage: "She lived on the folly of one man's love . . . and felt the fury of another's!"

Wanger capitalized on salacious screen content to promote the film. Trade papers from the 1940s observed that the sex, violence, and censorship controversy over *Scarlet Street* aided the film's publicity and box-office receipts. In a telling April 2, 1946, letter Fox's Darryl Zanuck complained to Breen that he was "furious" not only about Howard Hughes's lewd publicity for *The Outlaw* but also about Walter Wanger's "capitalizing on censorship trouble with *Scarlet Street*." Zanuck explained, "I don't blame him [Wanger] for making money . . . he will eventually pay for it." However, Zanuck called Wanger's exploitation of censorable red-meat material in, and profitable scandal over, *Scarlet Street* (as in Hughes's *The Outlaw*) a "disgrace to the industry." With such disregard for censorship, Zanuck argued, "I have a hell of a job keeping my boys in line." He added that the major studios did not "resort" to "such cheap vulgarity."[28]

Clearly, Hughes and Wanger exploited the fact that these were independent productions not subject to the same kind of censorship pressures that the PCA could enforce with the major (MPPDA member) studios. The inflammatory vulgarity (to which Zanuck referred) related to red-meat promotion strategies. The Universal press book for *Scarlet Street* sensationalized the film's sex and violence as "realistic." The film's publicity called it a "stark melodrama," the "most graphic ever attempted." A press book feature notes: "As the *femme fatale* in 'Scarlet Street,' Joan Bennett carries on a volatile amour with the sinister Dan Duryea. Dan's no gentleman, and during one of their frequent quarrels, he lets go with his right and more than messes up Miss Bennett's makeup. He's sneaky . . . He blinds her first, by blowing a cloud of cigarette smoke into her eyes!" It heralded: "'Scarlet Street' Pulls No Punches," and "Drama sets pace in Candid Realism," heightening "natural" scenes. The film was lauded as a "miracle of realism" with a violent theme and then asserted, "Theatregoers are too smart to accept artificiality." A series of the film's frames provide a graphic how-to photo illustration and diagram: "Movie Shows How to Slap a Girl in the Jaw," below the feature, "Dan Duryea Finds Fun in Sadistic Tough-Guy Role." Universal's press book notes Bennett's role as a producing business "executive" serving as treasurer for Diana Productions, yet it cites "Cruel Movie Punishment Endured by Joan Bennett," who is "Mauled and Slapped for Picture Thrill." This sensational publicity naturalized the violence by claiming the actress "likes wicked role." It quoted Bennett: "There are hundreds of glamor girls in Hollywood, but actresses who are willing to let down their hair are always in demand. Getting a meaty role is like finding an old friend." The promotional piece then concluded: "Trends are quick to develop in filmland and the gals are hoping that the pastings handed out to Rita and Joan aren't indicative of things to come."[29] While males in these narratives "sock" their female counterparts, the violence is promoted and exploited as a selling angle. Even more than *Gilda,* the physical violence is readily shown in *Scarlet Street* and is as lethal as MacMurray's Neff gunning down Stanwyck's Phyllis in *Double Indemnity.* However, unlike *Scarlet Street*

Breen's "compensating moral values" ensured that Neff did not get away with his murderous crime and adultery—he dies or does time—after a mutual dual-shooting strategy of violence for both male and female parties, with Stanwyck's cold, calculating femme, like Neff, also murderous and reprehensible to Hollywood censors. This was clearly not the case in Lang's film.

Bogart, Hawks, *To Have and Have Not*, and *The Big Sleep*

One of the most powerful creative forces at wartime Warner Bros. was producer-director Howard Hawks, who was also actively involved in the writing and adaptation of his films. Hawks effectively functioned as an in-house independent producer-director at Warner Bros. during the war. His hyphenate status coincided with the industry-wide rise in hyphenate and independent production in Hollywood throughout World War II. Hawks had considerable creative power with *To Have and Have Not* and *The Big Sleep* in purchasing the stories, setting up the production deal, selling the properties at a tidy profit to Warner Bros., and then refusing to allow anyone to act as producer on the films he directed. In the wake of Warner. Bros.' success with *Casablanca*, Hawks was savvy enough to recognize the lucrative potential of adapting the fiction of Ernest Hemingway and Raymond Chandler as ideal masculine star vehicles for Humphrey Bogart and new female discovery Lauren "The Look" Bacall.

Bogart embodied gritty American masculinity on 1940s Hollywood screens. Following *The Maltese Falcon* and *Casablanca*, Warners cast him as a patriotic war hero / fatal martyr in *Passage to Marseille* (released in 1944) but not before the studio cast him as a heavy who murders his estranged wife (after eyeing her younger sister) in *Conflict*, a bizarre hybrid of female gothic and investigative detective thrillers (Greenstreet switches roles with Bogart, piecing together the murder case). *Conflict* was a non-war-related mystery-thriller, originally *The Pentacle*, written by émigré Robert Siodmak (in an effort to negotiate a Warners directing job with producer Henry Blanke in the early 1940s) and Alfred Neumann. It was sold to Warner Bros. in August 1942, shot shortly after *Casablanca*, then stockpiled by the studio until it was premiered for "100 rain-soaked and mud-spattered G.I.'s" of the 137th Infantry Regiment in a "cold barn some 1,500 yards away from the front lines" in France on November 3, 1944, prior to its June 1945 release.[30] (It was also one of the first red-meat films noir shown later that November 1944 night in Paris.) It is significant that *Conflict* was withheld from release while Bogart's wartime hero persona was developed in *Sahara* and *Passage to Marseille* during the war (as "un-American" gangsters were censored and

narratively reformulated). Warners let Columbia take the risk of putting
Bogie in its war film, then capitalized on his *Sahara* success in *Passage to
Marseille.* Bogart's masculine image changed as his star power increased.
The conflicted male in *Casablanca* and *Conflict* became an increasingly pa-
triotic wartime hero in the latter two films.

When Warner Bros. finally released *Conflict* on June 20, 1945, the *Los Angeles Evening-Herald Express* found "no scarcity of red meat in *Conflict.* This
muscular meller packed with gusto and Movieville's dramatic Vitamin A-
1" featured Bogart as a wife murderer.[31] (The irony of the star's real-life conflict and violence at home with jealous, hot-tempered, and soon-to-be former wife, Mayo Methot, is noteworthy here; the couple was known as the
"Battling Bogarts.") The film's clinical realism is emphasized in a June 27,
1945, *Los Angeles Examiner* article noting "psychiatry in its relation to crime
is vividly described" in *Conflict,* which "points out that certain mental fix-
ations can become obsessions and in some cases lead to violent crime."[32] A
June 10, 1945, *Saint Paul Pioneer Press* piece called Bogart "menace man de
lux who returns to his evil ways again and murders his wife" but noted that
the masculine star "tops all rivals in his home studio as the 'pin up' favorite
of service women, including WACS, WAVES, SPARS and Lady Marines."[33]

A major problem posed by *Conflict* and *Marseille* was an ongoing concern for Warners and Bogart: finding a sufficiently strong female star to cast
opposite Bogart in his rising career with increasingly romantic roles. Warners had to borrow Ingrid Bergman from independent producer David O.
Selznick for *Casablanca,* and the only heroine in Columbia's *Sahara* was a
tank! Absent Warners' borrowing Bergman from Selznick, Bogart had better chemistry opposite the tank than he had with his *Conflict* or *Marseille*
costars. (January 1943 PCA files for *Sahara* even noted censoring "keep your
pants on," referring to Lulubelle, the tank: "She's just like a woman—she
won't say yes the first time.")[34] This casting problem was solved for star and
studio by the increasingly powerful producer-director Howard Hawks (and
wife "Slim"), who discovered and groomed nineteen-year-old model and
cover girl Betty (renamed Lauren) Bacall and then cast her opposite Bogart in *To Have and Have Not* and *The Big Sleep.* This pairing was a significant improvement over other actresses—even better than female weaponry
in *Sahara.*

Hawks's discovery of Bacall and casting of the ingenue with Bogart in
To Have and Have Not and *The Big Sleep* accelerated Bogart's masculine
screen reformulation. Like *Casablanca, To Have and Have Not* and *The Big
Sleep* were pivotal narratives for Bogart, transitioning his male persona from
destabilized patriotic wartime (anti)hero to gritty, hard-bitten professional.

Bogart's reformed star image opposite Bacall paralleled Warner Bros.' shift from wartime to non-war-related narratives toward the end of World War II in the studio's effort to target a postwar viewing audience. *To Have and Have Not* refined Bogart's rough hero supporting the war effort, and *The Big Sleep* moved his persona back to urban, hard-boiled terrain, recasting him as a cynical *noir* individualist. The reforming and romanticizing of Bogart's character throughout the war (from *High Sierra* and *Casablanca* onward) left an indelible imprint in his masculine armor, as did his amour with Bacall. Thus, the sentimental heart of *High Sierra* and *Casablanca* was invigorated by the sexual rapport of *To Have and Have Not*. Its Bogart-Bacall precedent would romantically inform the male star's tough hide in *The Big Sleep*—as an A professional, despite an unsavory criminal milieu, no longer doing B roles as a heavy.

Hemingway's *To Have and Have Not* was cleaned up considerably to appease the PCA and infuse wartime topicality. Red-meat brutality (directed toward women) was rife in A. E. MacKenzie's August 17, 1937, Warner Bros. synopsis of the original story (from advance galleys of Hemingway's novel) about rum-running between Cuba and Key West, where life is cheap amid a Depression setting. Writing in a style much like Hemingway's, MacKenzie called Harry "hard and trained to kill when an occasion demanded ruthless action." The character was married, with three daughters:

> young bitches at an age when they were liable to lay any one with the price of a movie they wanted to see badly enough. That came from their mother's side of the family honest enough. Marie had been a whore before Harry married her, but he was the only man she ever found capable of subduing her physically and so she stuck to him with a more avid loyalty than any moral principle could have induced. By conventional civilized standards the Morgans were scum; but in terms of their background and jungle surroundings they were a worthy family unit of "have-nots." One must do what is necessary to live in one's own world. Only sperm-less suckers try to kid themselves they're in another.[35]

Coupled with its provocative gender slurs, MacKenzie's synopsis of Hemingway's novel included repeated ethnic slurs—from "Chinks" to "Spiks" to "Niggers." All of this, along with shady rum-running, smuggling, gangsters, and Cuban revolutionaries, was duly reformed and sanitized for the PCA. However, changes for the Code and the war in Warners' *To Have and Have Not* adaptation used a patriotic framework not unlike *Casablanca*.

As in other *noir* films, it metaphorically suggested increased sex and violence as a means of gaining PCA approval. Like the Nazis in *Casablanca*, rather than gangsters or other unsavory characters, the villains were Vichy French. Warner Bros.' May 15, 1944, revised synopsis reeked of wartime espionage and duplicity, justified by overthrowing the Nazis: "Vichy 'loyalists' rule the French island of Martinique in the days following the fall of France. Under the calm surface, however, revolt brews in Fort de France, the capital, as Free French patriots continue to struggle for liberty."[36] And rather than the male protagonist having a whore wife and three slut daughters—capitalizing on Bogart's post-*Casablanca* appeal—the hero, Harry Morgan (a.k.a. Steve), and new female costar, "Slim," were decidedly single. Breen purged any suggestion of prostitution or adultery, although it's suggested in Slim's recurrent ability to procure large sums of cash and entire wallets by seductively enticing men at the bar. And unlike the book, Bogart doesn't die at the end of the narrative but sails off with the girl.

Enter Bacall. Howard Hawks had discovered Lauren Bacall and signed her up for a $100-per-week contract at his in-house independent H-F Productions to star opposite Bogart in *To Have and Have Not* and *The Big Sleep* at Warner Bros. After incorporating Ella Raines in B-H Productions (with partner Charles Boyer) and selling her contract to Universal for *Phantom Lady*, Hawks formed another independent company, H-F Productions, in 1943 with agent Charles K. Feldman. Hawks was shrewd in gaining three hot properties that he then sold to Warner Bros.: Ernest Hemingway's *To Have and Have Not*, Raymond Chandler's *The Big Sleep*, and nineteen-year-old Betty Bacall. Originally, Howard Hughes (who had worked with Hawks producing the gangster film *Scarface* in 1931) had purchased the rights to the 1937 novel *To Have and Have Not* from Hemingway on May 31, 1939, for $10,000. By September 7, 1943, a Warner Bros. memo outlined the "Howard Hawks deal" to pay Hawks $100,000 to direct the film for the studio, plus 20 percent of the gross up to three million and 30 percent thereafter, to star Bogart in the lead with newcomer Bacall—under contract to Hawks—on a fifty-fifty split contract basis with Warners, and to purchase *To Have and Have Not* from Hawks (and pay the director whatever he paid Hughes for it) for a price not to exceed $100,000. Interestingly, an October 22, 1943, contract stated that Hawks purchased the story from Hughes (for an unknown amount on an unknown day) in October 1943 and that Warner Bros. agreed to pay $92,500 to acquire the property from Hawks. A June 3, 1944, production budget confirms the sweet deal: a hefty $92,500 cost for story rights (with another $64,278 developing the continuity and treatment), no producer, and $200,000 paid to director Hawks—who insisted on producing his own films. After Warner initially opposed Bacall's casting in *To Have and Have Not* (with ads promoting Bogart and not even mentioning Bacall), her debut was so successful that Hawks then sold Bacall's contract outright to the major studio for future Warners projects—as relations between the stars and hyphenate director became strained because of Bogart and Bacall's off-screen romance and marriage (during filming of *The Big Sleep*). Production on *To Have and Have Not* ran sixty-two days, from February 29 to May 10, 1944 (following filming on *Double Indemnity* but before its release, and before Warners shot *Mildred Pierce*).[37]

The studio capitalized on sensational red-meat promotional strategies, hyping, heightening, and conflating sex and violence à la Bogart as tough, tormented male star in *Casablanca, Conflict, To Have and Have Not,* and *The Big Sleep.* Warner Bros.' October 20, 1944, press release for *To Have and Have Not* explained that the censorable "taint of rum running had been removed" from Ernest Hemingway's novel, but the "helping of gun powder and sex increased." It described Bogart as "hot as a Long Tom on the Siegfried front, after 'Casablanca' and the Academy Award." Publicity even credited Hawks's grooming of newcomer Bacall to Bogart. It called the male star a "veteran in timing, voice inflection and all the tricks of technique," who "generously passed on his experience gained knowledge" to ensure Bacall's "socko debut." Consistent with Bogart's combat roles and post-*Casablanca* star status, his screen opponents "fighting with pistols" lose to the patriotic masculine star. Drawing on his recognized crime roles at Warners, the release played up rugged romantic appeal: "Bogart dishes out violent death in the best Bogart tradition. Even so, the combustion crown for the film goes to tawny topped Bacall. She lighted the spark" and "whipped it to flame." It promoted Bacall as "sultry," the first woman Bogart "lived to keep" and "maintaining his lease on her love life through the currently filming 'The Big Sleep.'" Reversing gender roles, publicity cited Bacall having to be embarrassingly assertive in boldly initiating "sex charged situations" with "Bogey playing hard to get" in the screen effort to "prove that he can love like he can fight." This is not unlike the transitional strategy of easing men back from combat into relationships with women in the home—in a move from violence to love and toward sexual confrontations with transgressively assertive career women who were working during the war.

In fumigating the narrative for the PCA, Warners publicized how it "purified" Hemingway's Cuban revolutionists by "making them DeGaullists fighting the Vichy French for control of Martinique." In its efforts to duplicate the success of *Casablanca,* the studio described a shrouded wartime milieu: "Settings for the Hemingway story harmonized with the mood of smoldering sex and violent intrigue. A smoke hazed cabaret interior, more than vaguely reminiscent of 'Casablanca;' the dingy but picturesque waterfront of Fort de France" that was "duplicated from photographs" to ensure "authenticity" from an "Army regiment stationed in Martinique." It noted "fog shrouded island landings and open sea" with "narrowly sinister hotel corridors and a decidedly masculine bedroom."[38] Not surprising, in a cultural and production context growing out of the war, this trend toward authenticity often related to violence. Its hard-hitting milieu drew on wartime experience, realistic newsreels, and combat films. Realism proliferated well into the postwar era—onscreen (in Hollywood and abroad, as in Italian neorealism) and on the New York stage, and contributed to the development of film noir in a symbiosis between documentary and Hollywood narrative films related to the wartime psyche emerging in *noir.*

Warner Bros. publicity for *To Have and Have Not* read, "When Humphrey Bogart kills a man in a motion picture, he wants to do it right." It explained how the actor and director Hawks were "ballistics experts," having a lengthy "professional discussion" on "trajectory and deflection" because Bogart was "about to knock off one of the villains" and "wanted the execution to be boner proof" when firing a bullet through a table top. It capitalized on his experience with guns onscreen and off, stating "in real life, naturally," Bogart suggested a "laboratory experiment" conducted using a "real slug" according to "authentic specifications." Another piece (obviously aiming to target a male military or veteran audience) read, "Actor Qualifies as Machine Gun Expert" and "Bogart Demands Perfection in Film Gun Fight." Publicity exploited his earlier gangster roles and directed his tough-guy persona to wartime combat, weapons, and women. In "Pistol Packin' Bogart Changes Role, Not Weapon," the actor "escaped gangster roles but not tommy guns." But "since his reformation," Bogart was doing "more shooting" and "getting more romance," playing up the sex and violence angle. It quoted the star: "You can always find a Bogart set. Just follow the sound of gunfire." Citing "fusillades" using ".45 automatics to .30 caliber machine guns," he "couldn't remember doing a picture without firearms and shooting."[39]

The studio press book publicizes "action," "torrid romance," and—interchanging weapons and women—a "rivalry" that "matches the tommy guns in explosiveness" in an "exciting tale of love that smolders" in a "web of political intrigue that is woven" by the "hands of Vichy's Gestapo" in a "smoky cafe drenched in cigarette and gun smoke." It describes how the story involves a "dangerous night" and "running gun battle at sea" where an "underground leader is desperately wounded by Vichy machine gun bullets" and calls the couple "two Americans, sick with themselves and the rotten world that lay bleeding all about them." It refers to Bogart as a "lusty, gnarled sea wolf" who is "tough and nonchalant" and Bacall as "sultry," a "siren," and a "New York tough gal" who "slithers" as a "throaty serpentine blonde" and gets her "ears slapped back in Hollywood," recalling the violent slap Bacall receives from the Vichy police (while Bogart voyeuristically "watched"). The brutality continues: Hawks "said he was sorry. They had to do the scene again. They did it four more times. Miss Bacall took the slaps without flinching although they obviously stung."[40] Publicity pitched violence, often sexual violence, to sell and sensationalize, and also to justify and naturalize its narrative exploitation in the effort to increase verisimilitude and "realism." This promotion strategy related to the rough, tough, stark images of "raw" wartime violence in newsreels, documentaries, and combat footage—and studios' efforts to capitalize on a more lenient PCA.

Warner Bros. certainly accentuated the tight-paced action and Hawks's reworking of masculine crime and combat films to bump up the romance in *To Have and Have Not* and *The Big Sleep*. Warners reformulated Hemingway's story along the lines of the war and Code in its 1944 trailer advertising Hawks's film. The narrator begins: "Ernest Hemingway, soldier of fortune, who can always be found where adventure beckons, now takes you to the danger zone of the mid-Atlantic, where strange ships slip through the fog with even stranger cargos. Where every man has a price, and every woman a past. Where all barriers are down, and the only law is the law of the Caribbean." The preview emphasizes violence as Bogart yells: "Gimme that gun." Rummy sidekick Walter Brennan (in a remarkable transformation from his dignified university professor role in Lang's *Hangmen Also Die*, released the year before) warns: "You can't fight them guys, Harry." But publicity capitalizes on narrative violence, justified as a job and mission for the war. It played up the sex angle, suggestively quoting a provocative Bacall: "I'm hard to get, Steve. All you have to do is ask me." Later, Bogart (as tough guy breaking furniture and threatening two Vichy thugs) yells a macho threat: "That broke as easy as you will. You're both gonna take a beating till someone uses that phone. That means one of yuh's gonna take a beating for nothing, and I don't care which one it is!" The trailer segues to Bacall's sexual assertiveness in initiating a kiss, igniting repartee:

Bogart: What'd you do that for?
Bacall: I've been wondering whether I'd like it.
Bogart: What's the decision?
Bacall: I don't know yet . . . It's even better when you help.[41]

Steve (Humphrey Bogart), with his kind of woman: sultry "Slim" (Lauren "The Look"
Bacall) in *To Have and Have Not*.
Warner Bros., 1944.

Hawks's pairing of "The Look" opposite Bogart and turning up the heat
via suggestive innuendo was as phenomenally successful as the couple's
chemistry in real life. Warner Bros. capitalized on the stars' affair and exploited their offscreen romance all the way to the box office. Press books included double-full-page ads of the couple in a rough embrace: "It happens
this way," and "Bogart in love with his kind of woman!" in "A Howard
Hawks Production" of "Hemingway's daring story adapted for the screen!"
The *Hollywood Reporter* called it a "highly exciting, fast-moving, exotic
melodrama of the 'Casablanca' School . . . Bogart at his best . . . Bacall is
nothing less than terrific." *Showman's Trade Review* praised its "lustic,
comic, romantic, melodramatic" appeal, and *Boxoffice* observed, "In mood,
situations, suspense and adventure, this is comparable to 'Casablanca' . . . If
anything, this one moves faster than the other . . . Its romantic interludes
are more on the torrid side . . . Bacall delivers a performance which will cat-
apult her to certain stardom."[42] *To Have and Have Not* returned its
$1,684,000 cost, grossing $3,442,000 on its initial domestic release (with another $1,602,000 in foreign earnings, totaling $5,044,000).[43] Bogart and Bacall's sexual repartee sparked a second Warners project starring the couple:

in Hawks's *The Big Sleep* Warners hoped to duplicate the onscreen combustion of *To Have and Have Not.*

"My, my, my. Such a lot of guns around town and so few brains."

In "The Simple Art of Murder" Raymond Chandler described the dangerous urban environment and tough, resilient detectives in his crime fiction: "Down these mean streets a man must go who is not himself mean, who is neither tarnished nor afraid."[44] At age fifty-one Chandler wrote *The Big Sleep*—the first of four masterful detective novels creating an atmospheric Los Angeles—over three months in 1939 while residing in the City of Angels. The classic mystery story was a moody, brilliant labyrinth of the shady exploits of hard-boiled detective Philip Marlowe navigating through a complex, lethal setting—a duplicitous world of decadent estates, corrupt crime, crooks, con artists, gamblers, menacing cops, and deadly women. In the book and in the film tough-guy private dick Marlowe (Humphrey Bogart) tries to solve a case for his wealthy, dying, elderly client, General Sternwood (Charles Waldron), father of two wild, beautiful daughters, Vivian (Lauren Bacall) and Carmen (Martha Vickers), who become embroiled in an unsavory blackmail-murder ring run by hoodlum gambler Eddie Mars (John Ridgeley). By March 16, 1939, Chandler wrote of his desire to "make enough" to "move to England and to forget mystery writing ... if there is no war and if there is any money." World War II clearly preempted Chandler's plans and instead provided a "machine-gun burst of creativity" that resulted in four of his best mystery novels (*The Big Sleep, Farewell, My Lovely, The High Window,* and *The Lady in the Lake*) between 1939 and 1943, in adapting the screenplay for *Double Indemnity,* and in writing *The Blue Dahlia* in early 1945, while Chandler was living in wartime Los Angeles.[45] Remarkably *The Big Sleep* got only four reviews in 1939, and Chandler's books were out of print by the mid-1940s; it was his Academy Award–nominated script for *Double Indemnity* that revived interest in Chandler's novels, spreading his reputation by word of mouth.

On September 20, 1943, as Wilder and Chandler completed the script for *Double Indemnity* and as Breen okayed the project for production, Alfred Knopf published the paperback version of *The Big Sleep.* As *Double Indemnity* was released, Steve Trilling's August 2, 1944, memo to Jack Warner noted Hawks's effort to acquire the rights to Chandler's *The Big Sleep,* a "highly censorable detective yarn which, like *To Have and Have Not,* presents grave problems in adapting" the screenplay for Bogart and Bacall.[46] Hawks sent a memo to Roy Obringer regarding *The Big Sleep* deal on August 28, 1944.[47] By August 29 Hawks had secured the rights to Chandler's *Big Sleep* for $20,000, with Bogart to star in the picture, and requested $80,000 from Warners to direct and $55,000 to sell the story and completed scenario to the studio with a $20,000 advance as an option to buy the rights. The script was submitted to the PCA on September 26, 1944, with Breen haggling over reducing the violence, liquor, and sex in the story through October, when Shurlock intervened and phoned Hawks.[48] On October 10, 1944, a *Los Angeles Times* article (alongside a *Woman in the Window* review) read, "Lauren Bacall Selected to Portray Sinister Role in Bogart's 'Big Sleep.'" Originally, Bacall was to play the murderous femme fatale, Carmen, in *The Big Sleep*—a role that eventually went to Martha Vickers. Instead, Hawks cast Bacall as Carmen's maternal "rich bitch" older sister, Vivian, a less-meaty and more peripheral role. *The Big Sleep* was then reformulated into a costar vehicle, changing Bacall's role to retarget and capitalize on her star appeal on the tails of the enormous success of *To Have and Have Not* and publicize "The Look" portrayed as a comparatively benign, sympathetic character onscreen.[49]

Warner Bros. purchased the rights to make one film of Chandler's hot property from Hawks for $20,000 on October 27, 1944—with no rights to produce a sequel or a television broadcast version of *The Big Sleep*. After reading her 1944 book *No Good for a Corpse*, and thinking she was a man, Hawks hired writer Leigh Brackett to adapt *The Big Sleep*. It was her first script for Warner Bros. Author of numerous hard-boiled crime novels, Brackett, inspired by Bogart's performance in *The Maltese Falcon*, "conceived a mad passion for detective stories." She pursued crime writing, "studying Steinbeck, Hemingway, Kipling, Chandler and Dashiell Hammett because they got so much into so little," polishing her craft of "writing like a man" and penning tough women. Brackett and William Faulkner worked separately on the screenplay for *The Big Sleep*, adapting the seductive corruption of Raymond Chandler's story. Hawks and Jules Furthman then refined the script during production. Hawks admitted Brackett "wrote *[The Big Sleep]* like a man . . . Yeah. I hired her through an agent and I thought I was hiring a man. We had *Big Sleep* and Bill Faulkner wanted a job. Leigh Brackett knew screen formula and . . . how to write scenes. They did the script for that in eight days." Brackett recalled, "Hawks liked my dialogue and called my agent. He was somewhat shaken when he discovered that it was Miss and not Mister Brackett, but he rallied bravely and signed me on anyway, for which I have always been extremely grateful." Hawks remembered, "In walked a rather attractive girl who looked like she had just come in from a tennis match. She looked as if she wrote poetry. But she wrote like a man." Drafts and revisions for the script reveal Brackett's knack for cynical barbs. In fact, when Bogart wanted to toughen up the dialogue on the set, he realized the tame lines were written by Faulkner, not Brackett. Bogart called her "Butch" and sought Brackett to add grisly grit to the script.[50] Bogart's dialogue is supremely hard-boiled. Marlowe beats up a thug—sprawled bloody on the floor—then caustically tells police: "I have some cold meat set out that might interest you."

Newsreel realism influenced the rich imagery of Warner Bros. crime productions like *To Have and Have Not* and *The Big Sleep*. Cameraman Sid Hickox shot both Hawks films. The visual style in *The Big Sleep* was quintessentially film noir, even darker than *To Have and Have Not* or its predecessor *Casablanca*. In a famous murder scene the black exterior of the storm-drenched, tree-covered road outside menacing blackmailer (criminal-conman-turned-murdered-stiff) Geiger's house resembled the body-dumping sets in *Conflict* and *Woman in the Window* and the rain-pelted finale of *Ministry of Fear*. A November 9, 1944, Warner Bros. production memo from Eric Stacey to T. C. "Tenny" Wright described the tarped "outdoor" set, rigging the Brownstone Street exterior, and arranging for "necessary fog keys," which enhanced its murky atmosphere. The enclosed, tented sound stage enabled a more controlled shooting environment and accentuated claustrophobic *noir* style. A November 13 memo noted that filming was preempted because the script was being rewritten, and Warners' artificial rain had gotten the exterior set of Geiger's house too wet to continue.

Production was rough. There was tension between Hawks and Bogart over his romance with the director's discovery. (Relations between Hawks and Bacall even cooled but remained polite.) By November 24, 1944, "Bogart overslept" and had "not had a day off for thirty-six straight days," and Hawks was "seriously thinking of arranging his work so that Bogie can get a little rest."[51] The star's marriage to estranged Mayo Methot was falling apart. He was in and out of living at home and at the Beverly Hills Hotel, and in and out of an alcoholic stupor. And all the while he was seeing Bacall—on the sly initially; then he finally broke off his marriage and eloped with his costar during production of *The Big Sleep*. Hawks apparently was not amused. He refrained from congratulating his newlywed stars.[52]

By November 28 the picture was twenty days behind schedule, and Stacey noted "Hawks' practice" of "rewriting the entire scene on the set." In Bogart's absence Faulkner left the project and the studio. The writer's famous December 12, 1944, memo to Jerry Geller read: "The following rewrit-

Bacall's duplicitous "Girl Friday" Mrs. Routledge aids Bogart's Marlowe in *The Big Sleep*.
Warner Bros., 1946.

ten and additional scenes for THE BIG SLEEP were done by the author in respectful joy and happy admiration after he had gone off salary and while on his way back to Mississippi. With grateful thanks to the studio for the cheerful and crowded day coach which alone saved him from wasting his time in dull and profitless rest and sleep. With love, *WILLIAM FAULKNER*." (Many of Faulkner's revisions were not used in the film. In addition to Hawks's and Furthman's extensive rewriting on the set, and Chandler's contributing here and there, Brackett's caustic, witty dialogue was incorporated more often into the script.)[53] On December 29 "Bogart returned to work— apparently in good shape." Production was thirty days behind schedule, and completion was not anticipated until mid-January 1945. A January 13, 1945, memo notes that "a retake of the opening sequence in Vivian's sitting room" of Bacall "was finished. Incidentally, this sequence has already been retaken completely and this will be the second retake of this episode." Bogart, Bacall, and Vickers finished cast shooting. The film was thirty-four days behind schedule yet only $15,000 over budget, "with $35,000 budgeted for music" and "yet to be spent" it may "not go over budget much more than $50,000."[54] The film received a PCA seal of approval on January 31, 1945.[55]

With Hawks's increasingly awkward rapport with his stars, the producer-director focused considerable effort on grooming, lighting, and dialogue for female costar Martha Vickers, who plays the femme, Carmen—so much so that she upstaged Bacall in the film's initial release. The UCLA Film and Television Archive's recently discovered April 1945 print certainly bears this out. *The Big Sleep* (like *Conflict*) premiered for U.S. military troops, this time in the Pacific, in the spring and summer of 1945. Bacall's more minor role and lukewarm performance got less than enthusiastic reviews. Yet Hawks's *To Have and Have Not* surged in popularity. Newcomer Bacall was now an onscreen sensation. Warner Bros. smartly desired additional tough "insolent and provocative" scenes of the female star opposite Bogart (such as the classic harsh words in her bedroom, and the horse racing innuendo at the restaurant) to feature her more prominently in the narrative and draw on the immense success of the sultry pair in *To Have and Have Not*. As Warners rushed and prioritized the release of all its war-related pictures to capture the last of a wartime consumer market before the global conflict drew to a close, *The Big Sleep* was temporarily stockpiled. But a year later, a January 28, 1946, production report indicates six days of retakes beginning on January 21, 1946; the project completed filming on Monday the 28th. This new footage included Vickers's scenes in Marlowe's apartment and the district attorney's office, as well as numerous added scenes of Bacall.[56] Warner Bros. now owned Bacall's contract, and the studio wanted to maximize its investment in developing her star potential. In fact, so "insolent and provocative" was Bacall's dialogue that a year after the film had already received a PCA seal, Breen's January 25, 1946, letter to Warner nixed Bacall's salacious comeback: "A lot depends on who's in the saddle." The suggestive line, however, remained in the film.[57]

In the end *The Big Sleep* cost $1,562,000. Twenty months after the end of principal photography, its delayed August 1946 release brought in $3,493,000 in domestic grosses and $1,346,000 internationally, totaling $4,839,000.[58] Warner Bros. publicity called Bogart a "two-fisted, realistic private detective Philip Marlowe." Tapping into the studio's crime tradition and the star's earlier gangster roles, Warner Bros. promoted the unsavory milieu of tough-guy "bigshot racketeer and gambler" Eddie Mars and capitalized on the deviance of "real-life" gangsters. The press book heightened the picture's authenticity: "The dashboard gunflap in Detective Bogart's car was modeled after a similar utility arsenal that G-men found rigged up in the getaway car used by 'Pretty Boy' Floyd Hamilton." It emphasized: "Realism Plays Big Role in Filming 'The Big Sleep'" and "'Big Sleep' Aided Okinawa Storm Victims" as "Rehearsal Realism Assures Solitude." Warner promoted "new female faces" amid "sudden death" in Bogart's crime film, including "six other girls" and "husky-voiced Bacall." Red meat is abundant in Bogart's "tough private dick" leaving a "memorable study in black and blue" after roughing up female costar Vickers.[59] Studio publicity even recognized the growing crime trend in Hollywood, citing Raymond Chandler's involvement in screen crime adaptations (*Double Indemnity* and others), increasing interest in the hard-boiled writer's tough fiction as source material (*The Big Sleep, Farewell, My Lovely,* and others), and Hollywood's "increasing use of" filming in "its own California backyard," noting *Double Indemnity* and *Mildred Pierce.* (While many *noir* films primarily used enclosed studio back lots, blackouts made night locations in the Los Angeles basin "backyard" much darker during the war.) And the style of these films was noteworthy in the U.S. press. *The Big Sleep* was called a "violent smoky cocktail" where a "sullen atmosphere of sex saturates the film."[60] Such was the hallmark of film noir.

Black Film, Red Meat

The studios have gone in for these pictures because the Hays office is becoming more liberal . . . okaying treatments now which they would have turned down ten years ago, probably because they feel people can take the hard-boiled stuff nowadays. Of course, people have been reading about murderers, cutthroats and thieves in the newspapers . . . for years, but only recently has the Hays office permitted the movies to depict life as it really is.
—Raymond Chandler, *New York Times*, 1945

oward Hawks's successful pairing of Humphrey Bogart and Lauren Bacall in his wartime adaptations of Ernest Hemingway's *To Have and Have Not* and Raymond Chandler's *The Big Sleep* at Warner Bros. coincided with a broader trend. Midway into the war, Hollywood rechanneled earlier "patriotic" crime to depict the corruption of the American city—usually, Los Angeles, the film industry's home front. As wartime films like *Double Indemnity, Murder, My Sweet, Laura, The Woman in the Window, The Big Sleep, This Gun for Hire,* and *Gilda* hit Paris cinema screens, French critics, "long cut off from America, ill-informed about Hollywood's output during the war," applauded a new kind of American motion picture that boasted "an unusual and cruel atmosphere . . . one tinted by a very particular eroticism." Nino Frank noted that "what used to be known as the detective genre . . . from now on we'd do better to call 'crime adventure stories' or, better still, 'criminal psychology.'" Raymonde Borde and Etienne Chaumeton later observed "a new 'series' was emerging in the history of the cinema."[1]

In Hollywood's shift from wartime to postwar narrative film strategies, 1940s industry insiders and trade papers indicate a clearly observable cycle of crime films produced during World War II—affected, influenced, and enabled by war-related conditions—originating prior to 1946, when French critics coined the term *film noir*. World War II created a complex set of circumstances that converged in an intricate network of interacting production conditions. Rather than the war being a hiatus in the development of a primarily postwar film movement, fully articulated film noir emerged in the United States as an aspect of film production and spectatorship under wartime circumstances. *Noir* evolved as a dark style of "realism" and a wartime Hollywood crime trend described, and clearly identified by a term circulated widely, as *red meat*.

This crime cycle grew out of an industry need in Hollywood. By August

1943, in "Hiss-s-s-s through the Years: Styles in movie villains change, but whether Western desperadoes, city slickers or Japs, they're all bad men," Florett Robinson of the *New York Times* observed that in the earlier Prohibition years, "indifference to law and order brought . . . the most ruthless and brutal bad man the screen had yet known, *the gangster*. Contemptuous of the law, living by violence and dying the same way, he enjoyed a short hour of luxury in the big-time rackets. And the audience loved it. Maybe it was because he brought back some of the blood and thunder of frontier days, together with the added thrill that here was current history." When the war broke out, Robinson noted, Hollywood reformulated horror and gangster narrative conventions to combat and patriotic themes. As the conflict continued, weary audiences became tired of its incessant reminders and preferred a diversion. In the studio system's shift from wartime to postwar narrative film strategies many companies moved away from portraying simplistic "Nazi" or "Jap" combat enemies to a more complex criminal onscreen. "Lately the film fan has been seeking some escape from the war. He finds it by watching a novel kind of bad man—the *sympathetic villain*. More sinned against than sinning, this new menace is not cast in shades of black, but in more human, indeterminate grays of a real-life character. So a moviegoer looking at him might say, 'There but for the grace of God go I.' "[2]

Studios increasingly transferred screen narratives to non-war-related film topics that would appeal to home-front audiences yet be commercial in the long term. This was especially important with fewer films being produced and greater numbers of A pictures boasting substantial budgets for studios seeking to recoup their large expenditures as major studios eliminated low-budget, B-film divisions. The crucial need for motion picture companies to develop long-term narrative strategies and seek alternative non-war-related screen material arose because studios planned their release schedules at least a year in advance. As World War II progressed—and wore on—it became readily evident that a conclusion to the conflict was on the horizon. Within this changing cultural, political, and economic context by 1943, as combat events overseas began to suggest an end to the war, Hollywood's wartime industry keenly considered revamping its strategy with regard to its film output. As Hollywood transitioned from wartime to postwar American culture, film industry, studio production, and cinematic style, the motion picture industry projected beyond wartime and solicited stories for release after the war. Industry trades noted Hollywood's long-term strategies included fewer combat films because of their short-term appeal. Fred Stanley's *New York Times* article "Hollywood Peeks into the Future" outlined OWI propaganda, wartime censorship, and the ban on gangster pictures and considered future trends: "Guessing just what the American home front will be like a year or eighteen months from today is a ticklish task that confronts Hollywood producers and writers now preparing pictures that will not reach theatres until 1944." Stanley explains, "Though war subjects away from the home front, musicals and stories of eras before the war now in preparation are regarded as relatively safe bets, there are nevertheless a number of projected films which will deal with contemporary domestic subjects. In planning the latter, producers and writers are faced with the necessity of keeping a step or two ahead of the changing scene in order to avoid inadvertencies of dialogue or incidents which might cause audience derision twelve months hence."[3] Preproduction on *Double Indemnity* began just a few months later, initiating the red-meat *noir* trend that would ably fill this narrative need in Hollywood's transitional economy.

The *New York Times* and West Coast trades began to mention the decline in war films by January 1944 and in April reported that studios were scrapping many of their war stories. Fred Stanley observed, "Studio executives have estimated that the major companies will take a loss of at least $2,000,000 on war story properties that were acquired during the last two years and since have been shelved because of the fast-changing status of the conflict and decreasing theatre-going interest in war plots . . . The eagerness of Hollywood a year or two ago to bid for—and buy—almost any and every war story, particularly the factual 'I was there' type, has now changed to one of almost apathy to this kind of material." As *Double Indemnity* previewed in late spring 1944, the *Times* noted an increase in a "new horror cycle" that was "psychological." "Possibly as a breathing spell from war and 'hate Nazi' pictures, Hollywood, temporarily at least, has all but shelved martial projects in favor of films bulging with screams in the night, supercharged criminal phenomena and esthetic murder." By the end of May, in "Hollywood Shivers," Stanley recognized an inventive variation on horror films in female centered World War II–era *noir* thrillers *Phantom Lady, Laura, Gaslight, The Woman in the Window,* and *Spellbound.* Well aware of the growing Hollywood crime trend, he observed, "Every studio has at least one such picture in production and others coming to a witching boil. Meanwhile, war stories are at their lowest production ebb in months" with only four films "before the cameras" out of fifty-six "on the stages."[4]

The realism and violence of war-related combat pictures was expediently and profitably redirected—channeled into sensational crime narratives "ripped from the tabloids" and aimed at nonwar films coinciding with wartime anticipation of future reconversion to a postwar economy. Despite targeting future trends, however, these pictures were made during the war

(escalating in red-meat trends by 1943–45, and even continuing in "libera-
tion and occupation" abroad by 1946) and were nonetheless produced in
the midst of war-related circumstances, modified marketing demographics and distribution practices, military and national security considerations,
and material limitations. Amid this late-wartime reconversion to a postwar
industry, these crime films were lucrative and permissible after the PCA's
influential endorsement of *Double Indemnity,* lifting the bar and function-
ing as a censorship precedent laying the groundwork for *noir* during the
war. *Double Indemnity* was indeed a milestone. Philip K. Scheuer of the *Los
Angeles Times* claimed that *Double Indemnity* had made film history and
described the film as a "study of murder without bunk."[5] On July 17, 1944,
Time magazine ran Paramount publicity calling *Double Indemnity* a
"thriller" and Edward G. Robinson a "blood hound" after Stanwyck's femme
fatale: "The dame's poison . . . cold-blooded as a she-snake . . . especially
when she's after that 50-grand" in this "remarkably gripping murder-ro-
mance" billed as "doubly exciting, doubly deadly, doubly real."[6] By August
1944 the *Hollywood Reporter* described *Double Indemnity* as "realistic," one
of the most "gripping and exemplary crime films ever screened." It called
the film "grim and grizzly" with tense action, recommending it as a "crime
shocker with a moral," debunking the Hays Office's claim that the film was
a "blueprint for murder," showing, instead, the futility of a perfect crime.[7]
Louella Parsons of the *Los Angeles Examiner* called the film a "screen classic, . . . sheer brilliance, the finest picture of its kind ever made."[8]

Wartime Crime Trend: From Weapons to Women— Beating the Enemy

In 1945 Raymond Chandler was invited by the *New York Times* to share his
views on the Hollywood motion picture industry and to shed some light
on the burgeoning crime trend sweeping American cinema screens with
wild abandon. Chandler had been credited in part with fostering its growing popularity. Penning "The Simple Art of Murder" in 1944, Chandler, like
Cain and Hammett, was recognized for his mastery of the urban crime milieu and his contribution to Hollywood's shady, salacious films. Late in the
war Chandler acknowledged the significance of lapses in censorship and a
growing tolerance by the PCA in finally allowing tough, hard-boiled films
to thrive in Hollywood during the war—after a decade of banning the adaptation of pulp-fiction novels. By August 8, 1945, in "Crime Certainly Pays
on the Screen: The growing crop of homicidal films poses questions for psychologists and producers," Hollywood film industry analyst Lloyd Shearer
of the *New York Times* noted the heightened sex and violence of a definitive

crime trend emerging—and gaining momentum—during the war in adopting non-war-related narrative strategies anticipating a postwar society. "Of late there has been a trend in Hollywood toward the wholesale production of lusty, hard-boiled, gat-and-gore crime stories, all fashioned on a theme with a combination of plausibly motivated murder and studded with high-powered Freudian implication. Of the quantity of such films now in vogue, 'Double Indemnity,' 'Murder, My Sweet,' 'Conflict' and 'Laura' are a quartet of the most popular which quickly come to mind. Shortly to be followed by Twentieth Century–Fox's 'The Dark Corner' and 'The High Window,' MGM's 'The Postman Always Rings Twice' and 'The Lady in the Lake,' Paramount's 'Blue Dahlia' and Warner's 'Serenade' and 'The Big Sleep.'" As Shearer observed, this "quartet constitutes a mere vanguard of the cinematic homicide to come. Every studio in town has at least two or three similar blood-freezers before the cameras right now, which means that within the next year or so movie murder particularly with a psychological twist will become almost as common as the weekly newsreel or musical."

Shearer considered the impact of World War II on the cycle of "rough, tough murder yarns," describing Hollywood's wartime crime trend as "suspense-jammed," offering a "violent escape in tune with the violence of the times," and he recognized the war's capacity to alter "sensitivity to death." He cited 1940s psychologists: "because of the war the average moviegoer has become calloused to death, hardened to homicide and more capable of understanding a murderer's motives." He added, "the psychologists aver, each one of us at some time or other has secretly or subconsciously planned to murder a person we dislike. Through these hard-boiled crime pictures we vicariously enjoy the thrills of doing our enemies in, getting rid of our wives or husbands and making off with the insurance money . . . [T]he war has made us psychologically and emotionally ripe for motion pictures of this sort. That's why we like them, that's why we pay out good money each week to see them and that's why Hollywood is producing them in quantity." Shearer explained that "after watching a newsreel showing the horrors of a German concentration camp," narrative violence elicits "no shock, no remorse, no moral repugnance." Many of these *noir* crime films were produced before America viewed images of liberated camps. From 1943 to 1945, however, newsreels provided ample graphic depictions of violence and atrocities endorsed by the federal Office of Censorship for propaganda purposes, as influential to filmmakers—many of whom enlisted in military service and saw combat overseas—as it was to audiences. "These are times of death and bloodshed and legalized murder; these are times when, if an audience can stomach newsreels of atrocities, it can take anything."

Shearer even noted the studio bandwagon mentality fueling the growth of the trend. He explained the "main reason behind the current crop of hard-boiled, action-packed cinema murders is the time-honored Hollywood production formula of follow-the-leader. Let one studio turn out a successful detective-story picture and every other studio in the screen capital follows suit." The industry analyst concluded that the result was "a surfeit of motion pictures of one type." Noting consensus that *Double Indemnity* was "generally accorded" the "honor" of being recognized as the "first of the new rough, tough murder yarns" which "started the cinema's cycle of crime," Shearer—like 1944–45 Hollywood trades, publicity, production correspondence, and industry insiders—explained, "Forever watchful of audience reaction, the rest of the industry almost immediately began searching its story files for properties like 'Double Indemnity,'" a fine example of "a fast-moving story" that studios could "buy cheap," describing the escalating trend of Hollywood jumping on the bandwagon. As studios rushed en masse to emulate its visual style and taut narrative and to produce "tough, realistic homicide yarns," Shearer reported: "RKO suddenly discovered it had bought Chandler's novel, 'Farewell, My Lovely,' on June 3, 1941. If 'Double Indemnity' was so successful, why not make 'Farewell, My Lovely'? . . . Twentieth Century–Fox followed with 'Laura.' Warners began working on Chandler's 'The Big Sleep' for Humphrey Bogart and Lauren Bacall. MGM excavated from its vaults an all-but-forgotten copy of James Cain's 'The Postman Always Rings Twice.' The trickle swelled into a torrent and a trend was born."[9] It was not only "what" was produced, however, but "how" it was cinematically achieved—with stark newsreel style to maximize war-related production constraints—that began to attract attention.

Anticipating postwar *noir* criticism overseas, James M. Cain noted the industry film trend spurred by *Double Indemnity* in 1944, referring to increasingly "adult" wartime 1940s productions where a "new field for moving pictures has been opened up."[10] The Hollywood crime cycle was in full stride by December 1944, when the *Atlantic Monthly* published Raymond Chandler's famous mystery fiction essay "The Simple Art of Murder," describing how "the streets were dark with something more than night."[11] RKO released *The Woman in the Window* and produced Chandler's *Farewell, My Lovely;* Warner Bros. produced Cain's *Mildred Pierce;* and MGM announced plans to film Cain's *The Postman Always Rings Twice.* By February 1945, as international film distribution resumed toward the end of the war, London's *Reynold's News* called *Double Indemnity, Laura,* and *The Woman in the Window* outstanding examples of a "well-directed, well-acted thriller" trend in Hollywood, "brilliantly photographed" with universal appeal and suspense. Warner Bros. publicity, the *Los Angeles Evening-Herald Express,* Joseph Breen of the Production Code Administration, and the *New York Times* called films like *Casablanca, Conflict, Double Indemnity, Mildred Pierce, Murder, My Sweet, The Postman Always Rings Twice,* and *The Big Sleep* red meat.[12] Cain remarked in 1945 that "plenty of real crime takes place every day," and producers have "got hep" that it "makes a good movie." He added: "I think 'Double Indemnity' started the trend toward the production of fast-paced, hard-boiled, life-like pictures, and I think it will last as long as the story supply."[13] Journalistic crime writers like James Cain and Raymond Chandler, as well as 1940s trades, studio publicity, and industry analysts noted the trend's growing "realism" in the context of the war and in the wake of *Double Indemnity.*

Warner Bros.' radio publicity release by Jack Rosenstein featured the wartime *noir* cycle's male-centered brutality and described "what women really want" in surly Hollywood crime flicks. The newly expanded representational parameters allowed by the Hays Office were exploited to the fullest by studios wanting to capitalize on sex and violence. And they certainly took every opportunity to do so. These red-meat narratives were lucratively packaged by the industry to exploit male fantasy, yet they were powerfully "naturalizing" and attributed the wish-fulfillment of provocative sexual violence as satisfying the desire of women. While heightening the sensation of its commercial and promotional appeal, World War II's dark underside also manifested an ambiguous, somber wartime psyche in Hollywood's *noir* films simultaneously emerging as masculine nightmare (death, violence, and murder, to which war vets were exposed and could relate) and hedonistic "dream come true" (an abundance of rough, tough sex). In an effort to appease the PCA, criminal sex and violence would ultimately prove futile—or fatal. Onscreen perpetrators faced the unavoidable doomed fate of moral retribution (death, jail, misery). So narrative and cinematic indulgences did not come without a price.

Although films adhered to Code representational strictures by maximizing suggestion, the PCA became more lenient after sanctioning Cain adaptations and continued to grow increasingly liberal in the postwar era. As seen in *The Outlaw, Scarlet Street,* and *Gilda* publicity, the film industry often relied on explicit, comparatively raw sexual material in heightening graphic, sensationalized film promotions, exploiting a more lenient advertising code. These dark crime films and exploitation narratives combined a battle-worn brutality with abundant erotic appeal and titillating sensation—no doubt an effort to lure the deprived yet rugged combat-oriented wartime military (ex)soldier market. Studios certainly sought to recapture their male audience—whether it was returning to the home front from active duty or still enlisted in military fronts overseas to aid in the war-related Allied combat and occupation effort. Film images and publicity invoked the carnal, disheveled environment of sheer survival amid legalized murder in this World War II terrain. Indeed, in succeeding to promote effective wartime ideals, propaganda, and morale, tough guys still needed to blow the enemy away. The "raw hide," tough-exterior mentality prevailed. That is, sensitizing soldiers' "feminine side" was certainly not a desirable or effective objective for media narratives at this crucial point in wartime—particularly with the possibility of Allied victory so near. Thus, the message: "Courage, man—win the war!"

In adding sexual polemics to this mix, Jack Rosenstein's 1944 Warner publicity release read: "What the women want, what really makes them weak and willing, is a guy with guts who treats 'em mean and tough. They're just mad about being mauled. As a matter of common fact," he notes, "the number of fainting femmes in the audience is in direct ratio to how unkempt Humphrey Bogart dresses and how savagely he slaps around his leading ladies." For example, Rosenstein explains, "Bogie's newest picture, Warner Bros.' 'To Have and Have Not,' should certainly score a sock, since he has hardly a single civil word to say in the script to Lauren Bacall, Howard Hawks' sultry find, who plays opposite." Empowering the male in a position of mastery in these publicity narratives, Rosenstein describes Hollywood's growing meaty crime trend: "There are almost a half-score of forthcoming mystery melodramas à la 'Double Indemnity' in which boy gives girl a thorough working over. Even Dick Powell, always before the perfect soul of circumspection with the gentle sex, does a complete turnabout as the detective in RKO's 'Farewell, My Lovely.' Claire Trevor and Anne Shirley are the lucky little ladies who get their pretty phizzes shoved around." As in other 1940s trades and industry press, the crime trend's stylistically dark films and cynical, antiheroic characters are detailed: "a bad guy with the beauty in this sort of murder thrillers is Dana Andrews, the plain clothesman opposite Gene Tierney in Twentieth Century–Fox's 'Laura.' Warners are going to team Bogart and Bacall again in just this sort of script in 'The Big Sleep,' with him as the sleuth who slugs around the love-hungry little murderess, and in 'Conflict,' which the Bogey man completed some months ago, he plays the sort of guy who simply bumps off a babe when she begins to bore him." He adds, "Of course, at Paramount Alan Ladd has always been 'the velvet hand in the iron glove' ever since his click in 'This Gun for Hire.'"[14] Hollywood industry insiders and 1940s film critics in the United States recognized the trend's emergence. Studio publicity exaggerated the provocative gender images and violence in these sexy narratives even more and showed how the wartime crime cycle was swiftly gaining momentum.

Violence Bred by War:
The Blue Dahlia and *The Stranger*

Hollywood narratives, including *noir* films, responded to the conclusion of fighting overseas by adapting topical stories to target a changing market and audience. In May 1945 Fred Stanley of the *New York Times* wrote:

> The end of the war in Europe has given added impetus to Hollywood's year-long interest in stories with post-war themes. That movie patrons may expect a definitive cycle of screen dramas dealing with various problems and phases of the post-bellum period is indicated by the more than twenty-five subjects of this genre now in preparation, or being filmed, at the major studios . . .
>
> For the most part, the current studio-favored plots deal with the home front, the rehabilitation of returned servicemen, their readjustment to changed economic conditions, and personal domestic problems. In some of the proposed films even such delicate themes as marital unfaithfulness are to be treated. However, none of the pictures planned deals with serious European post-war topics. Hollywood appears content to leave this matter . . . to the more factual screen reporting of the newsreel cameras.

Citing Alfred Hitchcock's *noir* thriller *Notorious* "with the experiences of a European who seeks refuge in South America" as an example, Stanley also mentioned RKO's *Cornered*, starring Dick Powell, "about a discharged aviator who goes to Argentina to wreak vengeance on a former Nazi collaborator who had murdered the serviceman's wife, a worker in the French Underground."[15]

Whereas many earlier World War II–era *noir* pictures avoided mentioning the war altogether, several crime films at the end of the war featured tormented military men and shady surroundings. Raymond Chandler's first original script, *The Blue Dahlia* (1946), is a fascinating *noir* released in the final days of the conflict—with unstable returning veterans, wild unfaithful female spouses, and a corrupt crime-infested California home front. The war influenced and motivated the making of the film. In early 1945 Paramount was especially eager, even frantic, to produce another *This Gun for Hire* crime vehicle for its lead male star, real-life veteran Alan Ladd, who had just returned from overseas. Ladd had made no films during his leave and soon had to resume military service. After the success of *Double Indemnity* Paramount offered Chandler a contract. At the behest of producer John Houseman and Paramount executive Joseph Sistrom (who had produced *Double Indemnity*), Chandler agreed to rework an unfinished novel into a script for the project and tailored the lead role, Lieutenant Commander Johnny Morrison, for Ladd.

Chandler's story of three discharged navy buddies returning to America's home front and starting new lives in Los Angeles was certainly topical. Johnny discovers that in his absence his assertive entrepreneur wife, Helen (Doris Dowling), who owned a Beverly Hills business, has become an adulterous alcoholic who throws wild parties, consorts with other men (even in front of him), then laughs and viciously tries to hurt him by revealing she killed his young son while driving home drunk from a party she took the boy to. Her lover, Eddie Harwood (Howard da Silva), owns the Sunset Strip club The Blue Dahlia, employs gangsters, and has a criminal past. When Johnny leaves Helen on a dark rainy night and she is found murdered the next morning, the law is after him. Although he has an alibi—Eddie's beautiful, estranged wife, Joyce (Veronica Lake), gives Johnny a ride in the rain past Malibu—rather than tell the police he is innocent, like a hard-boiled detective, Johnny is compelled as a man of honor to find his wife's killer. Helen had called Eddie to her apartment that night and met Johnny's buddy Buzz Wanchek (William Bendix) in a bar. Buzz is a bit crazy—physically wounded and mentally scarred from combat, suffering from shell shock, sporadic amnesia, and a volatile "short fuse" because of a head injury and a steel plate in his brain. Like a female detective Joyce is dubious of her husband and suspects Buzz's bizarre behavior. But seedy house detective "Dad" Newell (Will Wright), a former cop and crooked voyeur "after a buck" under his umbrella outside Helen's apartment, blackmails everyone in the movie. He turns out to be the killer, pulls a gun, and is shot by police captain Hendrickson (Tom Powers, Phyllis's ill-fated husband in *Double Indemnity*).

Chandler originally scripted Buzz as the murderer. He wanted to show the brutality bred by war in a veteran desensitized to violence as a result of the conflict and now psychopathically flawed. As Chandler explained, "What I wrote was a story of a man who killed (executed would be a better word) his pal's wife under the stress of a great and legitimate anger, then blanked out and forgot all about it; then with perfect honesty did his best to help his pal get out of a jam, then found himself in a set of circumstances which brought about partial recall. The poor guy remembered enough to make it clear who the murderer was to others, but never realized it himself."

But in wartime Paramount had to submit the script to the navy—"at that time the conduct of servicemen in movies had to be cleared with Washington; and the Navy Department ruled that Wanchek, a wounded hero, could not be the murderer. Bad for morale; disrespect for the service." So the navy forced Chandler to change the murderer and "abandon the plot rationale" for his script. Federal censorship undercut the PCA in allowing an old thirty-year police veteran to be the killer rather than soil the image of the military. Director George Marshall and cinematographer Lionel Lindon began filming *The Blue Dahlia* without a finished screenplay in late March 1945. By April PCA censors were concerned about reducing violence. Principal photography ran through mid-May. Chandler completed the script in the final days of shooting with all-night writing sessions and ample quantities of alcohol. The conflict in Europe ended—and FDR died—during the film's forty-two days of production, and retakes continued into mid-July as the war drew to a close. (For Chandler quotes see n. 20.)

The Blue Dahlia opens in broad daylight before descending into a nocturnal world of rain storms and murder. It includes locations in Hollywood and greater Los Angeles, and many scenes use rear-projection shots of the city and even the ocean in the background. Like *Mildred Pierce* it is not clear whether the story is set during or just after the war, but in *The Blue Dahlia* servicemen are everywhere as the war itself and its effects on the West Coast's shady home front permeate Chandler's urban milieu. Reflecting the male labor shortage, many of the picture's heavies were older men, and Bendix—known for World War II pictures like *Wake Island* (1942), *Guadalcanal Diary* (1943), *Woman of the Year* (1942), Hitchcock's *Lifeboat* (1944), and *The Life of Riley* radio series—was an actor whose career really took off during the war. A rising star, Paramount even gave Bendix coveted third billing behind Ladd and Lake.

Publicity featured Ladd holding a cigarette, a sultry Lake, Bendix holding a gun, and Dowling with a cigarette dangling from her mouth beside the taglines: "THIS BEAUTIFUL BLONDE TRIES TO STEP IN . . . *where* THIS GORGEOUS BRUNETTE LEFT OFF *with* LADD But even a blonde like this has to wait till Ladd settles the score! It's a gun-blazing, fist-smashing drama of Ladd—smack up against the kind of trouble he knows how to deal with—but good!" and "TAMED *by a Blonde* . . . It's a tough job—but Veronica's the girl who can do it! FRAMED *by a Brunette* . . . She's the famous 'Natch' gal of 'The Lost Weekend'. BLAMED *by the Cops* . . . For a murder he wanted to commit . . . but *didn't!* Better Check your blood pressure at the door . . . because Raymond Chandler has written the year's fastest suspense-filled mystery of murder in full bloom!" Ads read, "THAT *LADD* IS MIXING IN MURDER! The

Returning vet Johnny Morrison (Alan Ladd, *center*) exchanges blows with thugs in
The Blue Dahlia.
Paramount, 1946.

Big Three . . . in a rough, tough socker by Raymond Chandler, one of the
greatest hard-boiled mystery writers that ever lived! *'You ought to know that
you can't take chances with a stranger . . .'"* "IT'S MURDER . . . *When you step
into* ALAN LADD's *private affairs . . .* you go out cold!" "When Ladd puts his
name on a woman—she keeps it—or else! His brand of revenge is packed
with a gun and his fists—as Ladd goes after the man who killed his girl—
with a beautiful blonde all-out after him!" and "'Hands-off, MINE!'—says
Alan Ladd. And if you don't listen to Ladd's cool . . . clear words . . . you'll
be hearing plenty from his blazing gun and smashing fists!" Paramount's
press book promised "DOUBLE DAME TROUBLE! DOUBLE-BARRELLED AC-
TION!" "WANTED by the cops . . . WANTED by a Murder Mob . . . WANTED by
a Beautiful Blonde! But before she can get him he's got a score to settle with
a murderous double-crosser!" and "LADD'S HOT . . . " "The way he handles
his gun and his fists—and the way he holds a woman!" Posters clamored,
"ONE'S OUT TO FRAME HIM . . . THE OTHER TO TAME HIM!" "Dead or Alive,
Dames Are Double-Trouble For Him!" "He's fast-talking when he tangles
with two dames, hard-hitting when he tackles a double-crosser, straight
shooting when he's framed by a murder mob!" Like *This Gun for Hire*, pub-

licity conflated sex and violence: "ALAN LADD Tempted by two women . . . to kiss one . . . to kill the other! VERONICA LAKE She's involved in a love-nest murder . . . and she's taking dangerous chances with a stranger! WILLIAM BENDIX Rounding out this thrilling threesome . . . and having no 'Life of Riley' in his rocking, socking role!"[16]

When the film previewed in January 1946, the *Hollywood Review* wrote: "Everything about the John Houseman production is top grade . . . with an authentic ring . . . Like *Double Indemnity, Murder, My Sweet* and *Mildred Pierce,* this hard-boiled thriller is also laid in Los Angeles and its environs. A returning war hero walks in on a drunken brawl at his home and finds his wife in the embrace of a stranger." It praised "Raymond Chandler writing at his fascinating best, and you know that's good! . . . Lionel Lindon's expert camera marksmanship knocks off a number of stunning scenes and the process photography, particularly the Los Angeles backgrounds and the ocean shots, are masterfully matched with the interiors by [process photographer] Farciot Edouart and Lindon." It added:

> The new type of hard-boiled motion picture, which the public cinched with Raymond Chandler's *Murder, My Sweet* early last year, gets an expert going-over by George Marshall in the first original Chandler has written directly for the screen, *The Blue Dahlia.* The same author's *Big Sleep* is on the way from Warners and MGM, which has completed filming on James Cain's *The Postman Always Rings Twice,* also plans to film Chandler's *Lady in the Lake. Mildred Pierce* was in the same exciting category and, to a lesser degree, so was RKO's *Cornered.* Exhibitors will know what to do with it in booking and all they need to be told about Paramount's *Blue Dahlia* is that it is a fast and mile-a-minute package of guaranteed excitement. Also, that it brings back to them after more than a year's absence from the screen—Alan Ladd—one of the chosen marquee few whose names never fail to draw.[17]

Variety called it a "smooth, suspenseful murder thriller":

> Ladd's fans, awaiting his first screen appearance since his stint in the armed service, won't be disappointed by his return. Playing a discharged naval flier returning home from the Pacific first to find his wife unfaithful, then to find her murdered and himself in hiding as the suspect . . . In his relentless track down of the real criminal, Ladd has cold, steel-like quality that is potent. Fight scenes are stark and

brutal, and tremendously effective . . . Bendix, playing a tailgunner
suffering occasionally from shellshock, brings a gruff, hearty quality to
his role that is in excellent contrast to Ladd's . . . Howard Freeman [is]
an icily ruthless gangster.[18]

The film was released in April 1946 to positive reviews. The *New York
Herald-Tribune*'s Howard Barnes described "Ladd's dead-pan ferocity" and
"Lake's brazen coyness" in the "tough and tensile murder melodrama." *The
Blue Dahlia*, he wrote,

> spins a tightly integrated tale of killings and sluggings into an arrest-
> ing film of its kind, [despite] muffled love scenes between a navy flier
> and the wife of the cabaret operator whom he suspects of having
> killed his no-good wife . . . The mystery element is not nearly as im-
> portant . . . as the overt violence. Raymond Chandler, who has consid-
> erable know-how in making homicides and beatings entertaining, has
> fashioned a savage script . . . Ladd is beaten to a pulp so many times
> that he might have shown some slight contusions from his various or-
> deals [with] fancy in-fighting to remind us that veterans of the Pacific
> War learned well how to play dirty in a jam.

Eileen Creelman of the *New York Sun* compared *The Blue Dahlia* to Ladd's
"gangster of 'This Gun for Hire' who now is a naval officer returned from
the wars" to find "his wife involved with some unsavory . . . odd characters
wandering in and out of the drama . . . Buzz, whose head was badly injured
in the war; Corelli, the night club owner's shady partner; Joyce Harwood,
the night club owner's estranged wife, and a slimy hotel detective called Dad
Newell." Creelman observed, "The film is told indirectly in the manner of
the modern thriller," and she welcomed Alan Ladd "back to the screen in a
sympathetic role."[19]

Like *Laura, The Blue Dahlia* begins with the slaying of a woman. But responding to changes in movie audiences by the end of the war, the latter
film was a much more masculine narrative. It was a formula for success.
Bosley Crowther of the *New York Times* wrote, "To the present expanding
cycle of hard-boiled and cynical films, Paramount has contributed a honey
of a rough-'em-up romance." Its "floral fracas" featured "leading tough guy,
Alan Ladd," and

> equally dangerous and dynamic lady V-bomb, Veronica Lake. What
> with that combination in this Raymond Chandler tale, it won't be

simply blasting that you will hear in Times Square for weeks to come. For bones are being crushed with cold abandon, teeth are being callously kicked in and shocks are being blandly detonated at close and regular intervals on the Paramount screen. Also an air of deepening mystery overhangs this tempestuous tale which shall render it none the less intriguing to those lovers of the brutal and bizarre. In the manner of previous Ladd pictures, the rough stuff begins at the start, when our hero returns from the Pacific and finds his wife something less than true.

Like the reviewers, audiences seemed keen on this timely male-oriented murder mystery, registering their approval at the box office. *The Blue Dahlia* recouped its $900,000 cost, grossing more than $2,750,000 and earning Chandler a second Academy Award nomination, this time for best original screenplay.[20]

Although *The Blue Dahlia* was a topical *noir* film about the late war years and coming home, it was not a "message" picture advancing a social theme. Paramount's Chandler-Ladd vehicle was undeniably a hard-boiled crime picture. Just a few months later, however, another *noir*—made after the war was over—took a slightly different tack. *The Stranger* (1946), an independent production for International Pictures (released through RKO), produced by Sam Spiegel, scripted by Anthony Veiller, with uncredited writing by John Huston and director Orson Welles (who also starred in the film), conveyed more of a social-political message, but it, too, was a stylish, atmospheric *noir* crime picture. Welles and cinematographer Russell Metty (who also shot Dmytryk's *Hitler's Children*) created a disturbing visual milieu using abundant skewed and extremely low camera angles, shadows, smoke, geometric patterns, and wonderful elliptical cutting, especially in the film's finale. Shot from late September to late November 1945 and released in July 1946, *The Stranger* was clearly a postwar endeavor and less hard-boiled than earlier World War II era *noirs*. Yet it centered on the violence brought about by war and even incorporated shocking actual footage of the Nazi death camps into the picture—the first time many American audiences saw these brutal real-life atrocities outside of newsreels.

The Stranger combines several earlier *noir* preludes and genres, including espionage spy pictures and the female gothic thriller. It features wartime *noir* leading man Edward G. Robinson—fresh off his *Double Indemnity, Woman in the Window,* and *Scarlet Street* success—as a determined pipe-smoking Washington G-man catching Nazi war criminals and solving crime. Like *Gilda* and *Notorious* released that same year, *The Stranger* deals with former-Axis criminals. In Welles's topical *noir* film, however, action moves quickly from South America to the United States. Like *The Blue Dahlia, The Stranger* brings the war home to America. But rather than an urban Los Angeles filled with gangsters, loose women, and returned servicemen, the story takes place in a peaceful Connecticut community, where an American delegate to the Allied War Crimes Commission, Wilson (Robinson), tracks a former Nazi death camp commander, who leads him to the elusive Nazi mastermind behind the entire death-camps operation, Franz Kindler (Welles), who has unassumingly blended into rural main-street America by posing as a history teacher at a boys' school and marrying Mary Longstreet (Loretta Young), the daughter of a liberal Supreme Court justice.

From the very opening of the picture Bronislaw Kaper's riveting music captures the feel of a tense radio drama. Reviewer Herb Sterne called *The Stranger*

> the type of horrendous melodrama that woos and glues pre-puberty listeners to the family radio. Orson Welles, as director and star of this fright wig opera, capably visualizes the standard ingredients of thriller broadcasts, though never for a split second can one credit the frenetic events that revolve around a fat Nazi spider that weaves his noxious web in a small Connecticut town. A visit to the film will disclose that Mr. Welles struts and storms in his customary style; that Loretta Young's appearance has begun to belie her surname; and that Edward G. Robinson remains one of the more reliable actors working before the cameras.[21]

Like *The Blue Dahlia* and *Gilda, The Stranger* taps into gender distress at the end of the war, but its dysfunctional relationship shifts from the hard-boiled to a gothic premise, with a beautiful young ingenue trusting and betrothing a mysterious enemy that persists even after the war is over. The Nazi menace lurks in simple everyday life, where no one expects it—in broad daylight in the town square, at home, in a child's classroom, a school gymnasium, or a tranquil walk in the sun through the woods.

Rather than a nocturnal, enclosed urban environment, much of the film is shot outdoors during the day, on a bright uncovered sunlit studio back lot (at the Goldwyn and Universal studios), with huge sets (some of the biggest since Griffith's *Intolerance*) doubling as a small village. Even shots of the woods reveal stark sunlight filtering through the branches of the trees. By late October 1945, during filming for *The Stranger,* industry analyst Fred Stanley of the *New York Times* reported "a revival of typically Hollywood pre-war 'colossal' sets, luxurious costumes and expensive crowd scenes, all of which will be made possible by the anticipated easing of wartime shortages of costume and building material." Studios were planning more "spectacular" color pictures for 1946. "But the plans, for the moment, are dependent to a great degree on the outcome of the thirty-one-week-old studio strike which, along with wartime restrictions, has been instrumental recently in keeping a number of heavily budgeted films from being started or completed . . . The imposing subjects which are listed for production next year . . . could not have been produced satisfactorily under wartime conditions." Stanley observed Hollywood "cutting the corners" for the duration, recycling (and cleverly disguising) used costumes and materials. "The shortage of fabrics during the war years had imposed many difficulties for the studio wardrobe departments. But it also brought about unprecedented studio innovations and economy . . . There was also considerable economy, scrimping and makeshift practice in set construction. Lumber was used over and over again. For a time the studios were straightening nails for reuse, and necessity compelled a more extensive use of plaster in place of wood."[22] At the close of the war *The Stranger* already anticipates later *noir* films, made without the many constraints of wartime production. The moody opening, however—featuring thick swirls of cigar smoke and Robinson, wearing a dark fedora, tailing a spy and slinking in shrouded corners—the grim documentary footage, and the elaborate *noir* finale are shadowy, violent, and impressive.

Welles reveals a duplicitous Nazi enemy incognito and capable of great brutality: Kindler murders his former colleague, poisons his wife's dog after the cocker spaniel digs up the body, and attempts to kill his spouse. Wilson intervenes in the gothic-espionage scenario. Like Robinson's World War II–era everyman, his postwar G-man picks up where Keyes's "little man" in *Double Indemnity* left off—following the Nazi's doomed desperate actions like a bloodhound and closing in with a vengeance. Robinson's detective, like his investigator in *Double Indemnity,* really drives the narrative forward and makes it work. He flips the lights out and runs the projector to screen death-camp horrors, from piles of actual bodies to gas chambers, showing Mary—and the viewing audience of this film-within-a-film—while explaining Kindler's deplorable role in devising these atrocities. Wilson also handily becomes a shrink, explaining Mary's psychological conflict and her refusal to believe these crimes are true and that her lover is responsible. The film includes a fascinating reversal. When Mary realizes Kindler planned to murder her, she overcomes her denial and boldly shifts to a stronger lethal femme resolute on killing him. While Wilson engages Kindler in a fistfight, she grabs a gun and fires a flurry of shots, emptying the gun at her husband. Shown in a masterful chiaroscuro climactic montage sequence set against the crisscrossing beams and claustrophobic black bowels of the clock tower, Welles's Nazi meets his demise as a knight's statue rotates around the clock, spearing him with a blade through the heart. International spent $275,000 to promote the film with taglines like: "The most Deceitful man a woman ever loved!" "Bewitched . . . Bewildered . . . Betrayed . . . " The tagline above an image of Loretta Young reads, "After what you've done to me . . . KILL ME!" Press book publicity featured all three: Robinson "Hunter—or prey? Friend or Stranger?"; Young (with a more visceral spin) " . . . Tainted by the touch of the Stranger!"; and Welles " . . . Stranger to fear . . . master of deceit!"[23]

While filming *The Stranger* Welles told the *New York Times,* "I do not like being an actor and I don't acknowledge the existence of a job called producer. The only thing I like in films is directing. I think pictures are in a bad way. They need revitalizing . . . for private film experimentation and a chain of adult theatres free from Hays office code censorship." He added, "Films dealing with serious and important subjects should be produced, even if the big boys have to be taxed for them."

By June 1946 James Agee wrote, "Orson Welles' new movie, *The Stranger,* is a tidy, engaging thriller about a Nazi arch-criminal (Mr. Welles) who hides out as a teacher in a New England boys' prep school . . . In a quite modest way the picture is, merely, much more graceful, intelligent, and enjoyable than most other movies . . . plenty of reason to be glad that Welles is back at work. Although Mr. Welles takes a reasonable amount of care not to insist on it, *The Stranger* is an 'art' movie." A few weeks later Bosley Crowther observed, "Welles has directed his camera for some striking effects, with lighting and interesting angles much relied on in his technique. The fellow knows how to make a camera dynamic in telling a tale." Reflecting the desensitizing brutality audiences were exposed to in graphic documentary images of the war's devastation—preferring more violence and stark "reality"—Crowther complained, "The whole film . . . comes off a bloodless, manufactured show. The atom-bomb newsreels on the same bill are immeasurably more frightening." Crowther tellingly reveals that the atomic age brought a whole new, and different, era for *noir. The Stranger* is a fine example of how film noir was already beginning to change just after the war to address topical issues and cultural tensions burgeoning in the cold war. Welles's postwar *noir* conveyed a social message, albeit via a crime film. Sticking to a tight schedule, a disciplined Welles finished *The Stranger* on time and under budget—and after the studio cut the film from over two hours to a brisk hour-and-a-half, its abrupt ending (with Robinson waving good-bye to Young as he climbs down from the clock tower) certainly reflects cost-conscious haste to speedily wrap things up. The picture earned $2 million domestically and just under a million overseas—almost $3 million in all.[24] Quite a topical success.

If You Wanna Send a Message, Call Western Union: Changes and Decline in the Postwar Years

Whether examining the trauma of returning veterans, the atrocities of war, the danger of war criminals at home, or other social ills, many *noir* films made or released just after the war were "message" pictures. Even Billy Wilder's hard-hitting 1945 follow-up to *Double Indemnity* conveyed a social realist theme. Wilder's *The Lost Weekend* tackled the problem of alcoholism from a psychological perspective. It dealt with serious issues affecting many individuals and was shot on real locations—just as Italian neorealist films depicted war-torn devastation in Europe. By the mid-1940s, critics called Joan Harrison's immediate postwar production *They Won't Believe Me* (produced in 1946, released in 1947) an example of the *Double Indemnity* crime trend; this film was followed by Jacques Tourneur's classic *Out of the Past* at RKO. Robert Montgomery directed Raymond Chandler's *The Lady in the Lake* (produced in 1946, released in 1947) at MGM, moving to tighter-budgeted Universal to collaborate with producer Harrison and writers Ben Hecht and Charles Lederer on *Ride the Pink Horse* (1947). Film noir thrived at studios with limited resources, tight budgets, European personnel, and hard-hitting narrative and generic traditions such as RKO, Warner Bros., Universal, Paramount, Columbia, and minors such as Monogram, Eagle-Lion, and PRC. Sets were sparse and dark in lean pictures such as RKO's *Stranger on the Third Floor* and *Murder, My Sweet;* Paramount's *Street of Chance* and *This Gun for Hire;* Universal's *Phantom Lady, Christmas Holiday,* and *Black Angel;* Monogram's *When Strangers Marry;* and 20th Century–Fox's *Moontide,* and they were eliminated completely in Ulmer's *Detour* at PRC, the quintessential Poverty Row studio.

During and after the war RKO produced an immensely successful series of tightly paced, gritty films made with limited resources on shoestring budgets. Producer Val Lewton's cost-effective psychological thrillers and political potboilers were deftly reformulated into increasingly stylized *noir* and social-realist productions by the mid-to-late 1940s. Director Edward Dmytryk's inexpensive and immensely popular films illustrate the postwar narrative shift from battling "the enemy" in wartime to tackling hard-boiled *noir* crime and anti-Semitism issues. From the anti-Nazi B potboiler *Hitler's*

Children to the Raymond Chandler adaptation *Murder, My Sweet,* the antifascist *noir Cornered* (1945), and the definitive postwar antibigotry *noir*
"message" picture *Crossfire* (1947), Dmytryk's films drew on the violence
and permanent scars left by the war with returning veterans transitioning
to postwar society—reformulating trends that were part and parcel to the
same cultural and political impulses of wartime film noir, exposing its brutal aftermath. During the war Robert Wise directed psychological thrillers
in Val Lewton's modest unit after editing Orson Welles's *Citizen Kane* and
The Magnificent Ambersons at RKO. Wise infused social critique in postwar
noir thrillers *Born to Kill* (1947) and *The Set Up* (1949), exposing corrupt
crime in the boxing world. After the war Universal released director Robert
Siodmak and producer Mark Hellinger's *noir* film of Hemingway's *The
Killers,* and Bogart portrayed a psychologically tormented military man returning to a lethal milieu of gangsters, corruption, and a duplicitous femme
fatale in Columbia's *Dead Reckoning* (1947). Wartime film noir's legacy is
shown in the postwar plight of World War II veterans in *The Blue Dahlia,
Cornered, Dead Reckoning, Crossfire, Gentleman's Agreement* (1947), and *Act
of Violence* (1949), as studios eliminated B-film units. Like *The Blue Dahlia*
and *Dead Reckoning,* RKO's *Cornered*—directed by Edward Dmytryk, written by John Paxton (who adapted *Murder, My Sweet*) and John Wexley (who
wrote *Hangmen Also Die*), shot by Harry J. Wild (who shot *Murder, My
Sweet*), and starring Dick Powell as a Canadian airman who gets out of a
German POW camp and travels to Argentina looking for the Vichy French
administrator who had his wife killed—is another example of the return-
ing-vet genre of *noir* pictures that addresses the violence bred by war and
draws a connection between wartime violence and film noir.

From 1947 to 1948 RKO production chief Dore Schary championed social issues in hard-hitting *noir* message pictures, rechanneling realistic B
films from potboilers to take on postwar political issues in social-problem
pictures like the critically successful *Crossfire.* Schary left RKO (after
Howard Hughes bought the studio) to head production at MGM from 1948
to 1956, clashing with longtime studio boss Louis B. Mayer and later oust-
ing Mayer in 1951. As seen in *The Postman Always Rings Twice,* MGM's lavish, glossy, polished, big-budget A-film style, with its bright, high-key or flat
lighting—showcased in the studio's 1940s and 1950s popular musicals
filmed in glorious Technicolor by producers Arthur Freed, Joseph Paster-
nak, and Jack Cummings—would be counter to *noir.* MGM's traditionally
conservative policy of avoiding controversial, hard-hitting politics in lieu
of good, wholesome family entertainment was best expressed in Mayer's
telling director Elia Kazan, "Young man, you have one thing to learn. We

are in the business of making beautiful pictures of beautiful people, and anybody who does not acknowledge that should not be in the business."[25] Alongside MGM's comparatively slick, glossy escapist fare, by the late 1940s, under Schary, postwar MGM churned out grittier, more topical, tighter-budgeted social-realist *noir* films (at least "low-budget" by MGM's standards—comparable to A pictures at more modest studios).

At Poverty Row's Eagle-Lion studio director Anthony Mann and cinematographer John Alton shot B *noir* films *T-Men* and *Raw Deal* in 1948, before Schary recruited them at MGM for *Border Incident* in 1949. Abraham Polonsky scripted *Body and Soul* (1947, Enterprise Studio, released through United Artists), directed by Robert Rossen and starring John Garfield. Joan Cohen and Alain Silver have called the film "one of the last cries of liberalism before the House Un-American Activities Committee investigations were to crush many of its principals." Rossen and Polonsky's film dealt with corruption and the "ever present temptation of the dollar."[26] Polonsky cowrote and directed another independently produced social *noir, Force of Evil* (1948, Enterprise Studio, released through MGM) as a follow-up to *Body and Soul,* with star Garfield indicting organized crime in a milieu of urban corruption. Fred Zinnemann directed the powerful *noir Act of Violence* (1949, originally an independent Mark Hellinger project, then produced by MGM), in which an urban nightmare spills into a small suburban town in the postwar era. In allegory to Hollywood's red purges, guilt-ridden World War II veteran Van Heflin, tormented that he informed on his men—American POWs trying to escape a Nazi concentration camp, tortured and killed by the enemy because of his betrayal—flees menacing survivor Robert Ryan, vengeful to settle a score, who stalks his former commander to make him pay. By 1952 Stanley Kramer produced and Zinnemann directed the revisionist *noir* western *High Noon,* a legendary metaphor for HUAC's blacklist in the McCarthy era, written by Carl Foreman and released through United Artists.

Controversial adaptations had become increasingly acceptable to the PCA in wartime, and films noir proliferated as censorship restrictions continued to relax during the immediate postwar years. Hollywood's boom and the delayed release of stockpiled films contributed to record profits as box-office revenue peaked in 1946. The motion picture industry and *noir* films changed as Hollywood entered a peacetime market. As federal regulation eased, gangsters populated Hollywood screens in films like *Dillinger* (1945), *Kiss of Death* (1947; starring Richard Widmark in his notorious cackling psychopathic killer debut), Warner Bros.' *Key Largo* (1948; directed by John Huston with Bogart, Bacall, and Robinson as a mob boss), Raoul Walsh's

White Heat (1949; featuring James Cagney's virtuoso performance as a volatile soon-to-be-washed-up gunman), and Huston's *The Asphalt Jungle* (1950), in which Sterling Hayden, Louis Calhern, James Whitmore, and Marc Lawrence pull the ultimate heist. *Noir* reached its pinnacle at the end of the war, evolving into the 1940s and 1950s, before steadily declining amid new challenges in the postwar era. World War II–era *noir* changed after the war—as red-meat stories gave way to the "Red Scare." From 1945 through the late 1940s *noir* shifted to social-realist message pictures and by the 1950s to cold war *noir*.

Cold war *noir* is distinctive from wartime 1940s film noir, reflecting different cultural anxieties (xenophobia, organized crime, communism, the atomic bomb). Postwar *noir* took on a new tone—and ultimately a different, grayer *film gris* aesthetic, no longer the deep, shadowy blacks and flickers of light from the war years. Hollywood itself was changing as well. It was rocked by antitrust regulation, declining theater attendance, a postwar economy, new widescreen and color technologies, location shooting, independent and "runaway" production, freelance creative talent, competition from television, and burgeoning international markets. The film industry faced political challenges in a conservative cold war era that veered from Roosevelt's New Deal populism to the right. The national political and cultural landscape changed dramatically. After FDR's death in 1945, Harry Truman dropped the atomic bomb, and the Russians had the bomb by the end of the decade. The early 1950s faced federal HUAC investigations, crime hearings, the Korean War, Eisenhower, and the McCarthy era. Cold war fears included the alarming spread of communism in Stalin's Soviet Union, revolution in China, and Korea posing an ideological threat as a postwar arms race and dangerous nuclear capability was directed toward the United States. Once the Axis was defeated, absent the common enemy of Nazi fascism following World War II, many redirected their patriotic imperatives toward purging subversive communist elements—or dangerously liberal individuals—from the U.S. cultural landscape. The arts and media were targeted, particularly the film industry. Hollywood and black-and-white film noir would never be quite the same. As Washington's House Un-American Activities Committee investigations fueled the Red Scare and industry blacklisting of creative talent from late 1947 into the 1950s, cultural xenophobia and cold war paranoia encouraged major studios to be more conservative, pro-American, or upbeat—in films and in their labor force. The political climate following HUAC and the Red Scare led to blacklisting radical—often *noir*—talent, like the Hollywood Ten unfriendly witnesses (including Edward Dmytryk and Ring Lardner). In a climate discouraging liberal social-realist *noir* message pictures, the cold war changed crime films by the early 1950s. It was a death knell for *noir*.

By 1950 the psychic instability and destructive paranoia in such films—Humphrey Bogart's unstable veteran and screenwriter in Nicholas Ray's *In a Lonely Place*, Sterling Hayden's disturbed misfit in John Huston's *The Asphalt Jungle*, Gloria Swanson's delusional and suicidal past-her-prime silent star and William Holden's frayed, unemployed screenwriter in Billy Wilder's *Sunset Boulevard*, even disease-consuming gangsters in Elia Kazan's social *noir Panic in the Streets*—were wakeup calls signaling the end of a creative, economic, and political era in Hollywood. For the industry and for *noir* crime films growing out of the 1940s war years, the cultural, production, and reception climate was rapidly eroding. In 1950 industry executives revealed the state of the American film industry and the extent to which it had been transformed. In a telling example of the period's xenophobia, MGM's Louis B. Mayer publicly attacked Wilder, calling him a "foreigner" disparaging the industry at the premiere of *Sunset Boulevard* for studio executives. Gritty *noir* and downbeat social-realist pictures now became dangerous and were avoided. In a 1950 memo Darryl Zanuck of 20th Century–Fox cautioned Elia Kazan and John Steinbeck to make it "very clear" that film content "isn't Communism ... because, frankly, in the present script there is inadvertently a peculiar air about certain speeches, which might be interpreted by the Communists to claim that we are subtly working for them ... We will all get kicked below the belt if it does not turn out to be a commercial as well as an artistic success. *Sunset Boulevard* was a masterpiece until it was released throughout the country and failed to do business. It is not so big a masterpiece today."[27]

Zanuck sent a studio message marked "CONFIDENTIAL" to "All Producers and Directors" in 1950: "We have completed our third survey of audience and box-office reaction to all pictures released during the last quarter. It is always difficult to speak in broad or general terms about the *reasons* for the success or failure of individual pictures—or even of groups of pictures—because there are always certain exceptions. One thing stands out very clearly and that is the fact that the theatre-going public has been saturated with pictures of violence and films with underworld or 'low' backgrounds." In another confidential memo, to director Henry King, Zanuck wrote the epitaph for film noir: "Audiences today, particularly in America, do not want pictures of violence or extreme brutality," he opined. "In spite of the high quality of such pictures as *Panic in the Streets, Asphalt Jungle,* [Otto Preminger's 1950 *noir*] *Where the Sidewalk Ends*, etc., etc., these films and all films in this category have proved to be a shocking disappointment

... particularly, if they are 'downbeat' in nature or deal with sordid back-grounds, unsympathetic characters and over-emphasized 'suffering.'" He added:

> Pictures dealing even remotely with sickness or disease are not wanted. An exceptional picture of this nature manages to squeeze by occasionally. *The Men* is a disappointment and ... disease in *Panic in the Streets* is one of the elements that contributed to the poor returns on this fine picture, which received unanimous praise from the critics ... Pictures dealing with psychopathic characters have also outlived their usefulness *at this time*. There have been twenty-three pictures re-leased in eighteen months in which one or more characters are moti-vated by psychopathic or psychiatric disorders. It has gotten so that this has become the standard motivation for practically all evildoers. Of course, again, there is always an exceptional picture that for other reasons may be able to survive at the box-office in spite of this handi-cap. But you cannot with any sense of security depend on this. Pic-tures in this category are certainly a very high risk.[28]

James M. Cain's depiction of middle-class malaise and adultery—like the "adult" 1940s *noir* films of the war years—was at ironic odds with this postwar 1950s climate, its baby boom, suburbanization, and domestic con-sumerism. Penned in 1937, Cain's *Serenade,* purchased for $35,000 by Warner Bros. after the critical and box-office success of *Double Indemnity,* was planned during World War II. It was another Cain novel rumored to be in production by late 1944–45—many trades even included it in Holly-wood's wartime crime cycle. But it never came to fruition in the 1940s. Banned by Breen, the project was delayed by PCA censors for more than a decade, and the film wasn't released until 1956. By this time the industry, its production context, censorship circumstances, creative talent, and cast had changed. Rather than sultry 1940s *noir* innuendo, the provocative story was watered down beyond recognition. Warners' film diluted Cain's salacious fiction into tame, romantic soap opera in the style of *Love Is a Many Splen-dored Thing* (released the year before). The film not only lost its hard-boiled edge, but it also transformed into a big-budget musical melodrama—cost-ing a hefty $2,010,000—shot in WarnerColor on location in Mexico, where churches are "used primarily for praying and marriage, rather than candle-light meals of iguana soup and lovemaking by the altar."[29] It showcased 1950s genres, new technology, exotic travelogue locales, and runaway pro-duction filmed outside Hollywood. It became a Mario Lanza star vehicle—

seeking a singer rather than an actor to revolve the narrative around (and promoted RCA Victor's high-fidelity sound-track album in hopes of milking profits from ancillary merchandise). Void of *noir* style, sets were bright exteriors and places of worship—capitalizing on the resurgent popularity of religion in the 1950s. The couple does not run off together, nor do they shoot each other; instead, she gets hit by a bus!

Noir took a hit after the war, especially by the 1950s, as motion picture studios produced more color films—made increasingly affordable with cheaper Eastman Kodak "monopack" color systems, which replaced the expensive three-strip Technicolor process—with widescreen technologies and stereophonic sound to compete with the growing popularity of small-screen black-and-white television (offering much more cost-effective entertainment in the comfort of suburban living rooms). Even Alfred Hitchcock's 1950s adaptation of a hard-boiled Cornell Woolrich novel, *Rear Window* (1954), was a big-budget, widescreen Technicolor production. Its shadowy visual design, dramatic low-key lighting, and claustrophobic confines of voyeuristic wheelchair-bound photographer L. B. Jeffries' (James Stewart) apartment building reveal film noir's influence. Hitchcock originally intended to film on location in New York City but, dissatisfied with the lighting and color tests, instead created a massive studio replica set on a grand scale and cast moody hues on the walls and courtyard. Hollywood's predilection for big, color, widescreen films was counter to the appeal of more modest black-and-white *noir* films—which offered neither the color nor the expanded image as an alternative to monochrome television. Many B films were economically reworked into telefilms. Playing it safe, escapist and politically unrisky genres like breezy color musicals, comedies, westerns, melodramas, science fiction, fantasy, and TV cops were popular by the late 1940s and 1950s. Broadway adaptations soared as "pre-sold commodities" to further minimize the risk of controversial content while competing with television and live Broadway theater productions.

If Cain's *Serenade* had been another tough World War II–era Warner Bros. (or Universal, Paramount, RKO, Columbia, or PRC) black-and-white crime film, cast with Bogart and Bacall (or Rita Hayworth), written, designed, shot, and directed by Hawks, Curtiz, or Dmytryk—or hyphenate émigré stylists like Wilder, Siodmak, Lang, or Ulmer—after the release of *Double Indemnity* when it was purchased by the studio to capitalize on the red-meat bandwagon, it would likely be a *noir* film consistent with the 1940s period style. Instead, the 1950s picture, though still a Warners adaptation of a Cain novel (even with *noir* veteran Anthony Mann directing), little resembled a film noir. The censorship circumstances that made *noir* possible—

moderate easing of the PCA to allow filming of hard-boiled fiction while still requiring creative aesthetic handling and suggestive innuendo—were absent here. The PCA banned Cain's story outright for over a decade because of homosexuality and a host of other taboos. When Warner Bros. finally shot the project (after several false starts, cancellations, and different casts since the 1940s), the PCA was greatly liberalized and Breen had left, Warners had become far more conservative after the war, and the industry was in post-HUAC, antitrust decline. By the 1950s, World War II's constrained filmmaking circumstances and 1940s cultural climate were gone, the Code censorship so vital to *noir* had changed, and the gritty bite of Cain's novel was replaced by color musical-sappy melodrama with Lanza instead of Bogart. Warner Bros. promoted it not like a *noir* red-meat story but as "the story of a farm-hand who won fame as a singer and nearly lost his soul as a man," yet he "sings as never before!"[30]

Events by the late 1950s effectively undermined the unique production climate so crucial to film noir. Government efforts to regulate the film industry (HUAC, the Paramount decision, the *Miracle* case) complicated and compromised the studio industry's self-censorship. While Washington in effect dismantled Hollywood's oligopoly that had enabled PCA enforcement, and studios in a cold war "Red Scare" blacklisted undesirable or "uncooperative" members from its workforce, a different latitude was allowed on salacious topics (formerly taboo to the PCA) as the film industry focused on ideological and political concerns in the McCarthy era that made racy screen sex, violence, and cleavage look like tame transgressions. The postwar era influenced narrative strategies, genre conventions, and film style. As PCA censorship eased, a growing cold war national and industry political agenda changed Hollywood crime cycles, who was filming them, how they were stylistically achieved on film, and the *noir* trend, as readily evident in the screen adaptation of James M. Cain fiction. The red-meat cycle was long over by the time Warners produced *Serenade.* The filmmaking climate transformed an industry now more inclined to shy away from liberal, hard-hitting creative talent as the cold war era eclipsed the New Deal social and cultural climate of the 1930s and war years. As postwar audiences moved away from urban centers (farther from first-run theaters) to outlying suburban areas and raised families, many women resumed more traditional, domestic, gender roles (as Rosie the Riveter returned home), and the Red Scare's xenophobia countered a wartime synergistic creative climate where European émigré talent in Hollywood had honed *noir*'s aesthetic. The family-oriented baby boom of the postwar years also countered the adult themes of film noir and Cain's fiction.

Many postwar genres convey *noir*'s bleak cynicism and dark visual style. Don Siegel, who had created elaborate *noir* psychological montage sequences for *Blues in the Night* and *Casablanca* and would later gain fame with *Dirty Harry* (1971), directed sci-fi *noir* cult classic *Invasion of the Body Snatchers* (1955, Allied Artists / Walter Wanger), starring Kevin McCarthy in a paranoid allegory of the Red Scare, and low-budget social prison gang *noir Crime in the Streets* (1956, Allied Artists), starring James Whitmore, John Cassavettes, Sal Mineo, and Mark Rydell. Gangsters, ex-cons, and a corrupt former police captain pull a bank heist in Edward Small's *Kansas City Confidential* (1952), released through United Artists. Police detective and war veteran Dave Bannion (Glenn Ford) takes on the mob and settles a score after they kill his wife in Fritz Lang's *The Big Heat* (1953). Ex-boxer longshoreman Terry Malloy (Marlon Brando) informs on mob union racketeers who murder his brother, Charley (Rod Steiger)—one of their own—in Kazan's *On the Waterfront* (1954). From the claustrophobic venetian blinds splintering Terry's cab ride as his brother pulls a gun on him to the screeching cars and black alleys where Terry flees and Charley is killed, Kazan uses exquisite *noir* visual style in his cold war–era social realist crime picture that deals with urban corruption, working-class struggles, gangsters, organized labor, and federal detectives persuading Brando's conflicted antihero to rat on his gang of thugs. (In cutting corners director of photography Boris Kaufman had to craftily light the blinds and improvise in "the contender" scene when independent producer Sam Spiegel forgot to budget for rear-projection in the back window of the taxi—Columbia's Harry Cohn apparently had little faith in the provocative "message" project.)[31]

In a new breed of espionage and red-hysteria pictures, "commies" took the place of gangsters. Anti-commie *noirs* included *The Woman on Pier 13* (1950, a.k.a. *I Married a Communist*), produced at RKO under Howard Hughes's stewardship; Harry M. Popkin's independent production *The Thief* (1952, United Artists), starring Ray Milland as a nuclear scientist turned communist spy; and Samuel Fuller's *Pickup on South Street* (1953, 20th Century–Fox), starring Richard Widmark as a pickpocket embroiled in espionage and Thelma Ritter as the commie-hater killed by a red spy. Even Warner Bros. was no longer the risk-taking, hard-hitting, progressive-minded "liberal" proponent of social change that it had been during the 1930s and World War II. Jack Warner was disgusted by labor union discord in 1945 and, like many moguls, spoke out against the "red threat" at the HUAC hearings. By the 1950s Warners was getting into TV westerns and *Dragnet* in a big way and produced the patriotic crime fighting *I Was a Communist for the F.B.I.* (1951)—the *Confessions of a Nazi Spy* for a new era.

Inspired by Washington's crime hearings, Warners released United States Pictures' *The Enforcer* (1951), with Bogart starring as a savvy G-man cleaning up the mob and trying to foil the brutal crime business Murder, Inc., while protecting an informer witness testifying against the gang. Warner Bros. proudly unveiled John Wayne and Robert Fellows's right-wing, pro-HUAC *Big Jim McLain* (1953), in which Korean War veteran and HUAC investigator Duke combats the "red menace" at Pearl Harbor.

At 20th Century–Fox Zanuck wrote in July 1952:

> I have tried to analyze *why* every anti-Communist picture made so far has proven to be a box-office flop . . . [T]hey were so violently anti-Communistic . . . [R]ather than emphasizing entertainment and showmanship . . . they all managed to turn themselves into "message" pictures. In most instances, they failed because they were "obvious" . . . [P]eople are going to the theatre today to escape lectures, propaganda, politics and constant talk, talk, talk which they get on television and the radio. I doubt very much whether [liberal message pictures] *Snake Pit, Gentleman's Agreement,* and *Grapes of Wrath* would be successful if released today. Like everything else, audiences change . . . I cannot think of a picture on the market today which deals with a "thinking problem" and which is also successful.[32]

Wartime *noir* films were provocative and challenging. They demanded thinking from filmgoers just to figure them out. Their elaborate, even convoluted plots, foggy mysteries with open questions, oblique dialogue, murky shadows, and adult themes for viewers to actively piece together, like psychologically flawed criminals and detectives investigating a problem, would change in the face of challenges in the postwar years.

American culture, Washington, and Hollywood studios had come a long way from World War II to the cold war climate of the 1950s. Facing new challenges and different concerns in a film industry that in many ways had really been transformed, cold war crime films often drew on 1950s melodrama and television police procedurals—conventions that ultimately overshadowed and replaced earlier, shadier, and seedier hard-boiled fiction influences; rather than featuring a criminal or dubious protagonist as in the war years, *noir* antiheroes were more likely to be on the other side of law and order, portrayed as crime-fighting enforcers experiencing domestic trauma (even anticommunist red hysteria). Postwar *noir* films like Fritz Lang's *The Big Heat,* Robert Aldrich's *Kiss Me Deadly* (1955), and Orson Welles's *Touch of Evil* (1958) dealt with cold war anxieties, psychological instability, paranoia, fear of the A-bomb and atomic trauma. Cold war *noir* featured a different kind of tormented masculinity from that of the war years. Its G-men, war veterans, and detectives had other lives; many were also fathers, family men, virile and patriotic. Women, often molls, mistresses, or wives, more frequently adopted nurturing roles in domestic spaces. Perhaps a sign of the apocalyptic atomic age, augmenting the hand-to-hand combat and gun battles of World War II–era *noir,* sabotage and cataclysmic explosions blasted automobiles, igniting and destroying spouses and big-ticket personal property items in cold war *noir.* Ford's wife dies in a fiery boom behind the wheel (as he reads "The Three Little Kittens" bedtime story to his little girl), and Lee Marvin's gangster scalds and disfigures moll Gloria Graham's face with boiling coffee, invoking the psychic fears of nuclear trauma in *The Big Heat. Kiss Me Deadly* closes with an unforgettable, and apocalyptic, atomic blast. *Touch of Evil* wrapped the classic *noir* cycle with Welles's fluidly moving long take, shot on location and ticking away, ending in the deafening bang of a car bomb. Jazz melodrama, corruption, informing, and brooding *noir* documentary style resurface in *Sweet Smell of Success* (1957), starring Tony Curtis and Burt Lancaster, shot by James Wong Howe. Hollywood B-film production was successfully rechanneled into *noir* television crime dramas like Blake Edwards's *Peter Gunn* (1958–61) and Quinn Martin's *The Fugitive* (1963–67) by independent tele-film production companies. By the early 1960s Jack Warner personally produced anticommunist propaganda films for the U.S. government. *Red Nightmare* (1962), for example, featured *Dragnet* star Jack Webb warning folks, with documentary-style "voice of God" authority, how to thwart Reds in the suburbs. The moody duplicity and cold war paranoia in John Frankenheimer's spy thriller *The Manchurian Candidate* (1962) reveals the legacy of World War II–era *noir* as tormented Korean War veterans Frank Sinatra and Laurence Harvey return home to nightmares—battling insanity, communist plots, and psychological demons after being brainwashed. As the Hollywood film industry, its self-regulated PCA censorship, and American culture changed, so, too, did film noir, eventually tapering off by the late 1950s and early 1960s.

Wartime *Noir*'s Enduring Legacy

The impact of the war on 1940s Hollywood advanced the evolution of film noir style and narrative conventions. Unique World War II conditions influenced studio production practices, available materials, opportunities (and authority) of wartime creative personnel, and how these films were produced and marketed. Hollywood filmmaking techniques enabled and accelerated the development of *noir* style. Wartime shooting capitalized on constraints by relying on stark newsreel style to emphasize its graphic, red-meat topics and racy content and to maximize visual suggestion via "sordid" milieu in the effort to transcend Production Code restrictions. As 1940s *noir* cinematographers John Seitz and James Wong Howe and director Billy Wilder suggest, the film industry's war-related economizing emulated the realist style of documentary newsreels in the midst of tremendous studio production shortages. Hollywood's wartime production environment—with rationed electricity and lighting, recycled sets (disguised in low-key shadow, smoke, artificial fog, and rain), tarped studio back lots, enclosed sound stages, and blackouts—would later be countered by increasing postwar location shooting and lighting conventions that subsequently redefined *noir*'s realist aesthetic (as a lighter, grayer *film gris* in the absence of these war-related limitations) during the postwar period.

Rather than World War II interrupting the development of film noir, the war was a catalyst that accelerated the definitive "look" in these films and narrative elements (visual flashbacks, voice-over narration, and unique story structures), conveying an overwhelming sense of fatalism and doom that complied with PCA censorship. Filmmakers tried to avoid OWI regulation by using nonwar—that is, not combat-related or home-front-related—story cycles. While the OWI and PCA both endorsed positive views of American society and culture during World War II, within this wartime context these regulatory strictures contributed to *noir* screen images showing a dark underside to the war. As World War II enabled greater opportunity for new studio talent, film noir was shaped by exemplary individuals—including women, European émigrés, and older men ineligible for military duty—who were film stylists with distinctive aesthetic concerns in privileged positions of authority as a result in large part of wartime conditions in this industrial setting. Women and émigrés were given creative rein throughout Hollywood's wartime period. *Noir* evolved as a definitive style used by certain filmmakers both to comply with and to avoid regulation altogether during the war.

World War II–era films noir from the 1940s have become enduring classics. These "red meat" pictures, provocative in their day, are fascinating because they live on as outstanding artistic works. Their rich, brooding style and tough stories are all the more impressive today and continue to be popular among film fans and scholars decades later. They remain a remarkable, innovative, and unique phenomenon—perhaps even a historical anomaly. They capture a different time, place, and spirit in 1940s American culture and wartime Hollywood. Produced as commercial projects in a commerce-oriented American film industry at the height of the classical studio system, they endured the pressures and the stresses of war during a period of motion picture censorship. It was vital that these films were made during this time in history, like vivid time capsules and cultural products of 1940s America and classic Hollywood. The climate of this time in many ways cultivated *noir*. The movie industry's studio system was necessary for the development of these films, as was PCA censorship. Film noir may never have been possible, however, without the war. In regulating screen content and for producing *noir* films, World War II filmmaking conditions somehow struck a balance, neither too restrictive nor too lax, to foster creative freedom and ingenuity that, in retrospect, was ideal for the development of these masterworks. As the studio system and PCA censorship eroded over the 1950s, *noir* films and the conditions that produced them declined. The beautifully black cinematography of *noir,* especially those films from the 1940s World War II era, is often described as a lost art form that remains unsurpassed in style, vivid design, elaborate lighting, stark photography, and stunning composition. These extraordinary pictures—their wit, pacing, indelible stars, and unforgettable legacy—still excite and dazzle moviegoers, whether film fans, students, art house connoisseurs, or late night insomniacs discovering film noir for the first time (much like critics and other film lovers did many years ago). It is inspiring that many filmmakers today strive to emulate these 1940s films and to keep their spirit and their timeless black-and-white cinema art alive for new generations of filmmakers, fans, and scholars.

Notes

Abbreviations

AC   *American Cinematographer*
AHC   Alfred Hitchcock Collection, Margaret Herrick Library
CGC   Cary Grant Collection, Margaret Herrick Library
HR   *Hollywood Reporter*
JWC   Jack Warner Collection, University of Southern California Cinema-Television Library
LAT   *Los Angeles Times*
MHL   Margaret Herrick Library, Academy of Motion Picture Arts and Sciences
MPAA-PCA Files Motion Picture Association of America Production Code Administration Files, Margaret Herrick Library
MPH   *Motion Picture Herald*
NYHT   *New York Herald-Tribune*
NYT   *New York Times*
PBC   Press Book Collection, University of Southern California Cinema-Television Library
PCA   Production Code Administration (also the Hays Office)
PCPF   Paramount Collection Production Files, Margaret Herrick Library
PCSF   Paramount Collection Script Files, Margaret Herrick Library
SA   David O. Selznick Archives, Harry Ransom Humanities Research Center, University of Texas at Austin
USC   University of Southern California Cinema-Television Library
WBA   USC Warner Bros. Archives, School of Cinema Television, University of Southern California, Los Angeles
WSC   William Schaefer Collection, University of Southern California Cinema-Television Library, Los Angeles

Chapter 1. Introduction

1. Paul Schrader, "Notes on Film Noir," *Film Comment* 8, no. 1 (1972): 8–9.
2. Andrew Sarris and Raymond Durgnat, cited in Austin Whitten, "The Phantom Lady" Program Notes (Film Buff Series) at Academy of Motion Picture Arts and Sciences, Margaret Herrick Library (MHL), Beverly Hills, California, undated, 2.
3. Paul Fussell, *Wartime: Understanding and Behavior in the Second World War* (New York: Oxford, 1989), preface, 1–2, 195.
4. Raymonde Borde and Etienne Chaumeton, *A Panorama of American Film Noir, 1941–1953*, trans. Paul Hammond (San Francisco: City Lights, 2002), 9. Originally published as *Panorama du film noir Américain, 1941–1953* (Paris: Editions du Minuit, 1955).
5. Janey Place, "Women in *Film Noir*," in *Women in Film Noir,* ed. E. Ann Kaplan (London: British Film Institute, 1980), 35, 41–42.
6. Fred Stanley, "Hollywood Turns to 'Hate' Films: Government Lifts Ban on Showing Jap Brutality—Various Other Matters," *New York Times* (*NYT*), Feb. 6, 1944.
7. Schrader, "Notes on Film Noir," 8–9.
8. See Robert Sklar, *Movie-Made America* (New York: Random House, 1975); Thomas

Schatz, *Boom and Bust: American Cinema in the 1940s* (New York: Scribner, 1997); Thomas Schatz, *Hollywood Genres: Formulas, Filmmaking, and the Studio System* (New York: Random House, 1981); Raymonde Borde and Etienne Chaumeton, *A Panorama of American Film Noir*, trans. Paul Hammond (San Francisco: City Lights, 2002), originally published as *Panorama du film noir Americain, 1941–1953* (Paris: Editions du Minuit, 1955); Paul Schrader, "Notes on Film Noir," *Film Comment* 8, no. 1 (1972); Alain Silver and Elizabeth Ward, *Film Noir: An Encyclopedic Reference to the American Style* (Woodstock, NY: Overlook, 1979); David A. Cook, *A History of Narrative Film* (New York: Norton, 1981); Robert Porfirio, "No Way Out: Existential Motifs in the Film Noir," *Sight and Sound* 45, no. 4 (1976); Robert B. Ray, *A Certain Tendency of the Hollywood Cinema, 1930–1980* (Princeton: Princeton University Press, 1985); Frank Krutnik, *In a Lonely Street: Film Noir, Genre, Masculinity* (New York: Routledge, 1991); Brian Neve, *Film and Politics in America: A Social Tradition* (London: Routledge, 1992); James Naremore, "Film Noir: The History of an Idea," *Film Quarterly* 49, no. 2 (winter 1995–96), repr. in James Naremore, *More Than Night* (Berkeley: University of California Press, 1998).

9.   Naremore, "Film Noir: The History of an Idea," 14–17.
10. Frank Krutnik, *In a Lonely Street: Film Noir, Genre, Masculinity* (New York: Routledge, 1991).
11. Borde and Chaumeton, *Panorama of American Film Noir*, 6–12, 16, 21, 29.
12. Nino Frank, "Un Nouveau genre 'policier': L'Aventure criminelle," *L'Ecran Français* 61 (Aug. 28, 1946): 8–9, 14–16.
13. Jean Pierre Chartier, "Les Américains aussi font des films noirs," *Revue du cinéma* 2 (Nov. 1, 3, 1946): 66–70.
14. Sklar, *Movie-Made America*, 253.
15. Thomas Schatz, *Boom and Bust: The American Cinema in the 1940s* (New York: Scribner, 1997), 204–6, 232–39; Thomas Schatz, *Hollywood Genres: Formulas, Filmmaking, and the Studio System* (New York: Random House, 1981).
16. David A. Cook, *A History of Narrative Film*, 4th ed. (New York: Norton, 2004), 377n6.
17. Tom Flinn, "Three Faces of Film Noir," in *Kings of the Bs: Working within the Hollywood System*, ed. Todd McCarthy and Charles Flynn (New York: Dutton, 1975), 155.

Chapter 2. The Elements of *Noir* Come Together

Epigraph. Josef von Sternberg, *Fun in a Chinese Laundry* (San Francisco: Mercury House, 1965), 325.

1.   Cook, *History of Narrative Film*, 94.
2.   Ibid.
3.   Ibid., 94, 291–94.
4.   Rudolph Arnheim, quoted in Marilyn Yaquinto, *Pump 'Em Full of Lead: A Look at Gangsters on Film* (New York: Twayne, 1998), 20.
5.   Richard B. Jewell and Vernon Harbin, *The RKO Story* (London: Arlington Press, 1982), 150.
6.   Ibid., 120.
7.   Brian Neve, *Film and Politics in America: A Social Tradition* (London: Routledge, 1992), 4; Brian Neve, personal correspondence, July 6, 2004.
8.   Don Miller, *B Movies* (New York: Ballantine, 1973), 131–33.
9.   Neve, personal correspondence, July 6, 2004.
10. Joseph Breen to Joseph Nolan, re. *Stranger on the Third Floor*, May 7–July 24, 1940, Motion Picture Association of America Production Code Administration (MPAA-PCA) file, MHL.
11. *Blind Alley* memoranda, 1935–39, MPAA-PCA file, MHL.
12. Ibid.
13. Breen to Nolan (see note 10 above).
14. Flinn, "Three Faces of Film Noir," 156. Lynd Ward would design *This Gun for Hire*.
15. Edwin Schallert, "Gallup to Conduct Poll on Double Bill Issue," *Los Angeles Times* (*LAT*), May 16, 1940, A11.
16. Edwin Schallert, "Betty Field, Preston 'Shepherd of Hills' Duo," *LAT*, May 17, 1940, A10.
17. Edwin Schallert, "RKO Signs Lorre for Two Leading Roles," *LAT*, May 29, 1940, 15.
18. Edwin Schallert, "Beery, Carrillo Again Pals in Wyoming Tale," *LAT*, June 28, 1940, 16.
19. Philip K. Scheuer, "Town Called Hollywood: Matter of Bearing (False) Witness!" *LAT*, June 30, 1940, C2–4.

20. Jewell and Harbin, *RKO Story*, 140.

21. Richard B. Jewell, interview by author, July 15, 2004.

22. RKO Radio Pictures budget and final cost for *Stranger on the Third Floor*, Dec. 28, 1940, UCLA Arts Library Special Collections, Young Research Library, University of California, Los Angeles.

23. RKO press book for *Stranger on the Third Floor*, Aug. 16, 1940, Research Collections, New York Public Library for the Performing Arts.

24. Ibid.

25. "'Argentine Nights' Okay; 'Stranger' Interesting: Fine Performance By John McGuire," *Hollywood Reporter* (*HR*), Aug. 30, 1940, 3.

26. Philip K. Scheuer, "Ingenious Film Shown," *LAT*, Aug. 30, 1940, A11.

27. Jimmie Fidler, "In Hollywood," *LAT*, Sept. 4, 1940, 15.

28. Bosley Crowther, "Stranger on the Third Floor," *NYT*, Sept. 2, 1940, 19:2.

29. "Stranger on the Third Floor," *Harrison's Reports*, Sept. 7, 1940, 142.

30. "Stranger on the Third Floor," *Variety*, Sept. 4, 1940, 18; "Stranger on the Third Floor," *Variety*, Sept. 13, 1940, MHL; "Stranger on the Third Floor," *Motion Picture Herald* (*MPH*), Sept. 7, 1940, 40.

31. Richard B. Jewell, "RKO Film Grosses, 1929–1951: The C. J. Tevlin Ledger," *Historical Journal of Film, Radio, and Television* 14, no. 1 (1994): apps. 2–3; H. Mark Glancy, "MGM Film Grosses, 1924–1948: The Eddie Mannix Ledger," *Historical Journal of Film, Radio, and Television* 12, no. 2 (1992): 134, app. 1. (RKO's higher-budgeted A pictures ran $500,000 to $1,000,000, MGM's $900,000 to $1,500,000.)

32. RKO Radio Pictures budget for *Stranger on the Third Floor* (see note 22 above); Jewell, personal correspondence, 2000.

33. Jewell and Harbin, *RKO Story*, 144.

34. Jewell, "RKO Film Grosses," app. 1.

35. Schatz, *Boom and Bust*, 236.

36. Frank, "Un Nouveau genre 'policier,'" 8–9, 14; Borde and Chaumeton, *Panorama of American Film Noir*, 30–33.

37. *Suspicion* publicity, Dec. 1941, Cary Grant's personal scrapbook #13, Cary Grant Collection (CGC), MHL.

38. Joseph Breen to Alfred Hitchcock, Oct. 4, 1941, Alfred Hitchcock Collection (AHC), MHL; Jewell and Harbin, *RKO Story*, 167; Jewell, "RKO Film Grosses," app. 1; Jewell, interview by the author, Feb. 22, 1996. *Suspicion*'s bright, polished production values were similar to those of Selznick's prestige picture *Rebecca* the year before.

39. Hitchcock to George Schaefer, Aug. 18, 1941, telegram, production file, AHC, MHL; Cary Grant, interview by James Monaco for "Grant on Hitchcock Films," *Take One* 5, no. 2 (May 1976): 20; Leonard Leff, *Hitchcock and Selznick* (New York: Weidenfeld and Nicolson, 1987), 93; Jewell and Harbin, *RKO Story*, 167; Jewell interview, Feb. 22, 1996.

40. Joan Fontaine, interview by Gregory Speck for *Interview*, Feb. 1987, 64–65.

41. Eric Ergenbright and Jack Smalley, "Star Factory," *Ladies' Home Journal*, July 1937, 14–15, 54–55.

42. Fontaine to Hitchcock, undated memorandum, preproduction file, *Suspicion*, AHC, MHL.

43. David O. Selznick to Joan Fontaine, Aug. 15, 1940, 1–2, David O. Selznick Archive (SA), Harry Ransom Humanities Research Center, University of Texas at Austin.

44. Ibid.

45. Figures on Fontaine's salary, contract, talent files, Sept. 8, 1939–Aug. 1, 1944, and the Selznick wire to Danny O'Shea, Oct. 10, 1941, all in SA.

46. Thomas Elsaesser, "Tales of Sound and Fury: Observations on the Family Melodrama," in *Film Theory and Criticism*, ed. Gerald Mast, Marshall Cohen, and Leo Braudy, 4th ed. (New York: Rutgers University Press, 1992), 526. See also Schatz, *Boom and Bust*, 236; and Diane Waldman, "Horror and Domesticity: The Modern Gothic Romance of the 1940s" (PhD diss., University of Wisconsin, Madison, 1981).

47. Preview-audience survey cards for *Suspicion*, June 13–23, 1941, AHC, MHL.

48. *Suspicion* Publicity, Dec. 1941, CGC, MHL.

49. "Grant Changes Type in Picture," undated Los Angeles trade clipping, CGC, MHL.

50. George Schaefer to Hitchcock, telegram, Nov. 24, 1941, AHC, MHL.

51. Jewell, "RKO Film Grosses," app. 1.
52. Raymond Chandler, quoted in Dorothy Gardiner and Kathrine Sorley Walker, *Raymond Chandler Speaking* (Boston: Houghton Mifflin, 1977), 52.
53. Domestic gross earnings, Warner Bros. Cost and Income Figures for 1926–1936 Films, Aug. 31, 1944, William Schaefer Collection (WSC), USC Cinema-Television Library, University of Southern California; story and production files for *The Maltese Falcon*, 1930–31, USC Warner Bros. Archives (WBA), University of Southern California, Los Angeles; Darryl Zanuck to Jason Joy, Jan. 6, 1931, MPAA-PCA file for *The Maltese Falcon*, MHL.
54. Warner Bros. production correspondence for *The Maltese Falcon*, 1931, WBA; PCA correspondence for *The Maltese Falcon*, Jan. 6–June 25, 1931, MPAA-PCA file, MHL.
55. Schatz, *Boom and Bust*, 237–38.
56. John Huston, memoranda, March 31, 1947; June 20, 1941, WBA.
57. "Hays Purity Coder Adamant on Resigning," *Variety*, June 25, 1941, 4. See also Gregory D. Black, *Hollywood Censored: Morality Codes, Catholics, and the Movies* (Cambridge, UK: Cambridge University Press, 1994), 292; Breen to Hays, March 25, 1941, MPAA-PCA file, MHL; Breen to Hitchcock, Oct. 4, 1941, AHC, MHL; Jewell and Harbin, *RKO Story*, 141; Leonard J. Leff and Jerold L. Simmons, *The Dame in the Kimono: Hollywood, Censorship, and the Production Code from the 1920s to the 1960s* (New York: Doubleday, 1990), 110, 121.
58. Breen to Hays, May 31, 1941, MPAA-PCA files, MHL; see also various letters from June 3 to Oct. 18, 1941, in the WBA archives; and PCA letters from May 22 to Sept. 10, 1941, in the MPAA-PCA files, MHL.
59. John Huston, *An Open Book* (New York: Knopf, 1980), 79.
60. Al Alleborn to T. C. Wright, budget correspondence, June 2–Oct. 18, 1941, WBA.
61. Warner Bros. Cost and Income Figures for 1941–1946 Films, Aug. 31, 1955, WSC.
62. Ibid.
63. Warner Bros. press book for *The Maltese Falcon*, 1941, WBA.
64. Bosley Crowther, "The Maltese Falcon," *NYT*, Oct. 4, 1941, 18:2.
65. Fred Stanley, "Hollywood Peeks into the Future," *NYT*, Feb. 21, 1943.
66. Ibid.
67. Thomas Doherty, *Projections of War: Hollywood, American Culture, and World War II* (New York: Columbia University Press, 1993); Schatz, *Boom and Bust*.
68. Budget and story files for *This Gun for Hire*, 1941, Paramount Collection production file (PCPF), MHL.
69. Ibid.; Gene D. Phillips, *Graham Greene: The Films of His Fiction*, excerpt from Los Angeles County Museum of Art Program Notes for "This Gun for Hire," Sept. 18, 1980, MHL.
70. "Windfall for the Salvagers," *NYT*, Oct. 26, 1941.
71. Beverly Heisner, *Hollywood Art: Art Direction in the Days of the Great Studios* (Jefferson, NC: McFarland, 1990), 166; John Hambley and Patrick Downing, *The Art of Hollywood: A Thames Television Exhibition at the Victoria and Albert Museum* (London: Thames Television, 1979), 37.
72. Budget and story files for *This Gun for Hire*, 1941, PCPF, MHL.
73. PCA to Luigi Luraschi (Paramount Censorship Department), "RE: note changes and improvements made," Oct. 23–30, 1941, MPAA-PCA file, MHL; PCA to Luigi Luraschi, "RE: Happy to report script meets the requirements of the Production Code," Nov. 7, 1941, MPAA-PCA file, MHL.
74. PCA to Luraschi, Dec. 8–9, 1941, MPAA-PCA file, MHL.
75. Paramount preproduction file, Aug. 1–Dec. 12, 1941, MHL.
76. Preliminary cost of $488,295 eventually totaled $512,423. Budget, 1941, PCPF, MHL.
77. *Variety Weekly*, Jan. 6, 1943.
78. Paramount press book for *This Gun for Hire*, 1942, USC Press Book Collection (PBC).
79. Edward Greif, "This Gun for Hire," *Motion Picture Daily*, March 17, 1942; "This Gun for Hire," *MPH*, March 21, 1942.
80. "This Gun for Hire," *Look*, April 12, 1942; Philip Hartung, "This Gun for Hire," *Commonwealth*, May 29, 1942; "Movie of the Week: *This Gun for Hire*, Ladd and Lake Make an Unusual Melodrama," *Life*, June 22, 1942, 48, 50, 53.
81. Warner Bros. press book for *All through the Night*, 1942, WBA.
82. Story Department correspondence for *Everybody Comes to Rick's*, Dec. 8, 1941, WBA; "West Coast Lights Dimmed," *Saint Louis Star-Times*, Dec. 8, 1941, 20.

Chapter 3. Hollywood in the Aftermath of Pearl Harbor

1. James Anderson, quoted in the Associated Press (AP), *World War II* (New York: AP, 1989), 56–57.

2. Fussell, *Wartime*, ix.

3. John Keegan, *The Second World War* (New York: Penguin, 1990), 591; Harold Rabinowitz, ed., *America in the '40s* (New York: Reader's Digest, 1998), cites 405,399 casualties, 670,846 injuries.

4. William Styron, quoted in AP, *World War II*, 143.

5. Raymond Chandler to Mrs. Alfred Knopf, Aug. 23, 1939, in *Selected Letters of Raymond Chandler*, ed. Frank MacShane (New York: Columbia, 1981), 9.

6. Navy official history, quoted in AP, *World War II*, 64.

7. Tom Bradley, quoted in Ibid.

8. "Los Angeles Blacked Out: Bombs Fire Jap Battleship," *LAT*, Dec. 11, 1941, 1.

9. Richard E. Osborne, *The "Casablanca" Companion: The Movie Classic and Its Place in History* (Indianapolis: Riebel-Rogue, 1997), 143; Federal Bureau of Investigation Confidential Files, *Communist Activity in the Entertainment Industry:* FBI *Surveillance Files on Hollywood, 1942–1958*, ed. Daniel Leab (Bethesda, MD: University Press of America, 1991).

10. James M. Cain, quoted in Roy Hoopes, *Cain: The Biography of James M. Cain* (New York: Holt, Rinehart, and Winston, 1982), 316, 320.

11. Schatz, *Boom and Bust*, 132–34.

12. Fussell, *Wartime*, 4, 195.

13. Chandler to Alfred Knopf, Feb. 8, 1943, quoted in MacShane, *Selected Letters*, 24.

14. Leff and Simmons, *Dame in the Kimono*, 125–26.

15. *Variety*, Oct. 28, 1942, 5; also cited in Schatz, *Boom and Bust*, 173. Schatz (169–74) notes that Warner Bros. focused on producing A pictures while others—Disney, Hal Roach, and Fox's old B-picture studio (on Western Ave.)—retooled entirely, redirecting operations to produce war films.

16. *Variety*, Nov. 10, 1943, 2; also cited in Arthur Lyons, *Death on the Cheap: The Lost B Movies of Film Noir* (New York: Da Capo, 2000), 18.

17. Schatz, *Boom and Bust*, 132–34.

18. John Morton Blum, *V Was for Victory: Politics and American Culture during World War II* (San Diego: Harcourt Brace Jovanovich, 1976), 31.

19. Koppes and Black explain that taking the cue from Washington, studios "gave the public" what Hollywood—and the government—"wanted the public to have." Claiming to give American moviegoers what they wanted, justifying the claim with box-office popularity, the studio system cartel actually "controlled the range of choice." In reality popular culture was not "popularly determined"; rather, the public "bought what it was given." The OWI's Bureau of Motion Pictures wanted to be the "sole spokesperson" for the government with the studios but was undercut by the military, which did not share OWI's objectives. Wartime films "fused two powerful myths" with "deep roots" in American popular and political culture: (1) the "division of the world into slave and free," with forces of either "ultimate evil or righteousness," and (2) the "universalized version of the idea of regeneration through war," which produced unity. In messages promising that the war would bring "internal and international harmony," wartime propaganda "coincidentally helped prepare America for the Cold War" (Clayton R. Koppes and Gregory D. Black, *Hollywood Goes to War* [New York: Free Press, 1987], viii, 113, 324–28). See also Schatz, *Boom and Bust;* Robert James Maddox, *The United States and World War II* (Boulder: Westview Press, 1992), 186; Aljean Harmetz, *Round Up the Usual Suspects: The Making of "Casablanca"* (New York: Hyperion, 1992), 287.

20. Stanley, "Hollywood Turns."

21. Richard B. Jewell, "History of the Sound Film in America" (manuscript on file at School of Cinema-Television, USC, 1997), 46–59.

22. "Hangmen Also Die," *Motion Picture Daily*, March 23, 1943; "Hangmen Also Die," *Daily Variety*, March 23, 1943; "Hangmen Also Die," *Variety*, March 24, 1943; Alton Cook, "*Hangmen Also Die* Shows Czechs' Hatred for Nazis," *New York World-Telegram*, April 16, 1943; James Agee, "Hangmen Also Die," *Nation*, May 1, 1943; press book for *Hangmen Also Die*, 1943, PBC; Freddy Pressburger to Henry Brash, Aug. 3, 1942, Fritz Lang Collection, Box 1:12, USC Cinema-Television Library.

23. "*Film noir*, its development stunted by the PCA's aversion to certain stories by 'hard-boiled' writers like James M. Cain, became established during the war years when censors countenanced their screen adaptation" (Jewell, "History," 46–59); Sheri Chinen Biesen, "Censorship, *Film Noir*, and *Double Indemnity*," *Film and History* 25, nos. 1–2 (1995): 40–52; Sheri Chinen Biesen, "Raising Cain with the Censors, Again: *The Postman Always Rings Twice*," *Literature/Film Quarterly* 28, no. 1 (2000): 41–48.

24. Robert Mitchum, interview, in Lyons, *Death on the Cheap*, 2. Mitchum starred in Monogram's wartime B *noir When Strangers Marry* (1944, later retitled *Betrayed*, produced by the King Brothers, Maurice and Franklin, and directed by William Castle) before his success in *The Story of G.I. Joe* (1945), *Crossfire* (1947), and *Out of the Past*.

25. Mark Robson, interview in *Velvet Light Trap* 10 (1973); also quoted in Lyons, *Death on the Cheap*, 41.

26. "Cinematographers Show How to Achieve Production Economies," *American Cinematographer (AC)* 21, no. 8 (Aug. 1940): 360–62; Harry B. Warner speeches, 1941, Jack Warner Collection (JWC), USC; Harry B. Warner, "Waste More Deadly Than Sabotage," *International Photographer* 14, no. 2 (March 1942): 25; Jack Warner to Peter Lorre, Sept. 27, 1943, JWC.

27. Treatment for *Uncle Charlie*, May 5, 1942, AHC, MHL; Alfred Hitchcock to Joan Fontaine, telegram, June 8, 1942, AHC, MHL.

28. "$5,000 Production: Hitchcock Makes Thriller under WPA Order on New Sets," *Life*, Jan. 25, 1943, 70–73, in Joseph Cotten Collection, USC. Costs for set construction on *Shadow of a Doubt* totaled $2,979. One reason the film is bright is Hitchcock concluded filming well before the dimouts each night in Santa Rosa; the opening scene was filmed in Newark.

29. James Wong Howe, "Visual Suggestion Can Enhance 'Rationed' Sets," *AC* 23, no. 5 (June 1942): 246–47; see also Joseph Valentine, "Using an Actual Town Instead of Movie Sets," *AC* 23, no. 10 (Oct. 1942): 440–62.

30. James Wong Howe, "Documentary Film and Hollywood Techniques," lecture presented at 1943 Hollywood Writers Mobilization and University of California Conference Proceedings, UCLA (Berkeley: University of California Press, 1944), 94–96; repr. as "Documentary Technique in Hollywood," *AC* 25, no. 1 (Jan. 1944): 10, 32.

31. Howe, "Documentary Technique in Hollywood," 10, 32, 246–47; see also Fred Stanley, "Blast at Hollywood: Life Is Real," *NYT*, July 30, 1944; "Cinematographers Show How," 360–62 (see note 26); Warner, "Waste More Deadly," 25; Paul Kerr, "Out of What Past? Notes on the B Film Noir," *Screen Education* 32/33 (autumn/winter 1979–80): 45–65.

32. James Agee, "Sahara," *Nation*, Oct. 8, 1943. A *Hollywood Reporter* review called *Sahara* a "hard-bitten drama of fighting" with "stunningly realistic battle action," commending Maté's photographic style ("Sahara," *HR*, Sept. 27, 1943). Hungarian director Zoltan Korda (brother of British producer Alexander Korda) worked in Britain; Maté shot films in Germany and France (including Carl Dreyer's 1927 *The Passion of Joan of Arc*).

33. Stanley, "Hollywood Turns."

34. "By 1943 fiction and nonfiction war films were entertaining a stage of remarkable symbiosis, with combat dramas providing a (belated) fictional counterpart to the newsreel and documentaries, all of which not only depicted major military engagements but also defined and dramatized the war experience for millions of Americans at home" (Schatz, *Boom and Bust*, 248). See also Doherty, *Projections of War;* and Rabinowitz, *America in the '40s*, 101.

35. Howe, "Documentary Technique in Hollywood," 10, 32.

36. Stanley, "Blast at Hollywood."

37. Ibid.; Joel W. Finler, *The Hollywood Story* (New York: Crown, 1988), 277.

38. Domestic gross earnings, Warner Bros. Cost and Income Figures for 1941–1946 Films, Aug. 31, 1955, WSC; Warner Bros. Story Department correspondence and production reports, Dec. 15–22, 1941, WBA.

39. Jack Warner to Warner Bros. publicity, telegram, May 22, 1942, JWC, USC. (Warner's praising Bogart as the studio's Gable is impressive, considering Warner made no secret that he disliked Bogart.)

40. Warner Bros. press book for *Across the Pacific*, 1942, WBA.

41. Warner Bros. Story Department correspondence, Dec. 11–27, 1941, April 2, 1942, WBA; A. M. Sperber and Eric Lax, *Bogart* (London: Weidenfeld and Nicolson, 1997), 177–92.

42. Warner Bros. Story Department correspondence, Dec. 11–27, 1941, April 2, 1942, WBA; Sperber and Lax, *Bogart*, 177–92; Harmetz, *Round Up the Usual Suspects*, 352; *Casablanca* PCA report, June 23, 1942, MPAA-PCA file, MHL.
43. Jack Warner, *Warner Club News*, March 1942; Harry B. Warner, "Waste More Deadly," 25, JWC; Harmetz, *Round Up the Usual Suspects*, 66.
44. Breen to Jack Warner, May 19, 1942, MPAA-PCA file, MHL.
45. Harmetz, *Round Up the Usual Suspects*, 66, 124.
46. "Windfall for the Salvagers," *NYT*, Oct. 26, 1941; see also Osborne, *"Casablanca" Companion;* Harmetz, *Round Up the Usual Suspects.*
47. Lee Katz and Francis Scheid, quoted in Harmetz, *Round Up the Usual Suspects*, 136.
48. Hal Wallis to Arthur Edeson, memoranda, May 26–June 2, 1942, WBA.
49. "Treacle and indigestible chunks of propaganda [in *Passage to Marseilles*] make it clear how much *Casablanca* gained by being made early in the war before the OWI put its weight behind symbolic uplift" (Harmetz, *Round Up the Usual Suspects*, 66, 124, 287).
50. Warner Bros. press book for *Casablanca*, 1942, WBA, 8.
51. Jewell, "History"; Stanley, "Hollywood Peeks."
52. Stanley, "Hollywood Peeks"; Osborne, *"Casablanca" Companion.*
53. Warner Bros. Cost and Income Figures for 1941–1946 Films, Aug. 31, 1955, WSC.
54. *MPH*, April 18, 1942, 609.
55. Bosley Crowther, "Moontide," *NYT*, April 30, 1942, 14:1.
56. Production correspondence for *Moontide*, in Mark Preminger, Fritz Lang, and 20th Century–Fox Collections, 1941–42, University of Southern California; Patrick McGilligan, *Fritz Lang: The Nature of the Beast* (New York: St. Martin's, 1997), 283–84.
57. Production correspondence and budget for *Street of Chance*, 1942, PCPF, MHL.
58. Press book for *Street of Chance*, Oct. 5, 1942, Special Collections, USC.
59. "'Street of Chance' Absorbs," *HR*, Oct. 3, 1942, 4; Hobe, "Street of Chance," *Variety*, Sept. 30, 1942; "Street of Chance," *Harrison's Reports*, Oct. 3, 1942, 160; "Street of Chance," *MPH*, Oct. 3, 1942, 933.
60. Crowther, "Street of Chance," *NYT*, Nov. 19, 1942, 31:3.
61. Production correspondence and budget for *Ministry of Fear*, July 6–Aug. 21, Nov. 4, 11, 1943, April 27, 1944, PCPF, MHL.
62. Paramount press book for *Ministry of Fear*, 1944–45, PBC.
63. Ibid.
64. "Ministry of Fear," *HR*, Oct. 18, 1944; Alton Cook, "Ministry of Fear," *New York World-Telegram*, Feb. 7, 1945.
65. Production correspondence, July–Dec. 1943, PCPF; PCA correspondence, Sept.–Nov. 1943, MPAA-PCA files, MHL.
66. Walter Baade, *Evolution of Stars and Galaxies* (Cambridge, MA: Harvard University Press, 1963), 44, 51; Walter S. Adams, *Annual Report of the Director of the Mount Wilson Observatory*, 1942–1943, 1943–1944, 3; Carnegie Institution of Washington Yearbook 43 (1943–44), 3; Charles A. Whitney, *The Discovery of our Galaxy* (New York: Knopf, 1971), 253.
67. "Baltimore, 62 N.J. Towns Take Blackout Seriously," *New York Daily Mirror*, Feb. 28, 1942, 5.
68. *LAT* (1940–41), National Weather Service (1945), and City of Pasadena (1943) records (www.wrh.noaa.gov/lox/climate/climate_intro.php); Warner Bros. production file records for *Air Force*, 1942, WBA.
69. Stanley, "Hollywood Turns"; Jewell, "History," 46–59; Biesen, "Censorship"; Biesen, "Raising Cain."

Chapter 4. Censorship, Hard-Boiled Fiction, and Hollywood's "Red Meat" Crime Cycle

Epigraphs. Fred Stanley, "Hollywood Crime and Romance," *NYT*, Nov. 19, 1944; James M. Cain, quoted in David Hanna, "Hays Censors Rile Jim Cain," *Daily News*, Feb. 14, 1944, 11.
1. Stanley, "Hollywood Crime and Romance."
2. Joseph Breen to Louis B. Mayer (MGM), "RE: Violations compelled to reject," Oct. 10, 1935, MPAA-PCA file, MHL. Copies of Breen's letter were sent to John Hammell (Paramount), David O. Selznick (MGM), Jack Warner (Warner Bros.), Nicholas Schenck (MGM Distributing), and Frances Manson (Columbia Reading Dept.).
3. Lawrence Cohn, "All-Time Film Rental Champs," *Variety*, Oct. 15, 1990, M-154.

4.   Billy Wilder, quoted in Philip K. Scheuer, "Film History Made by 'Double Indemnity,'" *LAT*, Aug. 6, 1944, 1, 3.

5.   *Double Indemnity* stirred up considerable fervor before it was approved and produced. Charles Brackett did not have anything to do with the screenplay—by his own choice: he refused to work on it. See Maurice Zolotow, *Billy Wilder in Hollywood* (New York: Harper and Row, 1977), 111.

6.   The major Hollywood studios at this time—Paramount, MGM, 20th Century–Fox, Warner Bros., and RKO—were known as the Big Five and owned 77 percent of all first-run theaters. See Raymond Moley, *The Hays Office* (New York: Bobbs-Merrill, 1945), 77–82. Along with the Big Five, other MPPDA member companies such as major-minor studios Columbia, Universal, and United Artists (known as the Little Three) also agreed to this industry policy of not releasing films without the PCA seal of approval.

7.   Joseph Breen, quoted in Leff and Simmons, *Dame in the Kimono*, 57–59. See also Lea Jacobs, *The Wages of Sin: Censorship and the Fallen Woman Film, 1928–1942* (Madison: University of Wisconsin Press, 1991), 25.

8.   Cain was incensed: "That it would also show them how to wind up behind the eight ball is not mentioned" (Cain, quoted in Hanna, "Hays Censors Rile Jim Cain," 11–13).

9.   "Double Indemnity," *Variety*, April 26, 1944, 12.

10.   Cain, quoted in Hanna, "Hays Censors Rile Jim Cain," 11.

11.   Breen's letter detailed specific Code violations for several pages. "Part I violations" included Cain's "details of the crime," such as the "plan of the murder" and the "offensive, cold blooded manner" of the murder. "Part II violations" involved "criminals avoid[ing] arrest and punishment" and the "decision and attempt to kill the accomplice" of the crime. Breen complained, "characters are murderers . . . who cheat the law and die at their own hands. They avoid successfully the consequences of their crime through a miscarriage of justice . . . [then] commit suicide." Neff is "glorified by confessing to save the girl" as he attempts to get away with the crime. Breen urged the studios to avoid "hardening audiences, especially the young who are impressionable to the thought of . . . crime" (Breen to Mayer, Oct. 10, 1935).

12.   Joseph Breen to Nunnally Johnson, "RE: Story outline treatment written by Col. Joy acceptable," Oct. 14, 1935, MPAA-PCA file, MHL. Production Chief Zanuck left Warner Bros. in 1935 to head production at the newly merged company of 20th Century–Fox. Johnson would later go on to become a writer-producer-director at 20th Century–Fox.

13.   Cain, quoted in Hanna, "Hays Censors Rile Jim Cain," 11.

14.   Billy Wilder, interview by John Allyn, *Literature/Film Quarterly* (spring 1978); repr. in Robert Horton, ed., *Billy Wilder: Interviews* (Jackson: University Press of Mississippi, 2001), 134.

15.   *Double Indemnity*'s inception illustrates the key role of producer Sistrom in initiating the project and the influence of wartime female studio personnel in decision making. See Lloyd Shearer, "Crime Certainly Pays on the Screen," *NYT*, Aug. 8, 1945.

16.   Joseph Breen to Luigi Luraschi (Paramount Censorship Department), "RE: Violations compelled to reject," March 15, 1943, MPAA-PCA file, MHL.

17.   Cain sardonically added that "no reports of any murders" had "been committed as a result . . . I have not yet heard of any such reports, though the story has since [1943] enjoyed a wide circulation in book form" (quoted in Hanna, "Hays Censors Rile Jim Cain," 11).

18.   Luigi Luraschi to Joseph Breen, "RE: Partial script outline with yellow sequences A, C, and outline for D for evaluation," Sept. 21, 1943, MPAA-PCA file, MHL.

19.   Cain, quoted in Hanna, "Hays Censors Rile Jim Cain," 11–13.

20.   Breen to Luraschi, "RE: Basic story seems to meet the requirements of the Production Code," Sept. 24, 1943, MPAA-PCA file, MHL.

21.   Cain, quoted in Hanna, "Hays Censors Rile Jim Cain," 11.

22.   Jacob H. Karp, "RE: Purchased motion picture rights for Double Indemnity story from Cain on May 15, 1943," Paramount Legal Department memorandum, May 27, 1943, PCPF, MHL; William Dozier to A. J. Lagage and Bill Cowitt, "RE: Story Fund number 8599," memorandum, March 19, 1943 [cc: Mr. Freedman, DeSylva, Ginsberg, Sistrom, William Karp, Garvey, Mrs. Reis, Mr. Frey], PCPF, MHL.

23.   Cain, quoted in Shearer, "Crime Certainly Pays."

24.   Schatz, *Boom and Bust*, 131–32.

25.   Fred Stanley, "News From Hollywood," *NYT*, March 21, 1944.

26.   Stanley, "Hollywood Turns."

27.   Thomas Brady, "Hollywood Clears Decks for Consent Decree: Four Studios Revise Production Set-Ups to Meet the New Selling Terms," *NYT*, March 2, 1941; Douglas W. Churchill, "Hollywood Changes: Quietly the Major Studios Reorganize Executive Staffs to Meet a New Era," *NYT*, July 6, 1941.

28.   "U.S. Renews Battle on Film Monopolies," *NYT*, Aug. 8, 1944.

29.   Koppes and Black, *Hollywood Goes to War*, 112. Lea Jacobs notes that "the system of self-regulation becomes complicated by the Office of War Information's attempt to monitor scripts through its Bureau of Motion Pictures" (*Wages of Sin*, 25). The wartime regulation climate was unique. Conflicting entities (OWI propaganda vs. Office of Censorship endorsing atrocity violence vs. PCA morality) enabled racier violence and crime to be produced, and Cain's sexy crime adaptations could also be exploited if eroticism was suggested—in visuals and dialogue. Wartime murder was increasingly "acceptable"—it was committed in combat every day, endorsed by the government, and shown to the public in wartime documentary combat newsreels. Sex could not be blatantly shown, however, because PCA censorship was still in place during the war (requiring an effort to comply with many of Breen's restrictions). The complexity of Hollywood's World War II production environment, an increasingly hard-boiled home front, and the necessary process of negotiation and compromise often enabled trendsetting lapses in PCA enforcement.

30.   Wilder and Chandler, *Double Indemnity* Release Dialogue Script (RDS), Feb. 22, 1944, Paramount Collection Script File (PCSF), MHL. Chandler was paid only $350 a week for 161 days from May 12 (just prior to the story's purchase) to Nov. 15, 1943 (almost the end of original shooting), before being paid $750 a week for only four days, Nov. 22–25, 1943. In all he earned $9,891.66 for his six months of writing. Wilder was paid $1,500 a week as a writer for forty-nine days from April 12 to June 7, 1943, and then $2,000 a week for ninety-five days from June 8 to Sept. 25, 1943, totaling $43,916.67—Paramount paid him another $2,000 a week, or $26,000, to direct from Sept. 27 to Dec. 25, 1943, totaling $69,916.67. The final cost for scenario writers was $54,708.33. See Paramount budget for *Double Indemnity*, 1944, PCPF, MHL.

31.   Zolotow, *Billy Wilder in Hollywood*, 111.

32.   Wilder and Chandler, *Double Indemnity* RDS (see note 30 of this chapter).

33.   Wilder and Chandler, *Double Indemnity* (unpublished film script draft [including revisions: Sequence D-32 (114): "Neff: 'At the end of that ... trolley line ... just as I get off ... you be there ... to say goodbye ... will you, Keyes?' " and Sequence E (115): San Quentin gas chamber]), Sept. 25, 1943, 67, Edward G. Robinson Collection, USC.

34.   Cain, quoted in Jeffrey Lane and Douglas Borton, eds., *A Salute to Billy Wilder*, Fourteenth Annual American Film Institute Life Achievement Award Booklet, Los Angeles, CA, March 6, 1986, 35.

35.   Jacobs, *Wages of Sin*, 20.

36.   "Budget #1375—Double Indemnity," 1944, PCPF, MHL.

37.   Breen to Luraschi, "RE: Whole sequence in the death chamber very questionable in present form," Dec. 1, 1943, MPAA-PCA file, MHL.

38.   John Seitz, quoted in Ella Smith, *Starring Miss Barbara Stanwyck* (New York: Crown, 1973), 177.

39.   Billy Wilder, interview by Cameron Crowe, in *Conversations with Wilder* (New York: Alfred Knopf, 1999), 53.

40.   Billy Wilder, interview by Gene D. Phillips, *Literature/Film Quarterly* (winter 1976); repr. in Horton, *Billy Wilder: Interviews*, 103.

41.   Stanley, "Blast at Hollywood."

42.   Norman Lacey to Frank Caffey, "RE: Existing dimout regulations will not permit such use of light," memorandum, Oct. 6, 1943, PCPF, MHL; see also "Budget #1375—Double Indemnity," 1944.

43.   James M. Cain, *Cain ×3; Three Novels by James M. Cain* (New York: Knopf, 1969), 412.

44.   Wilder and Chandler, *Double Indemnity* (unpublished film script, Revision B-60, Oct. 2, 1943, 62.

45. O. C. Stratton to Hugh Brown, "RE: Two plainclothes detectives and OPA officials," memorandum, Oct. 22, 1943, PCPF, MHL.

46. Wilder, quoted in Smith, *Starring Miss Barbara Stanwyck,* 177.

47. With fifty-one days of actual shooting, *Double Indemnity*'s total direct costs were $725,422.43, with indirect costs of $201,840.43—$52,737.14 under its $980,000 budget. See "Budget #1375—Double Indemnity," 1944.

48. Cain, quoted in Lane and Borton, *Salute to Billy Wilder,* 35. The film "does not depart from my story in any of the parts to which the Hays office took exception . . . The murder is committed in exactly the same way that it is accomplished in the book, down to the smallest detail . . . [T]he reaction of the preview audience was one of admiration, with no indication that one of them expected to go out and commit a murder. Indeed, I heard a number of remarks to the effect that it was a dreadful warning of the utter impossibility of getting away with murder" (Cain, quoted in Hanna, "Hays Censors Rile Jim Cain," 11).

49. "Budget #1375—Double Indemnity," 1944.

50. Paramount press book for *Double Indemnity,* 1944, PBC.

51. Scheuer, "Film History Made," 1, 3. See also W. H. M., "Tidings: Perfect Crime Myth Exploded," *HR,* Aug. 11, 1944; Howard Barnes, "On the Screen: 'Double Indemnity,' " *New York Herald-Tribune* (*NYHT*), Sept. 7, 1944, 18; Louella O. Parsons, " 'Double Indemnity' Gripping," *Los Angeles Examiner,* Aug. 11, 1944; L. E. R., " 'Indemnity' Movie Well Acted," *Los Angeles Citizen News,* Aug. 11, 1944; Philip K. Scheuer, " 'Double Indemnity' Study of Murder without Bunk," *LAT,* Aug. 11, 1944.

52. Although the Academy nominated *Double Indemnity,* it passed Wilder's film up in the final 1944 awards; as if to amend an oversight, the Academy seemingly made up for this by awarding Wilder's next picture, *The Lost Weekend,* the top three awards, including Best Picture, Best Director, and Best Actor (Ray Milland) in 1945.

53. Breen to Mayer, "RE: Violations compelled to reject" (see note 2 of this chapter).

54. The film's convergence of multiple adaptation levels and historical events is noteworthy—Wilder adapting German expressionism to America, Wilder adapting the distinctively moody milieu and witty dialogue of Chandler's hard-boiled fiction style to the screen, Chandler refining Cain's punchy streetwise phrasing, and Wilder adapting the staccato pace of Cain's hard-boiled story. *Double Indemnity* functions as a "cultural artifact" culminating from historical events of the war, wartime production constraints, PCA censorship, and the development and adaptation of hard-boiled fiction in relation to American wartime culture. It was tremendously influential in establishing a prototype for film noir style and consequently posing challenges to the Production Code. Its success produced a kind of snowball effect—encouraging other hard-boiled material and other Cain adaptations to be produced. Primary archival research indicates that not only was *Double Indemnity* seminal in transcending the Code's restrictions to establish a prototypical dark *noir* style, but it was also a definitive film spurring other red-meat crime and passion adaptations in Hollywood. See Stanley, "Hollywood Crime and Romance."

55. Shearer, "Crime Certainly Pays."

56. Breen to William Gordon (RKO Censorship Department), "RE: *Farewell, My Lovely* basic story seems to meet the requirements of the Production Code," April 13, 1944, MPAA-PCA file, MHL.

57. RKO Radio Pictures budget and final cost for *Farewell, My Lovely,* Nov. 25, 1944, UCLA Arts Library Special Collections, Young Research Library, University of California, Los Angeles. For *Farewell, My Lovely / Murder, My Sweet* and *Citizen Kane* budgets and revenue see Jewell, "RKO Film Grosses," app. 1; and Jewell and Harbin, *RKO Story.*

58. Edward Dmytryk, interview in Turner behind-the-scenes retrospective on *Murder, My Sweet* (*Murder, My Sweet,* videocassette, Turner Home Video, 1996); Jewell and Harbin, *RKO Story.*

59. RKO press book for *Murder, My Sweet,* 1945, PBC.

60. Jewell, "RKO Film Grosses," app. 1.

61. Biesen, "Censorship."

62. Stanley, "Hollywood Crime and Romance."

63. Robert E. Morsberger, Stephen Lesser, and Randall Clark, eds., *Dictionary of Literary Biography,* vol. 26, *Screenwriters* (Detroit: Gale Research, 1984).

64. Herschel Brickell, "This Is Strong Men's Meat," review of *The Postman Always Rings Twice,* by James M. Cain, *NYT Book Review,* Feb. 18, 1934, 8.

65. Breen, Production Code memorandum, March 9, 1934, MPAA-PCA file, MHL.

66. Will Hays, MPPDA (New York office), to Nicholas M. Schenck, President of MGM Distribution Company in New York (cc: Breen), March 15, 28, 1934, MPAA-PCA file, MHL.

67. "Exhibit A," correspondence between Gabriel L. Hess and Will Hays, March 22, 1934, MPAA-PCA file, MHL.

68. P. S. Harrison to Louis B. Mayer, March 30, 1934, MPAA-PCA file, MHL.

69. Correspondence between Will Hays and Joseph Breen, April 2–Sept. 4, 1934, MPAA-PCA file, MHL

70. Breen to Luraschi, "RE: Violations compelled to reject," (see note 16 of this chapter); Breen to Luraschi, "RE: rejecting *The Postman Always Rings Twice,*" March 15, 1943, MPAA-PCA file, MHL.

71. Breen to Luraschi, "RE: Basic story seems to meet the requirements of the Production Code," Sept. 24, 1943, MPAA-PCA file, MHL.

72. Luigi Luraschi to Joseph Breen, "RE: Denies interest in *Postman,*" April 4, 1944, MPAA-PCA file, MHL.

73. Hedda Hopper, "Looking at Hollywood," *LAT,* Aug. 3, 1944.

74. Revised scripts and Carey Wilson's story treatments for *The Postman Always Rings Twice,* April 4, 5, May 31, 1945, Tay Garnett and MGM Collections, USC; Breen to Luraschi, "RE: *Postman* basic story seems to meet the requirements of the Production Code," May 7, 17, 1945, MPAA-PCA file, MHL.

75. Leff and Simmons, *Dame in the Kimono,* 133.

76. "Love at Laguna Beach: Lana Turner and John Garfield Sizzle Sands in Making 'The Postman Always Rings Twice,'" *Life,* Aug. 20, 1945, 122–24.

77. Reverend H. Parr Armstrong to Dr. Roswell Barnes, Aug. 24, 1945, MPAA-PCA file, MHL.

78. Joseph Breen to Dr. Samuel McCrea Cavert of the Federal Council of Churches of Christ in America, "We believe the finished picture," Sept. 19, 1945, MPAA-PCA file, MHL.

79. Carey Wilson, quoted in Leff and Simmons, *Dame in the Kimono,* 132.

80. Carey Wilson, "'The Postman' Emerges as Torrid Movie," interview by Virginia MacPherson, *Los Angeles Citizen News,* Feb. 26, 1946.

81. James M. Cain, "Tough Guy," interview by Peter Brunette and Gerald Peary, *Film Comment* (May–June 1976): 57.

82. Shooting script for *The Postman Always Rings Twice,* April 27–May 4, 1945, 4, Tay Garnett Collection, USC.

83. MGM press book for *The Postman Always Rings Twice,* 1946, PBC.

84. Glancy, "MGM Film Grosses," app. 1; Finler (*Hollywood Story,* 277) gives *The Postman Always Rings Twice*'s domestic profit as $4 million.

85. Successful Cain adaptations proved red-meat film noir could also be quite lucrative. Stanley, "Hollywood Crime and Romance." "The Seal on *The Postman* would close the parenthesis on an era of Code enforcement; it would tell Hollywood to purchase the most salacious books and anticipate Production Code certification" (Leff and Simmons, *Dame in the Kimono,* 134–35, 138).

86. Schatz, *Boom and Bust.*

Chapter 5. Rosie the Riveter Goes to Hollywood

1. See "Rosie the Riveter" illustration in *Hygeia,* Sept. 1943, 635.

2. Fred Stanley, "Hollywood Takes a Hint From Washington: Two Big Negro Musicals Are Under Way," *NYT,* Feb. 7, 1943. This rather segregated screen strategy coincided with racial (military) segregation during World War II.

3. Stanley, "Blast at Hollywood."

4. Schatz, *Boom and Bust,* 144–49.

5. Maureen Honey, *Creating Rosie the Riveter: Class, Gender, and Propaganda during World War II* (Amherst: University of Massachusetts Press, 1984), 5–11.

6. Fred Stanley, "Hollywood Bows to the Ladies," *NYT,* Jan. 7, 1945.

7. Lizzie Francke, *Script Girls: Women Screenwriters in Hollywood* (London: British Film Institute, 1994), 55.

8.   Universal press book for *Phantom Lady*, 1944, PBC.
9.   Joan Harrison, quoted in Philip K. Scheuer, "Producer's Spurs Won by Woman," *LAT*, Feb. 23, 1944.
10. Universal press book for *Phantom Lady*, 1944, PBC.
11. Louis Black, "Phantom Lady," *CinemaTexas Program Notes* 14, no. 1 (Feb. 8, 1978): 79.
12. Review of *Phantom Lady, LAT*, March 29, 1944, USC.
13. "Ella Raines: The Pretty Young Star of 'Phantom Lady' Began Her Career by Being Incorporated for $1,000,000 by a Production Firm," *Life*, Feb. 28, 1944.
14. Universal press book for *Phantom Lady*, 1944, PBC.
15. Joan Harrison, originally quoted in *Time* (1944), cited in Francke, *Script Girls*, 59.
16. Harrison, "Why I Envy Men Producers," *HR*, Oct. 23, 1944.
17. Sarris and Durgnat, in Whitten (see note 2 of chapter 1).
18. Ibid.
19. George Amy, quoted in Black, "Phantom Lady," 76.
20. Universal press book for *Phantom Lady*, 1944, PBC.
21. Breen to Maurice Pivar, Sept. 3, 1943, MPAA-PCA file, MHL.
22. Breen to Pivar, Sept. 14–16, 1943, MPAA-PCA file, MHL.
23. Pivar to Breen, Sept. 21, 1943, MPAA-PCA file, MHL.
24. L. Greenhouse, PCA report for *Phantom Lady*, Dec. 7, 1943, MPAA-PCA file, MHL.
25. Universal press book for *Phantom Lady*, 1944, PBC.
26. Pivar to Breen, Jan. 6, 1944, MPAA-PCA file, MHL.
27. "Phantom Lady," *Motion Picture Daily*, Jan. 21, 1944, MHL.
28. Bosley Crowther, "Phantom Lady," *NYT*, Feb. 18, 1944.
29. Scheuer, "Film History Made," *LAT*, Aug. 6, 1944, 1.
30. "Siodmak Rebels," *NYT*, Feb. 17, 1946.
31. *Double Indemnity*'s screen adaptation influenced Jerry Wald's production of *Mildred Pierce*, particularly in employing a flashback *noir* suspense framework to what was originally a female melodrama (though Wald contended, in a plagiarism lawsuit a few years later, that it was his own idea all along, which he coincidentally came up with after Wilder and Chandler employed it to get Cain's *Double Indemnity* by the censors). Tom Chapman to Roy Obringer, legal correspondence for *Mildred Pierce*, March 4, May 12, Nov. 8, 1949, WBA.
32. Catherine Turney, quoted in Francke, *Script Girls*, 47–50.
33. Cain, quoted in Hoopes, *Cain*, 349–50. Turney's female contribution was heavily mediated by men. This male authority structure dictated and overrode Turney's creative involvement in the process.
34. Turney, quoted in Francke, *Script Girls*, 47–50.
35. Paramount publicity release, 1944, in Cain files, Library of Congress; Cain is also cited in Hoopes, *Cain*.
36. Hoopes, *Cain*, 348. In adapting *Mildred Pierce* Warners was making a keen effort, as were other studios, to capitalize on the momentum of *Double Indemnity*'s success. Industry trades note the significance of Hollywood's adaptation of Cain's controversial *Double Indemnity* in 1943–44, calling it a film that "rapidly became accepted as the start of a trend labeled 'red meat' by contemporary reviewers." Paul Jensen, "Film Noir: The Writer, Raymond Chandler: The World You Live In," *Film Comment*, Nov. 1974, 20.
37. Stanley, "Hollywood Crime and Romance"; Shearer, "Crime Certainly Pays."
38. Hoopes, *Cain*, 350.
39. Thames Williamson to Jerry Wald, Jan. 12–14, 1944, WBA.
40. Breen to Jack Warner, correspondence for *Mildred Pierce*, Feb. 2 and 22, 1944, MPAA-PCA file, MHL.
41. Jack Warner to Jerry Wald and Steve Trilling, telegram, May 15, 1944, WBA.
42. Francke, *Script Girls*, 50.
43. Jerry Wald, production memoranda for *Mildred Pierce*, Oct.–Nov. 21, 1944, Feb. 6, 1945, WBA.
44. Warner Bros. production correspondence re. permission from A. J. Bolton, U.S. Navy, to film coastal beaches for *Mildred Pierce*, Dec. 4, 1944–Feb. 5, 1945, WBA.
45. Alton Cook, "Warners Banish Three-Year Jinx: 'Mildred Pierce' Rings Bell in Non-War Category," *New York World Telegram*, Sept. 29, 1945.

46. Tenny Wright to Jerry Wald, budget correspondence for *Mildred Pierce*, Feb. 5–6, 1945, WBA; Warner Bros. Cost and Income Figures for 1941–1946 Films, Aug. 31, 1955, WSC.

47. Harold Heffernan, "Good Tag Line Can Do Lot for Movie," *Detroit News*, July 3, 1946, 6. By 1955 a reissue of the film brought only $13,000 in gross income. This marketing strategy did not encourage repeat viewing.

48. Francke, *Script Girls*, 63.

49. Stanley, "Hollywood Bows."

50. W. R. Wilkerson, "Tradeviews," *HR*, MHL.

51. "Gilda," *NYT*, Sept. 16, 1945; see also Bernard F. Dick, *The Merchant Prince of Poverty Row: Harry Cohn of Columbia Pictures* (Lexington: University Press of Kentucky, 1993), 67–68.

52. Silvia Stein to Gentlemen of the Association of Motion Picture Producers, Nov. 16, 1944, MPAA-PCA file, MHL; Breen to Harry Cohn, Nov. 20, 1944, MPAA-PCA file, MHL.

53. Correspondence for *Gilda* between Columbia's Silvia Stein and Joseph Breen, Aug. 4, 1945–Feb. 25, 1946, MPAA-PCA file, MHL.

54. Review of *Gilda*, *Variety*, March 13, 1946.

55. Dick, *Merchant Prince*, 67–68.

56. All quotes in this paragraph are from the Columbia press book for *Gilda*, 1946, PBC.

57. Ibid.

58. Heffernan, "Good Tag Line."

59. Universal press book for *Scarlet Street*, 1945, PBC; Columbia press book for *Gilda*, 1946, PBC.

60. Columbia press book for *Gilda*, 1946, PBC.

61. Bob Thomas, *King Cohn* (New York: McGraw-Hill, 1990), 232; Dick, *Merchant Prince*, 69; Gay Hayden, quoted in Francke, *Script Girls*, 61.

62. Dick, *Merchant Prince*, 69.

63. Francke, *Script Girls*, 61.

64. Van Upp, cited in Francke, *Script Girls*, 65.

65. Lang assistant and confidant Andries Dienum, quoted in McGilligan, *Fritz Lang*, 332; see also *HR*, April 2, 1946. (Émigré Lang, as well as Wilder, Siodmak, and Curtiz, certainly capitalized on this war-related labor need to advance their careers over the course of the war.)

Chapter 6. Hyphenates and Hard-Boiled Crime

1. Joan Lester, "Professor in Love with Picture," *Reynold's News* (London), Feb. 4, 1945.

2. Shearer, "Crime Certainly Pays."

3. See *Variety*, April 1, 1940, 3; *NYT*, Feb. 21, 1940, 5x; Stanley, "New Hollywood Units," *NYT*, March 17, 1946; see also Schatz, *Boom and Bust*, 46.

4. Darryl Zanuck, story conference notes on *Laura*, Nov. 1, 1943–March 22, 1944, 1–10, 20th Century–Fox Collection, USC.

5. *HR*, June 19, 1990; PCA correspondence, 1943–1944, MPAA-PCA file, MHL; 20th Century–Fox press book for *Laura*, 1944, PBC; *HR*, Oct. 11, 1944, 4; *Variety*, Oct. 11, 1944, 12; *Daily Variety*, Oct. 11, 1944, 3.

6. McCarthy and Flynn, *Kings of the Bs*, 149.

7. Joseph Breen to Leon Fromkess, PCA correspondence, Nov. 1, 1944–Feb. 13, 1945, May 29, 1945, MPAA-PCA file for *Detour*, MHL.

8. Jim Henaghan, review of *Detour*, *HR*, Oct. 29, 1945, 1, 9.

9. Edward G. Robinson, with Leonard Spigelgass, *All My Yesterdays: An Autobiography* (New York: Hawthorn Books, 1973), 261.

10. John Beck Jr., International Pictures and PCA correspondence for *Once Off Guard*, Nov. 15, 1943–April 3, 1944, MPAA-PCA file, MHL.

11. Art direction records, budgets, photographs, and design materials for *Once Off Guard*, Duncan Cramer Collection, April 12, 1944, MHL.

12. PCA seal for *Once Off Guard*, Sept. 21, 1944, MPAA-PCA file, MHL.

13. *Once Off Guard* publicity, *International Pictures Press Handbook* (Jack Mulcahy, publicity director), 1944, International Pictures press book collection, MHL.

14. Philip K. Scheuer, "'Woman in the Window': Adroit Exercise in Crime," *LAT*, Oct. 10, 1944.

15. International Pictures press book collection, 1944, MHL.

16. "Woman in the Window," *Variety*, Oct. 10, 1944.

17. Jewell, "RKO Film Grosses," app. 1.
18. Bert McCord, "Woman in the Window," *NYHT*, Jan. 26, 1945; "Woman in the Window," *NYT*, Jan. 26, 1945.
19. Fred Stanley, "Hollywood Bulletins," *NYT*, Nov. 18, 1945.
20. Partner-owner-investor Bennett named "Diana Productions" after her daughter from an earlier marriage.
21. McGilligan, *Fritz Lang*, 327. Like Wilder, whose parents perished at Auschwitz, Lang hated the Nazis. After fleeing Germany, Lang had depicted Gestapo torture, executions, and concentration camps in hard-hitting films based on real World War II events—films such as *Hangmen Also Die*, for example, about the Nazi slaughter in Czechoslovakia. As bleak wartime footage came back from the fronts, the émigré director recalled his torment as friends told him, "You are too close to it, Fritz, you are bitter." Lang's outrage over the war intensified amid stark documentary coverage.
22. Production also coincided with the U.S. dropping of the atomic bombs and the aftermath of their brutal destruction.
23. Fritz Lang, quoted in Lotte Eisner, *Fritz Lang* (New York: Oxford, 1977), 257.
24. Ibid., 259.
25. Production correspondence, story and budget material for *Scarlet Street*, Universal Collection, Fritz Lang Collection, Edward G. Robinson Collection, USC.
26. Universal financial budgets show a $50,000 to $80,000 margin cost over budget. One Universal budget cites an $82,579 overage, with costs totaling $1,232,179; another shows a difference of $53,000 with $1,202,000 in costs against a $1,149,600 budget (including direct costs of just over $1 million), but cites a potentially inaccurate $551,493 figure that does not add up. Budget #1454—Lang-"Scarlet Street," File #1, Box 133/Folder 7016 and Box 281/Folder 9976, Universal Collection, USC, 1945.
27. McGilligan, *Fritz Lang*, 327.
28. Darryl Zanuck to Joseph Breen, April 2, 1946, MPAA-PCA file, MHL.
29. Universal press book for *Scarlet Street*, 1945, PBC.
30. "'Conflict' Gets Its Preem Right on Fighting Line," Dec. 6, 1944 (anonymous trade news clipping), WBA; and "'Conflict' Premiere Held in France," *Los Angeles Citizen News*, July 2, 1945.
31. "There Is No Scarcity of Red Meat in *Conflict*," *Los Angeles Evening-Herald Express*, June 20, 1945.
32. "Conflict," *Los Angeles Examiner*, June 27, 1945.
33. "Conflict," *Saint Paul Pioneer Press*, June 10, 1945.
34. Breen to Cohn, PCA correspondence for *Sahara*, Jan. 1943, MPAA-PCA file, MHL.
35. A. E. MacKenzie, synopsis of *To Have and Have Not*, Aug. 17, 1937, WBA.
36. Synopsis of *To Have and Have Not*, May 15, 1944, WBA.
37. Production records, legal contracts, and budget for *To Have and Have Not*, May 31, 1939–June 3, 1944, WBA.
38. "Production Notes" press release for *To Have and Have Not*, Oct. 20, 1944, WBA.
39. Warner Bros. press book for *To Have and Have Not*, 1944, WBA.
40. Ibid.
41. Warner Bros. promotional trailer transcript for *To Have and Have Not*, 1944, WBA.
42. Warner Bros. press book for *To Have and Have Not*, 1944, WBA.
43. Warner Bros. Cost and Income Figures for 1941–1946 Films, Aug. 31, 1955, WSC.
44. Raymond Chandler, "The Simple Art of Murder," *Atlantic Monthly*, Dec. 1944, 57.
45. Raymond Chandler, *The Notebooks of Raymond Chandler* (New York: Ecco, 1976), 8–10; Lawrence Clark Powell, in Chandler, *Raymond Chandler: Four Complete Philip Marlow Novels* (New York: Alfred Knopf, 1967), xi.
46. Steve Trilling to Colonel Jack Warner, memorandum, Aug. 2, 1944, WBA.
47. Howard Hawks to Roy Obringer, memorandum, and contract between Howard Hawks/H-F Productions and Chandler re. *The Big Sleep*, Aug. 28–29, 1944, WBA.
48. Contract between Howard Hawks / H-F Productions and Warner Bros. re. *The Big Sleep*, Oct. 27, 1944, WBA; correspondence between Joseph Breen and Jack Warner re. *The Big Sleep*, Sept. 26–Oct. 1944, MPAA-PCA file, MHL.
49. "Lauren Bacall Selected to Portray Sinister Role in Bogart's 'Big Sleep,'" *LAT*, Oct. 10, 1944.

50.   Contract between Howard Hawks / H-F Productions and Warner Bros. re. *The Big Sleep*,
        Oct. 27, 1944, WBA; drafts and revisions of the screenplay for *The Big Sleep*, 1944–46,
        WBA; Howard Hawks, quoted in Joseph McBride, *Hawks on Hawks* (Berkeley: University
        of California Press, 1982), 138; Leigh Brackett, "From *The Big Sleep* to *The Long Goodbye*
        and More or Less How We Got There," *Take One* 4, no. 1 (1972); also cited by Francke,
        Script Girls, 81–82; Hedda Hopper, "They Call Her for Salty Dialogue," *LAT*, Dec. 28, 1965;
        correspondence between Breen and Warner, Sept. 26–Oct. 1944, MPAA-PCA file, MHL.
51.   Eric Stacey to T. C. ("Tenny") Wright, memoranda re. *The Big Sleep*, Nov. 9–13, 24, 1944,
        WBA.
52.   Lauren Bacall, *By Myself* (New York: Alfred Knopf, 1979), 118–20.
53.   Stacey to Wright, memorandum, Nov. 28, 1944, WBA; William Faulkner to Jerry Geller,
        Dec. 12, 1944, WBA.
54.   Stacey to Wright, memoranda re. *The Big Sleep*, Dec. 29, 1944, Jan. 13, 1945, WBA.
55.   Correspondence between Breen and Jack Warner re. *The Big Sleep*, Jan. 31, 1945, MPAA-
        PCA file, MHL.
56.   Warner Bros. production report for *The Big Sleep*, Jan. 28, 1946, WBA.
57.   Breen to Jack Warner, Jan. 25, 1946, MPAA-PCA file, MHL.
58.   Warner Bros. Cost and Income Figures for 1941–1946 Films, WSC.
59.   Warner Bros. press book for *The Big Sleep*, 1946, WBA. The film also marked the screen
        debut of nineteen-year-old Dorothy Malone, who would become a 1950s screen siren in
        Douglas Sirk melodramas.
60.   Warner Bros. press book publicity and production notes for *The Big Sleep*, quotes from
        reviews of *The Big Sleep* by James Agee (*Nation*, Feb. 20, 1945) and Richard Winnington
        (June 27, 1946), WBA.

Chapter 7. Black Film, Red Meat
Epigraph. Raymond Chandler, quoted in *NYT*, Aug. 8, 1945.

1.   Frank, "Un Nouveau genre 'policier,'" 14; Borde and Chaumeton, *Panorama of American
        Film Noir*, 1.
2.   Florett Robinson, "Hiss-s-s-s through the Years: Styles in movie villains change, but
        whether Western desperadoes, city slickers or Japs, they're all bad men," *NYT*, Aug. 15, 1943.
3.   Stanley, "Hollywood Peeks," *NYT*, Feb. 21, 1943.
4.   Fred Stanley, "Hollywood Shivers: The Studios Are Busily Stirring Up a Grade A Witches'
        Brew—Other Items," *NYT*, May 28, 1944. See also Fred Stanley, "Hollywood Activities:
        More Musicals and Comedies, Fewer War Films, in the Offing—Other Notes," *NYT*, Jan.
        16, 1944; Fred Stanley, "Hollywood Flash: Studios Scrap Many War Stories—The Horror
        Boys Convene—Other News," *NYT*, April 16, 1944, B.
5.   Scheuer, "Film History Made by 'Double Indemnity,'" *LAT*, Aug. 6, 1944, 1, 3. Scheuer,
        "'Double Indemnity' Study of Murder without Bunk," *LAT*, Aug. 11, 1944.
6.   "Inside Paramount: *Double Indemnity*," *Time*, July 17, 1944, MHL.
7.   W. H. M., "Tidings," *HR*, Aug. 11, 1944, MHL.
8.   Parsons, "'Double Indemnity' Gripping," *Los Angeles Examiner*, Aug. 11, 1944, MHL.
9.   Shearer, "Crime Certainly Pays"; see also Stanley, "Hollywood Crime and Romance."
10.   James M. Cain, Paramount publicity release, 1944, Cain files, Library of Congress, Wash-
        ington, DC; Cain cited in Hoopes, *Cain*, 348.
11.   Chandler, "The Simple Art of Murder," 57.
12.   Lester, "Professor in Love with Picture"; Warner Bros. press book for *Casablanca*, 1942, 8,
        WBA; "No Scarcity of Red Meat in *Conflict*," *Los Angeles Evening-Herald Express*, June 20,
        1945; Breen to Cavert (see note 78 of chap. 4).
13.   Cain, quoted in Shearer, "Crime Certainly Pays," *NYT*, Aug. 8, 1945.
14.   Jack Rosenstein, Warner Bros. publicity release, 1944, WBA.
15.   Fred Stanley, "Hollywood Crystal Ball," *NYT*, May 20, 1945.
16.   Paramount press book for *The Blue Dahlia*, 1946, PBC.
17.   Review of *The Blue Dahlia*, *Hollywood Review*, Jan. 28, 1946, 1–2.
18.   Review of *The Blue Dahlia*, *Variety*, Jan. 30, 1946, 12.
19.   Howard Barnes, review of *The Blue Dahlia*, *NYHT*, May 9, 1946; Eileen Creelman, "The
        New Movies," *New York Sun*, May 9, 1946.

20. Bosley Crowther, "'Blue Dahlia'... Proves an Exciting Picture," *NYT,* May 9, 1946. Final cost in May was $871,000; see Budget #11403, April 25, May 21, Aug. 3, 1945, PCPF and MPAA-PCA file, MHL. See also Chandler to James Sandoe, June 1946, Chandler Collection, UCLA Special Collections; also cited in Chandler, *The Blue Dahlia,* ed. Matthew J. Bruccoli (Carbondale: Southern Illinois University Press, 1976), 132–34.

21. Herb Sterne, "The Stranger," *Rob Wagner's Script,* July 20, 1946, 13.

22. Fred Stanley, "An Old Hollywood Costume," *NYT,* Oct. 21, 1945.

23. International press book for *The Stranger,* 1946, PBC.

24. Orson Welles, quoted in Stanley, "An Old Hollywood Costume"; James Agee, *Nation,* June 22, 1946, 765; Bosley Crowther, review of *The Stranger, NYT,* July 11, 1946. Foreign earnings for *The Stranger* were $935,000 and total earnings $2,935,000; see Jewell, "RKO Film Grosses," app. 1.

25. Finler, *Hollywood Story,* 133.

26. Alain Silver and Elizabeth Ward, *Film Noir: An Encyclopedic Reference to the American Style* (Woodstock, NY: Overlook, 1992), 38–39.

27. Darryl Zanuck to Elia Kazan and John Steinbeck, memorandum, Dec. 26, 1950, 20th Century–Fox Collection, USC.

28. Darryl Zanuck to All Producers and Directors, confidential memorandum, June 14, 1950, 20th Century–Fox Collection, USC; Zanuck to Henry King, confidential memorandum, Oct. 12, 1950, 20th Century–Fox Collection, USC; Rudy Behlmer, *Memo from Darryl F. Zanuck* (New York: Grove Press, 1993), 174–94. Many social-realist *noir* writers, directors, and creative talent were political liberals and intellectuals affiliated with social politics, progressive causes, Depression-era populism, the antifascist Popular Front in World War II, and even the Communist Party—and many were later labeled a "Red" postwar threat in the xenophobic cold war political climate. The influence of Italian neorealism was significant in Hollywood's progressive push toward realistic "message" pictures, and the liberal leaning of social-conscious creative talent was not unlike many social-conscious pacifist, humanist, Marxist writers and neorealist directors in Italy opposing wartime fascism.

29. Hoopes, *Cain,* 467; see also Warner Bros. story files for *Serenade,* WBA; and budget figures in WSC.

30. Warner Bros. press book for *Serenade,* 1956, WBA. The post-HUAC, post-antitrust, post-*Miracle* decision lapse of PCA enforcement led to a splintering and decline of *noir* by the late 1950s and 1960s. As the Code lost its bite and became more lenient, film noir also dissipated. Industry censorship by the PCA regulating Hollywood film content was collapsing by the 1960s—severely weakened after the *Miracle* decision, departure of Breen, and liberalization of the Production Code in the mid-to-late 1950s and later replaced entirely by a ratings system in Nov. 1968. Whereas 1940s *noir* embodied restraint, 1950s melodrama exuded excess. Over the course of this decade-long delay in filming Cain's *Serenade,* its production context, the industry, the historical wartime 1940s period, visual style, and narrative conventions were radically transformed, as was the political climate nationally, in Hollywood, and at Warner Bros. studio. *Serenade* could have had an entirely different fate, however. Originally, Leonard Bernstein composed a musical version of Cain's novel in 1953 and planned a Broadway play after scoring Elia Kazan's *On the Waterfront* in early 1954—even auditioning Stephen Sondheim, friend and protégé of Oscar Hammerstein II, as lyricist for the project in 1955; Bernstein was harassed by HUAC during this 1953–56 period and decided instead to collaborate with Sondheim, Arthur Laurents, and Jerome Robbins on the Broadway stage production of *West Side Story*—clearly influenced by the legacy of earlier films noir. Given the jazz-inflected realist *noir* edge of Bernstein's collaboration with Kazan, a dark musical stage score and more somber realist vision and milieu may have led to a very different film adaptation, as can be seen in the *noir* musical *West Side Story* onstage and onscreen.

31. Rod Steiger, in "Contender: Mastering the Method," retrospective documentary on the making of *On the Waterfront* (*On the Waterfront,* DVD, Columbia Tri-Star, 2001); Thomas, *King Cohn,* 341.

32. Zanuck to Robert Jacks and Robert Sherwood, memorandum, July 29, 1952, 20th Century–Fox Collection, USC; see also Behlmer, *Memo,* 215–16.

Index